A BOLD NEW VISION

Personal Enrichment Guide

A Bold New Vision

Personal Enrichment Guide

Floyd D. Carey and Hoyt E. Stone, Editors

CLEVELAND, TENNESSEE 37311

Unless otherwise indicated, all quotations are from *The New King James Version.* Copyright © 1979, 1980, 1982, Thomas Nelson Inc., Publishers. Used by permission.

Scripture quotations marked *TLB* are taken from *The Living Bible,* copyright © 1971 from Tyndale House Publishers, Wheaton, IL. Used by permission.

Scripture quotations marked *NIV* are from the Holy Bible, *New International Version.* Copyright © 1973, 1978, 1984 International Bible Society. Used by permission of Zondervan Bible Publishers.

ISBN: 87148-112-X
Library of Congress Catalog Card Number: 88-061202

Copyright © 1988
PATHWAY PRESS
Cleveland, Tennessee 37311

Printed in the United States of America

CONTENTS

January

DISCIPLESHIP, *Raymond E. Crowley*	11
SELF-HELP, *Hoyt E. Stone*	16
NURTURE, *Marcus V. Hand*	21
THE HOLY SPIRIT, *Lewis J. Willis*	26

February

WORSHIP, *Rebecca J. Jenkins*	31
PERSONAL ORGANIZATION, *Donald T. Pemberton*	36
FAMILY RELATIONSHIPS, *Sonjia Hunt*	41
PRAYER, *Benjamin B. McGlamery*	46

March

PARENTING, *W. A. Davis*	51
STEWARDSHIP, *Al Taylor*	56
OUTREACH, *Ray H. Hughes*	61
PERSONAL WITNESS, *Leonard Albert*	66

April

PRAYER, *J. Herbert Walker*	71
WORSHIP, *J. D. Golden*	76
SELF-HELP, *Robert D. Crick*	81
CHRISTIAN GROWTH, *Lance Colkmire*	86

May

PERSONAL DEVOTIONS, *O. W. Polen*	91
PERSONAL ORGANIZATION, *Julian B. Robinson*	96
SELF-HELP, *Mike Baker*	101
CHRISTIAN GROWTH, *James E. Humbertson*	106

June

DISCIPLESHIP, *Dorothy Jennings and Martha Wong*	111
NURTURE, *Daniel L. Black*	116
THE HOLY SPIRIT, *Clyne W. Buxton*	121
SOCIETAL RELATIONSHIPS, *Douglas W. Slocumb*	126

July

PERSONAL DEVOTIONS, *Delton Alford*	131
TIME MANAGEMENT, *O. Wayne Chambers*	136
COMMUNICATIONS, *Bob Pace*	141
OUTREACH, *John D. Nichols*	146

August

FAMILY RELATIONSHIPS, *Robert D. McCall*	151
SOCIETAL RELATIONSHIPS, *Thomas Grassano*	156
PRAYER, *Gary W. Sears*	161
CHURCH GROWTH, *Bill F. Sheeks*	166

September

DOCTRINE, *James D. Jenkins*	171
SOCIAL CONCERNS, *B. J. Moffett*	176
HELPING OTHERS (COUNSELING), *Esdras Betancourt*	181
STEWARDSHIP, *Gerald W. Redman*	186

October

COMMUNICATIONS, *Bennie Triplett*	191
PARENTING, *Junus Fulbright*	196
INVOLVEMENT, *Lamar Vest*	201
SELF-HELP, *Paul Conn*	206

November

CHURCH GROWTH, *W. C. Ratchford*	211

PERSONAL WITNESS, *Christopher Moree* 216
OUTREACH, *Hector Camacho* 221
SOCIAL CONCERNS, *Paul Duncan* 226

December

DOCTRINE, *L. Grant McClung Jr.* 231
HELPING OTHERS (COUNSELING), *Donald M. Walker* 236
NURTURE, *C. C. Pratt* 241
INVOLVEMENT, *Cecil B. Knight* 246

INTRODUCTION

Early pioneers of the Church of God, our forefathers, were inspired with a vision which has brought us to a unique position of leadership in today's world. It could be that we presently stand poised for growth of unbelievable and explosive dimensions, an opportunity which necessitates the involvement of every leader and every member in an unprecedented manner.

Concerned that this opportunity not be ignored, and surely inspired of God's Holy Spirit, the Executive Committee introduced Project 2000 at the 1986 General Assembly in Atlanta. There followed worldwide emphases on renewed involvement in prayer and the study of God's Word, appeals which have plowed deep furrows in our hearts and widened our vision of those miraculous possibilities through the power of the Holy Spirit.

We are now calling upon every leader and every member of the Church of God to develop a bold new vision for ministry, a new perspective which keys in on outreach and discipleship, an inspiration which will provide the force and the vehicle for implementing all aspects of Project 2000 during the coming Decade of Destiny.

With God's help and your full cooperation we plan to move into the Decade of Destiny with two giant steps—Outreach '89 and Discipleship 90.

This book, *A Bold New Vision—Personal Enrichment Guide*, is really the centerpiece of the first of these steps. It is an effort to unite our hearts around common weekly themes, to make us all more conscious of personal relationships within the Body of Christ, and to offer that spiritual strength necessary for making our new vision come alive.

A Bold New Vision—Personal Enrichment Guide, edited by Floyd D. Carey and Hoyt E. Stone, is designed to lead the reader through a daily regimen of mental and personal inner growth. It has been written by 48 respected church leaders, each sharing a week of five devotionals from his/her personal spiritual journey.

Within these pages you will discover 20 one-page guides per month, grouped by practical subjects, five devotions under each. The devotions each share a three-point outline for easy reading and continuity:

1. **Enrichment From the Word**—key passages of Scripture which offer guidance and strength for victorious living

2. **Enrichment From the Church**—testimonials, quotes, anecdotes, stories and illustrations drawn from the Christian fellowship and pertaining to present situations faced by believers

3. **Enrichment From the Heart**—prayers, commitments and personal affirmations of relationship with the heavenly Father.

All Bible passages are taken from the *New King James Version* of the Bible, except where noted and for some special emphasis chosen by the writer.

A Bold New Vision—Personal Enrichment Guide is designed to be read five days a week (we suggest your early morning devotions), but it also offers flexibility when and if your personal calendar demands a change. Just choose your subject and use in conjunction with what may be happening in your life at the moment.

For reference purposes we have provided a Table of Contents, listing the weekly themes and writers.

The printed Scripture passages are brief. We suggest, however, that larger blocks of text be read in order for you to fully understand the Bible setting. Included in the back of the book is a Bible Reading Guide designed to take you through the entire Bible during the year.

As you join us with your bold new vision for ministry in your "corner of the world" and as literally thousands of our brothers and sisters in Christ make the same commitment, we believe God's Spirit and grace will be manifest in an ever greater measure. That is why we ask your cooperation once again as we embrace Project 2000 and move in step toward the Decade of Destiny.

                        Church of God
                        The Executive Committee

Discipleship

January, Week 1

Raymond E. Crowley

DEVELOPING A BOLD NEW VISION

Scripture: But He [Jesus] needed to go through Samaria (John 4:4).

Enrichment From the Word: The Lord was starting on a journey from Judea to Galilee, and He decided to go through Samaria—even though this route was as much as 100 miles out of the way. Jesus knew there was a sinful woman who would be coming to Jacob's Well in Samaria, and He wanted to give her "living water" so she would never thirst again. When Jesus met this woman, He looked past the fact that she had been married five times and was now living with a man who was not her husband. Christ looked past her adulterous life—condemning her sin but not her—to save her.

Enrichment From the Church: The bold vision which God wants us to have arises out of a Christlike compassion—a compassion which sees past sin and prejudice to the lost people whom God loves.

As a young minister, I pastored a storefront church. One day a distraught woman came to the door. She was weeping, almost hysterical. "Brother Crowley," she said, "I was married, divorced and am now remarried. I have children by my first husband and by my present husband. My first husband is married again, and they have children. I wanted to be saved and visited a certain church. The people told me I would have to leave my present husband and go back to my first husband or I would go to hell." She burst into tears and wept uncontrollably.

I had the privilege of praying with that woman. I saw God's glory on her countenance; I heard praise from her lips. Jesus Christ gave her peace.

Enrichment From the Heart: May Christ's compassionate words of John 4:35 give me a bold new vision: "'Lift up your eyes and look at the fields, for they are already white for harvest!'"

Discipleship

Raymond E. Crowley

January, Week 1

READING THE BIBLE TO GROW SPIRITUALLY

Scripture: I press toward the goal for the prize of the upward call of God in Christ Jesus (Philippians 3:14).

Enrichment From the Word: The Apostle Paul's goal was eternal life. In his daily walk with God, he always strove to put the past behind him and press forward for what lay ahead. Paul was willing to do whatever was necessary to serve Christ only and to know Him fully—in "the power of His resurrection, and the fellowship of His sufferings, being conformed to His death" (v. 10).

In our continuing walk with God, victory will come only if we do not allow life's pressures to rob us of our daily time with God.

Enrichment From the Church: A scene in Madras, India, is imprinted forever on my mind. Brother Lovell Cary took me to a Hindu temple where I saw poor, starving people lined up to worship a Hindu god. They stood in the blazing sun with an orange, a tiny banana, and a rupee or two, hoping with their sacrificial gifts to appease the wrath of a god who did not even exist. Two-thirds of them were so malnourished you could count their ribs.

How pitiful our devotional lives often are when compared with the efforts of those Hindus! They gave out of their need to a god who was dead, yet we fail to give due time to the living God who died on our behalf. "Pressing toward the goal" through daily study and prayer is no easy task, but there is no substitute.

Enrichment From the Heart: Satan's opposing powers will do everything possible to deter us from having a strong devotional life, but let us seek to ever know Christ more until He comes.

Discipleship

January, Week 1

Raymond E. Crowley

RECOGNIZING GOD'S VOICE

Scripture: Jesus spoke to them, saying, "Be of good cheer! It is I; do not be afraid" (Matthew 14:27).

Enrichment From the Word: When Jesus appeared in the midst of the storm on the Sea of Galilee, the disciples cried out in fear, thinking Him to be a ghost or some type of apparition. The Lord spoke, "Be of good cheer! It is I."

What powerful words! Regardless of the storm, when Jesus speaks, His words bring relief from fear, depression and gloom. No matter the circumstances, where His voice is heard, there is hope, life and happiness.

Enrichment From the Church: When we get out of earshot of God's voice, fear is near. We are going under. The trials and storms of life are too great for human strength. We cannot make it alone.

On the little island where I grew up as a boy, there were a number of large fish trawlers, powerful oceangoing boats which were well-prepared for most ocean storms. But on one occasion severe storm warnings were posted. Boats were anchored, and everyone prepared to wait out the winds—all, that is, except one captain who had been drinking and announced he was going to take his boat out. Men begged him not to go, but he ignored them, saying, "I'll go out, or I'll go to hell."

Neither the vessel nor any of the men on board were ever seen again. Days later, salvage crews found one small piece of timber which could have been part of the boat.

Enrichment From the Heart: Whatever your circumstances, Jesus is trying to speak to you. Don't let the noise of sickness, financial troubles, sin or other problems drown out His voice. He has your answer. Listen and you will hear Jesus say, "It is I; do not be afraid."

Discipleship

Raymond E. Crowley

RESPONDING TO GOD'S PLAN

Scripture: Present your bodies a living sacrifice, holy, acceptable to God, which is your reasonable service. . . . Be transformed by the renewing of your mind, that you may prove what is that good and acceptable and perfect will of God (Romans 12:1, 2).

Enrichment From the Word: These two verses capture the essence of God's plan for our lives. We are to give ourselves completely to God, letting Him transform us through His Spirit. Then verse 3 adds this warning: We must not think of ourselves "more highly than . . . [we] ought to think."

Pride is devastating to God's plan for us. When Elijah was faced with Jezebel's threats, he proudly thought that he was the only one left who was right—that he was God's only standard-bearer. But God told Elijah he had 7,000 followers who had not bowed a knee to Baal (1 Kings 19:13-18).

Enrichment From the Church: I have known men who were at one time sound leaders. They established good churches and were a blessing to people. But as people gave them love, applause and honor, they forgot they were only human. They were not able to handle success.

When any man, in the slightest manner, begins to direct attention to himself, begins to put himself up as an equal to our Lord Jesus Christ, begins to toy around with the true meaning of Scripture, we had better turn from that leader and run.

Enrichment From the Heart: When we become self-centered, we had better take inventory. When we crucify the flesh and the affections thereof, letting God's Spirit transform us, we will find God's perfect plan for us.

Discipleship

Raymond E. Crowley

January, Week 1

DISPLAYING GOD'S POWER

Scripture: "Behold, I send the Promise of My Father upon you; but tarry in the city of Jerusalem until you are endued with power from on high" (Luke 24:49).

Enrichment From the Word: Jesus commanded His disciples not to depart from Jerusalem but to wait for the promised Holy Spirit. As they waited, a spirit of unity prevailed. "When the Day of Pentecost had fully come, they were all with one accord in one place. And suddenly there came a sound from heaven, as of a rushing mighty wind. . . . And they were all filled with the Holy Spirit and began to speak with other tongues, as the Spirit gave them utterance" (Acts 2:1, 4).

Enrichment From the Church: I'll never forget the spiritual power I saw displayed when W. T. Ainsworth and I visited a minister in Dallas, Texas. We walked into this very humble home, and I saw a brother who was struggling with cancer. There were medical devices all around him, and connectors from these machines seemed to go to every part of his body. The man could not have weighed a hundred pounds, but he greeted us with an exuberance I could hardly believe. When we prayed I heard the man give glowing expressions of worship and praise. The power of the Holy Spirit came upon him, and it seemed he would rise from the bed.

Brother Ainsworth and I had gone to minister to this brother, but he ministered to us instead.

Enrichment From the Heart: The Holy Spirit has been my Comforter for 50 years. When I haven't known how to pray as I ought, the Holy Spirit has prayed through me. When I have had problems I could not handle, the Holy Spirit has helped me. When I have not had the wisdom needed to make decisions, the Holy Spirit has given me wisdom.

Self-Help

January, Week 2

Hoyt E. Stone

ESTABLISHING PERSONAL GOALS

Scripture: I will lift up my eyes to the hills—From whence comes my help? My help comes from the Lord, Who made heaven and earth (Psalm 121:1, 2).

Enrichment From the Word: The psalmist was practical, cut from the cloth of today's entrepreneur, business adventurer or spiritual leader. He realized his need of help, he knew such help had to come from a source of strength beyond himself, and he had faith enough, courage enough, grit enough to spotlight inner spiritual values and call upon God.

Would that we today could show such wisdom! Self-help is a popular subject—respected, revered, splashed on every bookstore shelf across our nation and around the world—but no man must forget there are limits to human strength. Only God is in control, and like the psalmist, we help ourselves most by establishing that personal goal of an ever-renewing relationship with the heavenly Father.

Enrichment From the Church: The setting was the hospital room of an elderly parishioner. Frank Rostin was feeble, showing the scars of time and 35 years in the coal mines. "This is it, Preacher. God's going to take me home. Doc sez I'm dying."

The Holy Spirit must have prompted my answer. "Sure, you're dying. So am I. And so is Dr. Thomas . . . and everybody else around here . . . but only God knows exactly when."

Frank looked at me a moment. Reached out his arms. We hugged, and he laughed. Within two days he was home again, waiting with a big yellow apple for his pastor to come visit.

Enrichment From the Heart: Dear God, thank You for the presence and comfort of Your Holy Spirit, for knowing that the *first* of all my personal goals is the necessity of staying in touch with You.

Self-Help   January, Week 2

Hoyt E. Stone

BUILDING SELF-ESTEEM

Scripture: What is man that You are mindful of him, And the son of man that You visit him? For You have made him a little lower than the angels, And You have crowned him with glory and honor. You have made him to have dominion over the works of Your hands; You have put all things under his feet (Psalm 8:4-6).

Enrichment From the Word: Modern science, based on evolutionary concepts, sees us only as an animal. Even present environmental arguments set forth ecological claims as if animals of the wild have the same claim to this earth as do men. When it comes to self-esteem, some of us fall into this same error. We compare ourselves with other, what seem to be more noteworthy, individuals, and we look in the mirror with disappointment. The Bible tells us the truth—about our world and ourselves. Self-esteem begins with realization of the high and lofty position God has bestowed already upon us, His creation.

Enrichment From the Church: A child on the school playground was being bullied, plagued and put upon by classmates. They taunted him, abused him and finally brought him to tears. With smudged face, and just when his tormentors thought they had won the day, the boy pressed his lips into a determined line, wiped away his tears and said defiantly, "That's all right. No matter what you say or think, my mother loves me." A beautiful truth. No matter what, God loves us. This is a promise which can renew hope and bring strength during even the blackest hour.

Enrichment From the Heart: Help us, Lord, to remember that we belong to You and that You never fail in Your high and lofty purposes.

Self-Help January, Week 2

Hoyt E. Stone

BUILDING SELF-CONFIDENCE

Scripture: I can do all things through Christ who strengthens me (Philippians 4:13).

Enrichment From the Word: There is indeed a fine line between carnal self-confidence—presumptuous self-will which foolishly thinks youth is forever and life indestructible—and Christian faith in self as an instrument of God's service and grace to others. Paul understood this distinction and zeroed in on the latter when he wrote, "I can do all things through Christ who strengthens me" (Philippians 4:13). Our minds, our bodies, our senses and perceptions—they are limited; but God has no limitations. This realization is the cornerstone of all Christian accomplishments.

Enrichment From the Church: In his mid-50s, when others were reaping the fruit of their ministerial labors, A. E. Lewis found himself led of the Holy Spirit to begin a new church in Dale City, a suburb of Washington, D.C. He knew others had failed in that same location, he knew he himself didn't have great talent nor the educational advantages some possessed, but he also knew the burning of his heart. So through faith and the application of every available talent he possessed, he took a handful of people and built them into a thriving congregation (The **Church of God Evangel**, "Divine Orders: You Can Trust Them," June 1988).

Enrichment From the Heart: Teach us, O God, that You always do, and forever will, grant strength for the tasks You send our way. Our reliance on self rests in confidence in You.

Self-Help

January, Week 2

Hoyt E. Stone

FOCUSING ON MORAL STANDARDS

Scripture: Exodus 20:3-17

Enrichment From the Word: Through Moses, God revealed to us the Ten Commandments. Not suggestions, as someone has facetiously noted, but commandments. While some spoof the value of these, life confirms their relevance; and even those who verbally deny them are caught up in the penalty of disobedience. God's moral code reads: (1) Worship no other gods; (2) bow to no graven images; (3) don't use God's name in vain; (4) remember and respect the Sabbath; (5) honor your parents. Negatively God commands: (6) Don't kill; (7) don't commit adultery; (8) don't steal; (9) don't lie (or bear false witness); and (10) don't covet.

Enrichment From the Church: No individual can ignore God's moral standards with impunity. After watching our nation go through the sexual revolution of the 60s' and 70s', followed by the plague of AIDS and other sexually transmitted diseases, and after seeing the media so glaringly portray what happens to those in government, civic and church life who ignore honesty and uprightness, we have to realize this truth far more vividly than ever before.

Enrichment From the Heart: By Your grace, O Lord, I herewith commit myself again to respect for and adherence to, Your holy statutes, within which alone can be found happiness and peace of mind.

Self-Help   January, Week 2

Hoyt E. Stone

HONORING THE BODY AS A TEMPLE

Scripture: Your body is the temple of the Holy Spirit (1 Corinthians 6:19).

Enrichment From the Word: It is significant that Paul addressed these words to the church at Corinth, for in this congregation were men and women snatched from the slavery of heathenism at its worst. They lived in the heart of wicked Corinth, a city known for debauchery that would vie well with San Francisco or Miami today. Yet, in the midst of all this, Paul reminded believers the human body—not just the mind or the spirit but the whole being—is a temple of the Holy Spirit which must always reflect the love and righteousness of God.

Enrichment From the Church: In the winter of 1982 I met Todd Hafner, a teenage drug user, recuperating at Peniel Ministries outside Harrisburg, Pennsylvania. Last week I lunched with him in a local restaurant. He's now president of the senior class at Lee College, walking a new road, on his way to a life of ministry for Jesus Christ. No sermon however eloquent, no article however well-written can approximate the testimony of Todd's changed life. That miracle is the power of the gospel . . . in Todd's life . . . yours . . . and mine. It remains the central truth this world can't deny or escape.

Enrichment From the Heart: Our Father, who art in heaven . . . Thy kingdom come, Thy will be done, on earth (in my life), as it is in heaven. In Jesus' name. Amen.

Nurture   **January, Week 3**

Marcus V. Hand

GOD'S PROMISE FOR PEACE

Scripture: You will keep him in perfect peace, Whose mind is stayed on You, Because he trusts in You (Isaiah 26:3).

Enrichment From the Word: Against a backdrop of national distress and anguish, the prophet announces impending judgment. Broken covenants and forgotten commitments have brought the nation low: a sense of doom grips the people. In the midst of this prophetic message, there appears a liturgy of praise and promise. The heart of that promise—God's promise—is contained in this verse. It is a promise for peace in the midst of turmoil.

"The Lord . . . will speak peace To his people and to His saints" (Psalm 85:8). "The Lord will bless His people with peace" (Psalm 29:11). Jesus also promised, "Peace I leave with you, My peace I give to you" (John 14:27).

Enrichment From the Church: In 1939 British Prime Minister Neville Chamberlain met with German Chancellor Adolph Hitler and proclaimed, "Peace in our time." Within months Nazi troops had invaded Czechoslovakia. Six months later Hitler's forces attacked Poland, and the most catastrophic, worldwide war in history was under way. Man's search for world peace had failed again.

World peace can come only through personal peace, inner peace. Many today are using numerology, handwriting analysis, quartz crystals, biofeedback, palmistry, parapsychology, psychic readings, "pyramid power" and other "New Age" techniques to try to obtain peace of mind. They are being deluded by promises of holistic health and mind-stretching power.

Peace comes from the Prince of Peace. God promises peace to those whose hearts are fixed.

Enrichment From the Heart: Thank You, Father, because Jesus, the Prince of Peace, abides in my heart. I rest in You.

Nurture   **January, Week 3**

Marcus V. Hand

ACCEPTING GOD'S PROMISES FOR POWER

Scripture: To Him who is able to do exceedingly abundantly above all that we ask or think, according to the power that works in us (Ephesians 3:20).

Enrichment From the Word: Think of the awesome majesty of God's power. He who created worlds out of nothing and made man from the dust of the earth, He who raised up nations to do His will and destroyed the ones that rejected Him, He who stood beside Daniel in a lion's den and walked with the three Hebrew boys in the fiery furnace is alive in the world today. His power is at work in you!

Enrichment From the Church: George Washington Carver, an outstanding black leader, said he once prayed, "Lord, reveal to me the secret of the peanut." In his unique way Carver said the Lord answered back, "You got brains; figure it out yourself!" And Carver did.

I like that story. When God shows His power, He usually does it through a person. Whether making a scientific discovery, influencing a nation or changing the course of history, God works through men. He heals when men lay hands on the sick and pray the prayer of faith. He quickens, makes alive, our mortal bodies by the same power that raised Jesus from the dead.

God can do more than we ask or think; but He will do it through His power at work in us!

Enrichment From the Heart: Thank You, Father, for Your power in me through the Holy Spirit. It is **dunamis**, potential power. It is **energeia**, operational power. It is **ischys**, inherent power. It is **kratos**, controlled power. I submit myself to be used by You.

Nurture   **January, Week 3**

Marcus V. Hand

ACHIEVING VICTORY OVER DEPRESSION

Scripture: Why are you cast down, O my soul? And why are you disquieted within me? Hope in God (Psalm 42:11).

Enrichment From the Word: In happier times the psalmist went with the festive throngs to the house of God. Now he is depressed. He avoids people. He feels abandoned, forgotten by friends and God. Passersby see him weeping. They scornfully ask, "Where *is* your God?" Instead of despairing, however, the psalmist thirsts for the Lord (v. 2). He remembers God's love and God's song (v. 8). He concludes that with his trust and hope in God, "I shall yet praise Him . . . [my Savior] and my God" (v. 11).

Enrichment From the Church: Down times can be especially distressful to the human spirit. Everybody gets the blues sometimes. Our emotions, like the changing tides and shifting winds, echo an eternal rhythm. Peaks of activity and concentrated effort are inevitably followed by valleys of comparative melancholy and frustration. Why are we humans made this way?

Perhaps it is God's way of telling us there are times when we need to be refreshed, renewed. Periodically, we need to unwind the spring of our emotions. We need to relax, to break the taut, twisted strands of tension caused by certain kinds of effort, events and people. We need to be unleashed for greater service.

Enrichment From the Heart: I resolve to take advantage of my down times. I will use them as opportunities to draw closer to God, to renew my inner resources. I know the tide will change. And I know that the ebb and flow of my emotions do not affect God. He is my hope!

Nurture   **January, Week 3**

Marcus V. Hand

ACHIEVING VICTORY OVER FEAR

Scripture: You did not receive the spirit of bondage again to fear. . . . The Spirit Himself bears witness with our spirit that we are children of God (Romans 8:15, 16).

Enrichment From the Word: Romans 8 talks about life in the Spirit. The Christian is set free by the power of God's Son and is no longer a slave to the flesh and sin. Liberated, he lives according to the Spirit. This spiritual living produces life and peace, the opposite of the bondage of fear. The Holy Spirit frees from fear!

Enrichment From the Church: When its first cry shatters the air in the birthing room, a new baby comes equipped with two fears—the fear of falling and the fear of loud noises. All other fears, psychologists tell us, are learned. Some, like the fear of a rattlesnake, are healthy. Most, however, are deadly.

Sister Maude—pillar in the church, elderly, a widow—became ill and called her pastor. In her room I leaned close and heard her terrified whisper, "I've got cancer!"

"Have you been to the doctor?" I queried. "No," she confided, "but I know. Remember my best friend who died from cancer two months ago? I've got the same symptoms. I'm going to die, too."

For weeks Sister Maude was bedfast. Finally, we persuaded her to check into the hospital for a physical examination. She walked out four days later with a clean bill of health, feeling great! Fear had made her physically sick!

Enrichment From the Heart: "God has not given us a spirit of fear, but of power and of love and of a sound mind" (2 Timothy 1:7). Therefore, I will surrender my fears to Him.

Nurture   January, Week 3

Marcus V. Hand

ACHIEVING VICTORY OVER ANGER

Scripture: Let all bitterness, wrath, anger, clamor, and evil speaking be put away from you, with all malice (Ephesians 4:31).

Enrichment From the Word: Continual irritation causes resentment. Resentment, unresolved, leads to bitterness. The next step is wrath (**thumos**), a flare of temper, flying off the handle. If it continues, it becomes anger (**orge**)—long-lived and habitual. This in turn leads to loud talking and insulting language. Thus, in one short verse the Bible gives a technical description of the progression of the sin of anger. Put it away from you, the scripture says.

Enrichment From the Church: The news item said the man died from injuries he received while golfing on Easter Sunday! It seems the Chalmette, Louisiana, businessman became angry during a game at the City Park golf course and threw his club against the motorized golf cart. The club broke, boomeranged back into the irate golfer's neck and severed his jugular vein! Uncontrolled anger always boomerangs. Smoldering resentment exploding in an outburst of anger hurts the angry person much more than it hurts the object of his anger.

You will probably get angry sometime, Paul indicates in verses 26 and 27; but follow these guidelines: When you get angry, (1) do not sin, (2) get over it quickly, and (3) don't give place to the devil.

Victory is achieved through the fruit of the Spirit called self-control. Don't deny your anger; harness it, and use it for a creative purpose.

Enrichment From the Heart: Heavenly Father, I recognize misplaced anger as a burning fuse of hostility. Help me to get rid of anger in my life before it destroys me and everything dear to me. In Jesus' name!

The Holy Spirit   January, Week 4

Lewis J. Willis

GROWING THE FRUIT OF THE SPIRIT—LOVE

Scripture: But, speaking the truth in love, may grow up in all things into Him who is the head—Christ— (Ephesians 4:15).

Enrichment From the Word: All elements in the Fruit of the Spirit must spring from the ultimate source of love. God, of course, is the essence of and the source of love which is foundational to the believer becoming all he should be in Christ. Therefore, the "growing up" or maturing process whereby the believer takes on the identifying characteristics of a saint is to "walk in love" (Ephesians 5:2).

Enrichment From the Church: I saw him near the rear of the church. As I preached, I noticed how intently he looked toward me with anguished eyes. His face was rigid and hard. There was something forbidding about his countenance. Later I would be told he was one of the meanest men in the area. When the altar service began, he came forward very slowly but deliberately.

As he knelt and lifted his face with eyes closed, he didn't appear to pray any prayer for a long time. Then I saw it begin to happen. It was the miracle of God's love converting a soul. First, the tears squeezed from weary eyes to course down those taunt cheeks. As God's love washed his heart and infused his spirit, he changed before my eyes. Then came joy, peace and gentle countenance. As love did its perfect work, this scarred man developed into a worthy saint.

Enrichment From the Heart: Oh God, please help me to be yielded constantly to the processing of Your love in my life. Teach me more perfectly to think with Your love, to speak with Your love and to serve with Your love. Amen.

The Holy Spirit

January, Week 4

Lewis J. Willis

GROWING THE FRUIT OF THE SPIRIT—JOY

Scripture: You will show me the path of life; In Your presence is fullness of joy; At Your right hand are pleasures forevermore (Psalm 16:11).

Enrichment From the Word: There is absolutely no doubt that God intends that the "path of life" we each take will have sufficient wells of joy from which we may be refreshed. We grow in this element of the fruit of the Spirit by learning how to stay close to God. In the "presence" of God there "is fullness of joy" and also "pleasures forevermore."

Enrichment From the Church: It was a long journey that would involve weeks and would continue around the world. Quickly I felt alone and sad. She who was so much a part of me was on the other side of the universe and then I found the notes and she spoke to me and I was with her in spirit and I had joy. Again it was night and I was tired and lonely. Then by telephone I spoke to her thousands of miles away but her voice made her very near and I had joy. Eventually, the plane touched native soil again and she was there and the anguish of the weeks was gone and my joy was full.

We often feel very much alone in life and we struggle but Christ speaks to us through Holy Scriptures and because of his promises there is joy. When we are surrounded on every side by our evil adversary, we always have the opportunity to take our problem to God through prayer. God always answers and there is reason for joy. Christ is coming again—soon. That is reason for ultimate joy.

Enrichment From the Heart: Now to Him who is able to keep you from stumbling, And to present you faultless Before the presence of His glory with exceeding joy, To God our Savior, Who alone is wise, Be glory and majesty, Dominion and power, Both now and forever. Amen (Jude 24, 25).

The Holy Spirit   January, Week 4
Lewis J. Willis

GROWING THE FRUIT OF THE SPIRIT—PEACE

Scripture: And the peace of God, which surpasses all understanding, will guard your hearts and minds through Christ Jesus (Philippians 4:7).

Enrichment From the Word: The peace of God comes to the person who ceases to be at war with God. When a full surrender is made and Christ is acknowledged to be the one true Lord, then peace prevails and pervades. Also, the dimension of this peace is beyond all understanding for it brings tranquility of spirit that the individual never dreamed to be possible.

Enrichment From the Church: It was a very dark night and many strange noises echoed through the gloominess around us. Daniel, my small grandson, tugged at my hand and said, "Papa, I'm scared down here!" I lifted Daniel to my shoulders and we walked through the darkness until we arrived at the well lighted area. Daniel then announced proudly, "It was really dark out there but papa and I made it fine, didn't we, Papa?" Of course we made it! You and I will make it fine with our Heavenly Father also. Sometimes it is scary where we are and we feel very much alone. Our Lord knows where we are and what our circumstances are. If necessary, in our most terrifying storm our Lord will come walking on the very waves which seek to destroy us. Sometimes he speaks to the waves to be still and sometimes he lifts us out of the waves but we can be very sure that if we stay with Jesus "we will make it fine."

Enrichment From the Heart: Dear Lord, help us to understand that so long as we are in this wicked world, we will have some bad times. Also help us, Lord, to know that our worst times are the best times for You to speak peace to our hearts. Amen.

The Holy Spirit — January, Week 4

Lewis J. Willis

GROWING THE FRUIT OF THE SPIRIT— LONG SUFFERING (PATIENCE)

Scripture: But let patience have its perfect work, that you may be perfect and complete, lacking nothing (James 1:4).

Enrichment From the Word: Patience and/or long-suffering is the result of spiritual discipline. This very special grace comes when one is able to persevere in tribulations. Paul valued the outgrowth or harvest of this experience so much that he said, "tribulation produces perserverance" (Romans 5:3-5).

We see, therefore, that patience emerges from successful encounters with tribulation. Patience, thereafter, continues to effect within the believer a "perfect work" or a developing or maturing influence. According to our text the person who continues to develop patience will become complete, "lacking nothing."

Enrichment From the Church: He sat in a swing on the porch and taught me. I was young and eager to learn everything I needed to know quickly. Gently and patiently the good man dealt with my overzealous queries. He quietly spoke to my impetuous ideas. Soon my hurried, impassioned rush to gather bushels of information was tempered and I sat hushed and relaxed as he taught me patiently.

He talked about himself and his life's journey. He spoke of his feverish urgency to learn and to attain. Then he spoke of the painful times when he suffered a crucible, but said, "I learned that life is not simply a formula or quotient. Rather it is made of understanding, of sharing, of caring, and serving." The old man showed me that day the results of tribulation—it was patience to deal with a very immature young man.

Enrichment From the Heart: I pray "that you may have a walk worthy of the Lord, fully pleasing Him, being fruitful in every good work and increasing in the knowledge of God; strengthened with all might, according to His glorious power, for all patience and longsuffering with joy" (Colossians 1:10, 11).

The Holy Spirit   January, Week 4

Lewis J. Willis

GROWING THE FRUIT OF THE SPIRIT—GENTLENESS (KINDNESS)

Scripture: Therefore, as the elect of God, holy and beloved, put on tender mercies, kindness, humbleness of mind, meekness, longsuffering (Colossians 3:12).

Enrichment From the Word: Dr. Ralph W. Sockman correctly stated, "Gentleness is a divine trait; nothing is so strong as gentleness, and nothing is so gentle as real strength."

Gentleness and/or kindness is a consequence of a maturity in the Christian faith which expresses compassion in a proper attitude and action. Paul said, "And the servant of the Lord must not quarrel but be gentle to all," (2 Timothy 2:24).

Enrichment From the Church: He was the Assistant General Overseer of the Church of God and I was a struggling young preacher in Florida. One day when I was particularly overwhelmed with the responsibilities and stresses of Christian ministry I received the letter. It said, "Today I am thinking about you and I am praying for you to be the yielded servant of Christ. Be encouraged, God will see you through." It was signed, R. P. Johnson.

The awe and wonder of that great servant of God taking time to write me in Florida all the way from California amazed me. I didn't even know this extraordinary preacher even knew about me! But there it was—a warm, caring, gentle letter speaking to a very vulnerable young man. That special kindness made a significant difference in me and my ministry. I never forgot Brother Johnson, and I hope I never forget the example he gave me about the grace of kindness.

Enrichment From the Heart: Dear God, help me to do what I can do to change this ugly, harsh, selfish world by seeking opportunities to let Your gentleness and kindness flow out of my life to others.

Worship   February, Week 1

Rebecca J. Jenkins

WORSHIPPING IN THE CHURCH

Scripture: I was glad when they said to me, "Let us go into the house of the Lord" (Psalm 122:1).

Enrichment From the Word: However important we may feel at work or at home, in God's house there is a sense of His greatness and our smallness. As we meditate on His majesty, we want to bow down and worship Him. We can learn much about the attitude of worship from the prophetic vision recorded in Isaiah 6. The seraphim each had six wings. Of the six, four were used to indicate their sense of unworthiness in the presence of God. As we worship Him in church, we should come in honesty, in humility and with sincerity. Gratitude in our heart causes us to want to adore Him.

Enrichment From the Church: How long has it been since you were glad at the mention or thought of going to His house? Such gladness is rare today. We have all heard the question, "If you were accused of being a Christian, would there be enough evidence to convict you?" Ask yourself, "If a stranger came into my church on a typical Sunday morning looking for happy people, would he even glance at me?" No matter how much we try to conceal or pretend, true joy in worship will be detected. More importantly, the One who desires our worship is looking for our joy in worship.

Enrichment From the Heart: We can sense God's presence at home, at work or anywhere if our hearts are sensitive to the Holy Spirit; however, the house of God is a designated place set apart for this purpose.

Worship

February, Week 1

Rebecca J. Jenkins

WORSHIPPING WITH YOUR FAMILY

Scripture: Says the Lord. . . . "As the heavens are higher than the earth, So are My ways higher than your ways, And My thoughts than your thoughts" (Isaiah 55:8, 9).

Enrichment From the Word: Remember when your parents checked on Saturday to be certain your shoes were polished and your best outfit was clean and mended? You knew church on Sunday was something important. Worship was talked about all week long and the blessings experienced in the worship service were discussed around the table. They uplifted and encouraged. We went about our work each day of the week with a song in our hearts.

Families who worship together find it easier to desire God's will for their lives. As we worship Him and experience a renewed sense of the nearness and goodness of God, we can say, "Lord, replace my small thoughts with Your much higher thoughts. Not my way, heavenly Father, but Yours." As we gain this attitude, we will enjoy fullness of life.

Enrichment From the Church: I remember family reunions when all my brothers and sisters and their families were present. Our dad, a retired minister, was with us. We experienced warmth and gratitude as memories flooded our minds of growing up in the church and being taught by our godly parents to love and trust Him.

Enrichment From the Heart: Sunday is the most important day in the week for my family. Heavenly Father, please help me and each family member to always have a song of praise in our heart.

Worship

February, Week 1

Rebecca J. Jenkins

WORSHIPPING WITH FRIENDS

Scripture: "When he comes home, he calls together his friends and neighbors, saying to them, 'Rejoice with me, for I have found my sheep which was lost!'" (Luke 15:6).

Enrichment From the Word: While this verse refers to a sinner who repents, it points out how we like to include friends in our times of rejoicing. We also feel better when we can share our difficulties with friends. We are blessed when we have good friends.

Friends have differing ideas and viewpoints, but worship is one of the few things in which all can unite. That unity will extend to everyday life. God desires our praise; He merits our worship. Praise flowing from the heart blesses us, blesses our friends and blesses all who have assembled to worship.

Enrichment From the Church: At times I enter the church and feel disappointed when I don't see my closest friends. It is uplifting to see my friends in the church service. Worshiping with friends deepens the feeling of camaraderie. We feel each other's burdens in a deeper sense. As we praise God together for His tender mercy, as we worship our Ruler who guides us all "with His eye," and as we offer praise unto the Judge of all, we are strengthened. When we comprehend that God is love and sense His love, we are free to love our friends in a way we couldn't do before. Unified worship brings honor to Almighty God.

Enrichment From the Heart: Dear Lord, help me to never take for granted the friendships You have so graciously given me. Thank You for the privilege of worshiping with my friends.

Worship   **February, Week 1**

Rebecca J. Jenkins

WORSHIPPING THROUGH PRAISE

Scripture: Enter into His gates with thanksgiving, And into His courts with praise. Be thankful to Him, and bless His name (Psalm 100:4).

Enrichment From the Word: Why did God pronounce it good when man sprang forth from the dust of the earth? He was glad that man's eyes could behold God's glory, hear God's voice and praise Almighty God. Reflecting on His mercy, we now have no difficulty praising Him. Our very presence in church is an act of obedience and praise. We honor Him in silence and with a feeling of awe. We are thankful for His mercy and truth.

Enrichment From the Church: The New England colonists endured many privations and difficulties. They were distressed and became gloomy and discontented. A proposal was made to appoint a day of fasting and prayer. In the meeting a plain, common-sense old colonist remarked he thought they had brooded long enough over their misfortunes and that it seemed high time they should consider some of God's mercies. The colony was growing strong, the fields increasing in harvest, the rivers full of fish and the woods of game; the air was sweet, the climate salubrious and their homes happy. Above all, they possessed what they came for—full civil and religious liberty. Therefore, on the whole, he would amend their resolution for a fast and propose in its stead a day of thanksgiving. His advice was taken, and from that day to this the festival has been an annual one.

Enrichment From the Heart: An attitude of thankfulness helps us learn to make the best, not the worst, of our circumstances.

Worship February, Week 1

Rebecca J. Jenkins

WORSHIPPING IN SPIRIT AND TRUTH

Scripture: "God is Spirit, and those who worship Him must worship in spirit and truth" (John 4:24).

Enrichment From the Word: The human soul can worship the divine Spirit; there can be intimate communion between the two. Man's spirit was created in the likeness of the heavenly Father; therefore, he is capable of praising and thanking God. To enjoy this unique fellowship, we must worship Him in truth. God, our Creator, is spiritual in nature and is worthy of human worship.

"It is written: 'Eye has not seen, nor ear heard, Nor have entered into the heart of man The things which God has prepared for those who love Him.' But God has revealed them to us through His Spirit. For the Spirit searches all things, yes, the deep things of God. For what man knows the things of a man except the spirit of the man which is in him? Even so no one knows the things of God except the Spirit of God" (1 Corinthians 2:9-11).

Enrichment From the Church: I once heard a minister say, "Worship God's face, not His hands." He was telling us to worship Him for who He is, not for what He does for us. Our worship must be sincere with knowledge of the One we worship. True worship involves our lives as well as our voices. It is not merely lip service but comes from the heart. Worship exalts and perfects the affections. It purifies and dignifies the whole nature.

Enrichment From the Heart: No one knows the thoughts of God except the Spirit. What privileged people we are to worship Him in Spirit and in truth and to be assisted in worship by His Spirit!

Personal Organization   February, Week 2

Donald T. Pemberton

SETTING PERSONAL GOALS

Scripture: "Go, tell that fox, 'Behold, I cast out demons and perform cures today and tomorrow, and the third day I shall be perfected'" (Luke 13:32).

Enrichment From the Word: The exact meaning of Jesus' reply is not clear. The real idea is that His future is charted, He has set His goal, and Herod is powerless to divert Him from attaining His goal. He will complete what He has come to do. His decision to go to Jerusalem is not due to pressure brought by government officials but because of His commitment to attain to His goal, His destiny. He set His goal! No goal is reached that is not first set. Paul said in 2 Corinthians 5:9, "So we make it our goal to please him" (*NIV*). There are many personal goals we could set, but none more worthy.

Enrichment From the Church: It is said that Aldous Huxley was once on his way to attend a meeting of the British association in Dublin but arrived late at the station. Hurriedly he jumped into a jaunting car and ordered the coachman to "drive fast."

Away went the cab, jolting over the streets, and finally Huxley inquired of the driver, "Do you know where you are going?" He answered with a grin, "No, I do not know where we are going, but we are going fast."

Without setting personal goals in life which we hope to reach, we may be going in the fast lane, but not really getting anywhere.

Enrichment From the Heart: Lord, do not allow me to flounder aimlessly through life, but help me to reach toward the goals You want me to reach during this life.

Personal Organization   **February, Week 2**

Donald T. Pemberton

PLANNING THOROUGHLY

Scripture: "Surely, as I have planned, so it will be" (Isaiah 14:24, *NIV*). The noble man makes noble plans (Isaiah 32:8, *NIV*).

Enrichment From the Word: It is evident throughout Scripture that God thoroughly planned the Creation, completed in six-days with rest on the seventh. He meticulously planned the way, the method and the timing of the coming of His only begotten Son into this world to redeem fallen man. Each step, each episode of the great drama was thoroughly planned to include the many prophecies in the Old Testament and the pointing out of the fulfillment of those prophecies in the New Testament. The choosing of Mary to bring to this world the Christ child, the birth in the manger and events that followed were conceived in the mind of God.

Enrichment From the Church: Neaton, the great French surgeon, once said that if he had four minutes in which to perform an operation on which a life depended, he would take one minute to consider (to plan) how best to do it.

If matters of mundane life dictate that we should plan, how very much more should we plan the work of the Lord—matters of spiritual life, matters that impinge on the spiritual wellness of those we love!

Enrichment From the Heart: Lord, teach me to know the blessings of a well-planned day and a well-planned life so that my effectiveness for You will be maximized.

Personal Organization   **February, Week 2**

Donald T. Pemberton

REVIEWING REGULARLY

Scripture: I call to remembrance the genuine faith that is in you, which dwelt first in your grandmother Lois and your mother Eunice, and I am persuaded is in you also (2 Timothy 1:5).

Enrichment From the Word: Paul recalls specifically Timothy's sincere faith as he reviews their relationship. He further reviews Timothy's heritage. Timothy's grandmother and mother, whom Paul reveals further in a personal reference, were Timothy's forerunners in the faith. They testify, as have many others, to the importance of parental example in the instruction of children. From childhood they had taught Timothy from the Scriptures. It is good to review our heritage in the Lord, regularly remembering those who have contributed so much to our maturity in Jesus Christ. We need to take stock of how we have built upon that foundation which we have received.

Enrichment From the Church: Gypsy Smith was speaking to a Rotary Club meeting years ago. He lifted high his well-worn Bible. "How many of you men can recall a saintly mother and a godly father who loved this Book, read it, lived it and seeped it into you?"

Practically the entire group, with moist eyes, raised their hands. Then, quietly Gypsy swung home deftly this shaft: "With all your influence today, how many of you are so living that your children will remember you for your faithfulness to this same Book?" What a probing question!

Enrichment From the Heart: Lord, give us the grace and the ability to constantly review our lives and our heritage, and may we so live that our children can remember us because of the faith that we have instilled in them.

Personal Organization   February, Week 2

Donald T. Pemberton

LEARNING TO MAKE ADJUSTMENTS

Scripture: "Assuredly, I say to you, unless you are converted and become as little children, you will by no means enter the kingdom of heaven" (Matthew 18:3).

Enrichment From the Word: Jesus answered the disciples' question in verse 1 about greatness by means of an actual parable, placing a child in their midst. The requirement that those entering the Kingdom "become like little children" closely parallels the "birth from above" analogy in John 3:3. To "enter the kingdom" means that one must start life over with basically new attitudes, values, trust and commitment. In other words, learn to adjust to changes which God demands from time to time of all of us. Coping with life's problems and difficulties often demand that we make adjustment to our lifestyle, attitudes and views.

Enrichment From the Church: There was a team of horses pulling a very heavy load of logs. As they came to a hard place, they struggled and tried with all their force, strained every muscle to the highest tension, but they could not start the load. The driver took some of the logs off and tried to get them to start the load, but they would not. He rolled off some more, but those horses would not start. He rolled off still more and at last took off every log, and then they started up the road.

Those horses had been utterly discouraged. They had pulled with all their strength and failed. Neither man nor beast when utterly discouraged can accomplish half as much as one who has not lost heart. The challenge in trying circumstances is to learn to adjust to the difficulty and not to lose heart.

Enrichment From the Heart: Dear Lord, please give me the grace to be flexible in the crucibles of life and the wisdom to adjust to them.

Personal Organization February, Week 2

Donald T. Pemberton

MAINTAINING MOTIVATION

Scripture: For the love of Christ constrains us, because we judge thus: that if One died for all, then all died (2 Corinthians 5:14).

Enrichment From the Word: This is the view of Christ's death which made possible Paul's teaching on baptism in Romans 6. Baptism signifies not simply an acceptance that Christ died to set the believer free but that the believer participates in the death that Christ died.

Enrichment From the Church: Hudson Taylor was interviewing some young people who had volunteered for the Lord's service. He asked several practical questions to find out how well qualified they were for the life they were anticipating. "And why do you wish to go as a foreign missionary?" "I want to reach others across the sea because Christ has commanded us to go into all the world and preach the gospel to every creature," one replied. Another said, "I want to go because millions are dying without ever having heard of Jesus, the only One who can save them."

Taylor said, "All your motives are good, but I fear they will fail you in times of severe testing and tribulation—especially if you are confronted with the possibility of having to face death for your testimony. The only motive that will enable you to remain true is in Christ's love constraining you."

Enrichment From the Heart: Lord, may my motivation always come from love for You and the knowledge of Your love for me!

Family Relationships   **February, Week 3**

Sonjia Hunt

NURTURING WHOLENESS IN THE FAMILY

Scripture: Behold, how good and how pleasant it is For brethren to dwell together in unity! (Psalm 133:1).

Enrichment From the Word: Jews and Gentiles often came together in the early church as brothers and sisters in Christ. The Jews, however, sometimes separated themselves from the Gentiles. It was a case of "older" siblings disdaining the "younger" ones. After all, the Jews had a greater knowledge of the Scriptures. They also were the first and "true" children of Abraham. Unity, a feeling of oneness or wholeness, was impossible to achieve where this situation existed. Paul wrote specifically to the Ephesians about the unity of the church. He used the human body as an analogy of the church. Christ is the head of the church, and each member is part of the Body. Each member of the Body has a different function, but none is without honor.

Enrichment From the Church: Susanna Wesley, mother of John and Charles Wesley, shared the daily spiritual and academic nurture of each of her six younger children with each of her five older children. The very oldest was given the very youngest, and so on, to tutor for one hour each week with each one individually, sharing privately. She also was careful that no child, especially the girls, spent more time on chores than on studying. This was somewhat "extravagant" in her day; however, one could hardly say her children were spoiled. Each child's gifts were channeled into service to others, first in the home and then in the world.

Enrichment From the Heart: Uncontrolled sibling rivalry, hectic lifestyles, confused priorities and increased emotional demands can create jigsaw puzzle families that can't seem to fit together. Today I submit to the One who can bring order and harmony to the puzzle—the Prince of Peace. Amen.

Family Relationships

February, Week 3

Sonjia Hunt

SETTING FAMILY GOALS

Scripture: "But seek first the kingdom of God and His righteousness, and all these things shall be added to you" (Matthew 6:33).

Enrichment From the Word: Christ never lacked illustrations for His spiritual lessons. His object lessons irritated those whose inner selves were exposed. They confused His students who could not yet grasp what He tried to teach them. Logic simply would not work. Why should those who want to be great have to become servants? How does giving result in receiving? Why does trying to save your life result in losing it? How can sowing to spiritual things result in earthly needs being met?

Enrichment From the Church: Paul Yonggi Cho wanted to build the largest church in the world (*The Fourth Dimension*, Logos International, 1979). He learned several laws of faith as he prayed for God to help him reach his goals. "When you have a clear goal, and you have this desire burning in your heart to a boiling point, then you should kneel down and pray until you receive the substance, the assurance" (p. 24). "It could sometimes take two minutes, two hours, two weeks, two months, or two years; but whatever the length of time, you should pray through until you have this substance" (pp. 24, 25). For the assurance of receiving the funds to build his church, he prayed three months—sometimes night and day. "Suddenly those five million dollars had turned into a small pebble on my palm. I prayed with assurance. My faith reached out, and I grabbed hold of that five million dollars; it was mine" (pp. 27, 28).

Enrichment From the Heart: God, help us as a family to set goals that would be pleasing to You. Help us to be willing to pay the cost of seeking our goals Your way and in Your time Amen

Family Relationships — February, Week 3

Sonjia Hunt

READING THE WORD TOGETHER

Scripture: There was not a word of all that Moses had commanded which Joshua did not read before all the congregation of Israel, with the women, the little ones, and the strangers who were living among them (Joshua 8:35).

Enrichment From the Word: God's law, as it was given to Moses, was housed first in the tabernacle and then in the Temple. To hear the Law read, one had to go to the tabernacle at the times God appointed or on special occasions announced by Israel's leaders. All Israel would gather, every family standing or sitting together. Sometimes the readings would take hours, and there were no public-address systems to transmit the voice of the reader. Although Israel had no written copies of the Word of God which they could take to their homes, each family talked daily of God's law. When Israel failed to listen to the Word together and failed to rehearse God's law with their children, the knowledge of God virtually disappeared. Idol worship revived, and God judged the nation. One could say the fate of the nation hung on families reading the Word together.

Enrichment From the Church: The Bible lay in plain view on the coffee table. I noted its well-preserved cover and marveled since several young children played constantly around it. I complimented the mother on her children's obvious respect for the Word. Her pleasure turned to chagrin as the 7-year-old commented, "Oh, we know *never* to touch the Bible. Mom reads to us out of it on Christmas. That is the only time we can touch it."

Enrichment From the Heart: God, Your Word is such a valuable gift that I must share it with those I love the most. Thank You for its life-giving and life-changing power. Amen.

Family Relationships February, Week 3

Sonjia Hunt

PRAYING TOGETHER

Scripture: "Again I say to you that if two of you agree on earth concerning anything that they ask, it will be done for them by My Father in heaven" (Matthew 18:19).

Enrichment From the Word: Christ emphasized the strength of praying in unity. This praying, however, is more than merely praying together. Christ's emphasis was on agreement, honesty, mutual caring and asking according to God's will.

Enrichment From the Church: God was not finished with Catherine Marshall when her husband Peter died at age 46. Although she envisioned a more sedate life, God directed her path across that of Len Lesourd and his three children, ages 3 to 9. Her life and her prayer time took on a new sense of adventure as well as a new partner. Len's prayer notebook contained the following entries: "(1) that household help be found so that Catherine can continue the writing of her novel *Christy*; (2) that Peter will forget trying to be a playboy at Yale and find God's purpose for his life; (3) that Linda will stop rebelling against authority at home and at school; (4) that Chester will learn to control his temper and accept his new home situation; (5) that we can find the way to get Jeff out of diapers at night" (*Meeting God at Every Turn*, p. 200). Catherine wrote, "And so Len and I have grown over the years as parents, and our morning time together has set the tone and direction of over 21 years of marriage. As early morning prayer partners we have added assurance that 'where two or three are gathered together' in His name, our all-loving and all-wise Savior, Rescuer and Lord is indeed with us" (p. 213).

Enrichment From the Heart: Thank You, God, for my family. Help us together to seek life's answers from You. Amen.

Family Relationships February, Week 3

Sonjia Hunt

ATTENDING CHURCH TOGETHER

<u>Scripture:</u> I was glad when they said to me, "Let us go into the house of the Lord" (Psalm 122:1).

Enrichment From the Word: Would the psalmist have rejoiced had he been compelled to go to church alone? No one can answer that, but it is clear that attendance at worship includes others. Worship is corporate as well as individual. And happiness and joy are associated with going to God's house to worship together. In the Old Testament there were times when only the men came to stand before God at the tabernacle. Whole families, however, were expected to gather at the designated feasts of celebration. All family members would eat the sacrifice together, at the tabernacle or Temple if possible.

Enrichment From the Church: "Hurry! We're late!" It's Sunday morning again. Why can't anyone get out of bed! Why does getting ready take twice as long? Where's his other sock? Who borrowed her dress? Oh no, why did the cows choose today to get in the yard? Sunday is supposed to be calm and serene—birds singing, sun shining, children smiling. Why is Sunday never like that? The neighbors seem to be quite relaxed. He's reading the paper. The children are riding their bikes. She's having another cup of coffee. No one's yelling. That's the way things should be done. Wonder why they're not dressed yet? Oh, they don't attend church.

Enrichment From the Heart: God, for my family's sake, help me to make Sunday more the kind of day that You would be pleased with. Help me to model the anticipation described by the psalmist. Help us as a family to realize the joy of going to church together to worship You. Amen.

Prayer February, Week 4

Benjamin B. McGlamery

PRAYING WITH PURPOSE

Scripture: "But when you pray, do not use vain repetitions as the heathen do. For they think that they will be heard for their many words" (Matthew 6:7).

Enrichment From the Word: Some people pray to praise; some pray to confess; others, to intercede. The Pharisees prayed to impress others. When addressing conversation to God, perhaps everyone who does so has a definite purpose in mind. The Lord's Prayer flows beautifully with form and substance. When Jesus presented this prayer as a pattern, He was teaching His disciples, among other things, to pray with purpose.

Prayer cannot be aimless words void of meaning and direction. The praying person should name names, describe needs and "tell it like it is." Though the heavenly Father knows our thoughts and is aware of our needs before we ask, He said, "Ask. . . ." He is our Father who wants us to have purpose in our asking, as when a 16-year-old boy comes to ask his earthly father for the car keys.

Enrichment From the Church: One pastor was preparing his church for a revival meeting by asking the members to join in a prayer chain. Participants would come into the church at designated times to pray. While in his study one day, the pastor heard the prayers going up to God. One particular man not only prayed for the success of the revival, but he took time to mention every unsaved member of his family. His greatest purpose in prayer was to intercede for his lost loved ones. Intercession, a noble purpose in prayer, is best exemplified by Jesus, our high priest, who "ever lives to make intercession" (Hebrews 7:25).

Enrichment From the Heart: Father, even though our prayers lack poetic form, we do mean business when we come to You. Please hear us.

Prayer February, Week 4

Benjamin B. McGlamery

PRAYING WITH PRAISE

Scripture: Glory in His holy name; Let the hearts of those rejoice who seek the Lord (Psalm 105:3).

Enrichment From the Word: The Psalms are replete with examples of how praying and praise are used in combination. They are inseparable when conversing to our heavenly Father. Psalm 105:3 is a wonderful illustration of this hand-in-hand process. As with Old Testament seekers, believers of the New Covenant in the same prayer framework preface their petitions with praise to the Lord. Jesus illustrated this by precept and example. During one of the saddest experiences in His earthly life, the death of Lazarus, Jesus took to practice what He taught. As He approached the tomb of Lazarus, He gave praise to the heavenly Father for hearing Him and for always hearing Him.

The most familiar New Testament story about prayer and praise is the experience of Paul and Silas in the Philippian jail. In their moment of desperate need, they took time to praise the Lord. They could have despaired because of their circumstances, but they knew praise is not to be given only when things are going great. Praise is appropriate anytime under any circumstance. "In everything give thanks; for this is the will of God in Christ Jesus for you" (1 Thessalonians 5:18).

Enrichment From the Church: In the earlier days of the Church of God, fatigue did not preclude going to church for many of the faithful. Although tired in body after a hard day's labor, the desire to worship and praise the Lord in the congregation of the saints was not abated. A typical testimony would sound something like this: "I was tired when I got to church; but after worshiping the Lord, I feel refreshed."

Enrichment From the Heart: Father, You inhabit the praise of Your people. As we pray, we will not forget to praise You.

Prayer   **February, Week 4**

Benjamin B. McGlamery

PRAYING WITH OTHERS

Scripture: So, when he had considered this, he came to the house of Mary, the mother of John whose surname was Mark, where many were gathered together praying (Acts 12:12).

Enrichment From the Word: The early church was solidarity personified when together in prayer. On the occasion of the above scripture, Peter had been on the executioners' list waiting in prison for his scheduled demise. But the church met for prayer in his behalf (Acts 12:5). On the Day of Pentecost when Peter preached, the other apostles stood with him (Acts 2:14).

The Bible has much to say about the virtue of secret, or closet, prayer. But by the previously cited examples, there is much evidence to support the effectiveness of corporate prayer.

Enrichment From the Church: A few years ago the Christian world was awakened to the plight of seven Pentecostal believers in Soviet Russia who sought freedom by gaining refuge in the American Embassy in a Russian city. These people became known everywhere as the Siberian Seven. Several professors and students at Lee College in Cleveland, Tennessee, mounted a campaign of prayer and action directed toward gaining freedom of the Siberian Seven. Christians around the world were also involved in prayer. After months of praying and waiting, Christians everywhere rejoiced to learn of the release of these seven tenacious Pentecostals. The solidarity of Christians in prayer around the world touched the heart of God, who in turn changed the mind of evil men.

Enrichment From the Heart: Father, remind us of what can happen when we agree in prayer with others of like precious faith.

Prayer — February, Week 4

Benjamin B. McGlamery

PRAYING FOR THE SICK

Scripture: Now when Jesus had entered Capernaum, a centurion came to Him, pleading with Him, saying, "Lord, my servant is lying at home paralyzed, dreadfully tormented" (Matthew 8:5, 6).

Enrichment From the Word: When the centurion came to Jesus in behalf of his servant, he revealed some attitudes necessary when praying for the sick. It seems the centurion came in faith believing Jesus could heal his servant. His compassion is revealed in his descriptive language and in that he came for someone other than himself.

Some "healing services" are alive with assembly-line, quick-fix methods with a quick, short prayer and the lightning-fast touch. But there are times when it is necessary to go into a hospital room filled with the stench of death, to groan and agonize with a patient consumed with cancer or to sit with young parents as they watch life being torn from a child.

Enrichment From the Church: One beautiful Sunday afternoon a man lay dying in his home. Two ministers came to visit and pray for him, finding him delirious. They labored long in prayer on his behalf until they felt an answer from the Lord. In succeeding years the man testified of the healing power of the Lord. He recalled that in his delirious state of mind, he heard one of the ministers say, "Let's pray one more time." The man lived to enjoy many more productive and happy years.

Enrichment From the Heart: Lord, remind us that as we persevere in prayer for the sick, You said, "I am the Lord who heals you" (Exodus 15:26).

Prayer   **February, Week 4**

Benjamin B. McGlamery

PRAYING FOR PERSONAL NEEDS

Scripture: And my God shall supply all your need according to His riches in glory by Christ Jesus (Philippians 4:19).

Enrichment From the Word: The philosophy of prosperity so often blinds our minds to the reality of our neediness. All people regardless of income brackets have unique, personal needs—even children of a king. While some are more needy than others, there are some necessities all people have in common. Sunshine, rain, oxygen, food, clothing and shelter fit into the category of vital necessities of life. Never should we take these things for granted.

In regard to asking, Jesus taught that it should be a daily process in our prayer life. In the Lord's Prayer we are urged to ask, "Give us day by day our daily bread." When we ask, we have no fear of refusal, for "thine is the kingdom." He has made a way so that we do not need go away empty.

Enrichment From the Church: A story is told about a family that immigrated to America. As they journeyed to the new land of promise, they were eating cheese and crackers they brought. A steward observed this and asked why they were eating cheese and crackers. The father replied, "We spent all our money to pay for passage to America, and we have no money left to buy food. The steward answered, "Sir, when you paid for passage, the cost of all your provisions was included. Please feel free to eat with the other passengers."

The provision has been made for the righteous. We do not have to beg, but we certainly should pray to the Father each day concerning all our needs.

Enrichment From the Heart: Father, Your table is spread, and You do not want us to go away hungry. Thank You for supplying our need according to Your riches in glory.

Parenting March, Week 1

W. A. Davis

LOVING CHILDREN LIKE CHRIST

Scripture: And He took them [children] up in His arms, put His hands on them, and blessed them (Mark 10:16).

Enrichment From the Word: Christ gave us a forceful example of His love for children. People were bringing their little children to Christ to have Him touch them, but the disciples rebuked them. When Christ saw what was happening, He was indignant. Christ did three things: (1) He took the children in His arms, (2) put His hands on them and (3) blessed them.

Enrichment From the Church: I once saw a toddler venture away from his mother at the conclusion of a church service. He would go a short distance, then turn around and rush back to his mother's touch. The next time he went a little farther only to rush back into her arms. Love and security were represented in this mom's hand touching her son and her arms holding him.

Millions of children around the world today are starving for food and a loving touch. Are our own children starving for a loving touch? As parents we must make the effort to reach out to our children in love. Jesus put His love for children into action. Can we afford to do less today? Jesus said, "'"Inasmuch as you did it to one of the least of these My brethren, you did it to Me"'" (Matthew 25:40).

Enrichment From the Heart: We teach children about God by our actions as well as by our words. In the long run, our actions carry greater weight than our words. Take your child into your arms today, touch and bless him with Christlike love.

Lord, help me to love my children and all children like You do. Amen.

Parenting   **March, Week 1**

W. A. Davis

UNDERSTANDING YOUR CHILDREN

Scripture: Fathers, do not provoke your children, lest they become discouraged (Colossians 3:21).

Enrichment From the Word: Many agree wholeheartedly with the words of Scripture which state, "Children, obey your parents in the Lord, for this is right. 'Honor your father and mother, which is the first commandment with promise: that it may be well with you and you may live long on the earth'" (Ephesians 6:1-3). However, we must continue to read, "Fathers, do not provoke your children to wrath, but bring them up in the training and admonition of the Lord" (v. 4). Understanding is vital to good relationships. Correction can increase understanding, but overcorrection can destroy the spirit of a child and cause bitterness and discouragement.

Enrichment From the Church: Every family member should be accepted where he or she is. Remember that every child has his own rate of development. There ought to be a balance between parental supervision and a child's freedom to fail. Too much freedom will be interpreted by a child as rejection. But too much supervision will also be interpreted by a child as rejection.

A father must recognize the strong points and weak points in each member of his family. Listen for the message in what your children say. The words spoken by them may be the opposite of what they actually feel. Listen for feelings, and give them understanding which will make their life fruitful.

Enrichment From the Heart: Dear Lord, help me to earn the right to be heard. I never want to hurt or discourage. Grant me good relationships with my children so that I may gain the right to be heard and obeyed by them. Amen.

Parenting   March, Week 1

W. A. Davis

COMMUNICATING WITH YOUR CHILDREN

Scripture: "And these words which I command you today shall be in your heart; you shall teach them diligently to your children" (Deuteronomy 6:6, 7).

Enrichment From the Word: As parents there are a multitude of items we need to communicate. The most important are the principles found in God's Word. They must first be real in our own hearts, and then it is our full-time job to share these principles with our children.

Enrichment From the Church: Communication is a priority for parents. It is critical in the parent-child relationship. Strong families realize that good communication is essential for spiritual, emotional and social growth. Therefore, they set aside time to be together. They take time to listen to each other as individuals with needs, desires and goals. Listening and communicating is too important within the family to let other groups such as friends, the school and the church take the place of family time together.

The Sunday school, Family Training Hour, youth group activities, children's church and public worship are all a part of your child's spiritual support system. But the entire spiritual development of your child cannot be left to the church. Remember, your child is your responsibility, and the church supports your efforts.

Enrichment From the Heart: Daily, I must place God's truth in my heart. Then, Lord, with Your help, I will listen with my heart and talk with my children about the things that are important to You and them.

Parenting   March, Week 1

W. A. Davis

BEING A FRIEND TO YOUR CHILDREN

Scripture: A friend loves at all times (Proverbs 17:17).

Enrichment From the Word: The human family often faces adversity, but we have great hopes for our children. However, failures, misunderstandings and misconduct will rise up in the lives of our children from time to time. Whether our children are right or wrong, they need to know we will always love them. They may break our heart by doing evil, but our children must sense that we will never disown them. "A friend loves at all times." Unconditional love can outlast anything. Friendship motivated by love will patiently wait for God's victory. A friend loves in the good times and the bad times.

Enrichment From the Church: A recent survey regarding teenage suicide revealed one important factor that was consistent in most of the suicides. Young people who killed themselves did not have a significant relationship with an adult. They had friends their own age, but they had no friendship with their parents or any other adult. Children need time with their parents. Friendship is built through experiencing life together. Memories are important to friends.

Enrichment From the Heart: You make appointments to talk with important people, don't you? Make regular appointments to talk with your children. This says to them, "You are important to me. Let's be friends!"

Parenting   March, Week 1

W. A. Davis

BEING AN EXAMPLE TO YOUR CHILDREN

Scripture: "Only take heed to yourself, and diligently keep yourself, lest you forget the things your eyes have seen, and lest they depart from your heart all the days of your life. And teach them to your children and your grandchildren" (Deuteronomy 4:9).

Enrichment From the Word: Be careful! Watch your step! Someone important is following you, and it is your child. There are two contrasting examples of parental leadership in Scripture. First, "The Lord was with Jehoshaphat, because he walked in the former ways of his father David" (2 Chronicles 17:3). Second, "He [Ahaziah the son of Ahab and Jezebel] did evil in the sight of the Lord, and walked in the way of his father and in the way of his mother" (1 Kings 22:52).

Your influence as a parent is far-reaching. It extends not only to your children but also to your grandchildren. It may also extend to other children within your church and community. Therefore, keep your heart right with God, and walk before your family with integrity and uprightness.

Enrichment From the Church: A wise person observed regarding parent-child relationships that "often more is caught than taught." What we say and do should be consistent and righteous. A little boy was with his dad when a car illegally pulled in front of him. The dad hit his brakes, shook his finger at the other driver and yelled, "You must be crazy!" One day the family was driving to church. The little lad was sitting on the armrest in the front. As they approached a car, he shook his finger and yelled, "You must be crazy!" The dad immediately realized his son had caught something from him.

Enrichment From the Heart: What a responsibility You have given us, Lord! We affect our children by the way we act. Help us, Lord!

Stewardship   **March, Week 2**

Al Taylor

UNDERSTANDING STEWARDSHIP COMMITMENT

Scripture: "So likewise, whoever of you does not forsake all that he has, cannot be My disciple" (Luke 14:33).

Enrichment From the Word: Jesus was not reluctant to define the cost of belonging to Him. The cost is the same for everybody: *everything*. Apparently, there are not many who understand this requirement because so few have paid the price. How can I forsake all that I have?

The Apostle Paul described it in Romans 10:9 as confessing the lordship of Jesus. *Lord* means "owner." When we who love Jesus made our deliberate commitment to Him, we called Him our "owner" and master. At that very moment we changed the title of everything we possessed. We proclaimed that our time, talent, treasure and testimony no longer belonged to us but to Him. That is the first step in forsaking all to be His disciple.

Next comes the practice. If I have given everything to Jesus, then I am His steward. Now, when He calls me to give or serve, I simply fulfill a commitment already made. I do what the Owner commands with everything He has entrusted to me.

Enrichment From the Church: Stanley Tam was already a generous giver when God directed him to give his business and all of its profits to the Lord. Stanley did it. Then he watched as that business grew dramatically under its new ownership to become the biggest plastics company in America. Stanley experienced a new freedom. The company gives millions of dollars to the work of the church. The new Owner is doing a splendid job, and Stanley is free from the pressures of ownership.

Enrichment From the Heart: Yes, I have made Jesus the Lord of my life. Because He is owner, I will honor my commitment and do what He says with every possession today and every day.

Stewardship

March, Week 2

Al Taylor

MAKING A STEWARDSHIP COMMITMENT

Scripture: Now when He was in Jerusalem at the Passover, during the feast, many believed in His name when they saw the signs which He did. But Jesus did not commit Himself to them, because He knew all men, and had no need that anyone should testify of man, for He knew what was in man (John 2:23-25).

Enrichment From the Word: This is an extremely sad statement. Many people believed in Jesus' name, but Jesus did not commit Himself to them. Why not? Because He knew what was in their hearts. He knew they were not committed to Him.

Millions of people are now "believing" in Jesus' name, but they are not committed to Him. At one time it was reported that more than 50 million Americans professed to have been born again. Such a profession would indicate that these people believe something positive about Jesus. However, the lack of change in their lives reveals lack of real commitment.

How can we make certain we have made the commitment and that we are keeping the commitment? Jesus said if we would come after Him, we must deny self, take up our cross and follow Him.

Enrichment From the Church: Jim Jackson was instructed by God to give away his personal fortune of $6 million. As an act of obedience and self-denial, he did it. Since that time God has used His life to bless people in many parts of the world. He found that the cross we must take up is an instrument of death to self, but the life of Christ then follows through us and shares with others as we follow Him.

Enrichment From the Heart: Thank You, Father, for committing Your Son to us. I have chosen to follow Him, and I want to be changed to be like Him. Help me to take up my cross daily and deny myself so that I strengthen my commitment to Christ.

Stewardship   March, Week 2

Al Taylor

FOCUSING ON STEWARDSHIP PRIORITIES

Scripture: "But seek first the kingdom of God and His righteousness, and all these things shall be added to you" (Matthew 6:33).

Enrichment From the Word: The first priority of a good steward is to understand that relationship to the King is more important than relationship to things. We are seeking first the Kingdom when we love the Lord with all our heart.

Next, we are to acknowledge God's ownership of all that He has created. Because He is the owner, I am simply the steward or trustee of all that He has placed in my care. The only requirement of a steward is faithfulness.

God has commanded that I am to bring the first tenth of every increase promptly to His house for the support of the ministry. Then I am ready to give offerings to Him. I am to give to those people in God's church who minister to me and to those who are in need. Next I am to give to the poor outside the church—all under the direction of the Holy Spirit.

Enrichment From the Church: Jesus commanded His disciples to teach believers "'all things that I have commanded you'" (Matthew 28:28). He has placed teachers in the church. If the church obeys our Lord's command to teach what He taught, then we will hear much on the subject of stewardship. It was the Lord's most frequent subject. And just as He used stewardship to illustrate spiritual truths, our lives are to illustrate His truths as we faithfully follow Him.

Enrichment From the Heart: Dear Lord, I am thankful that You have invested in me and that You have made me Your child and Your steward.

Stewardship   March, Week 2

Al Taylor

BLENDING STEWARDSHIP AND PRAISE

Scripture: Beloved, I pray that you may prosper in all things and be in health, just as your soul prospers (3 John 2).

Enrichment From the Word: John the beloved was inspired of the Holy Spirit to tell us that it is pleasing to God for us to prosper and enjoy good health. He was also careful to communicate to us the controlling part of this blessed equation: "just as your soul prospers." Unless prosperity is balanced and controlled, it becomes a destructive force in our lives. "The prosperity of fools shall destroy them" (Proverbs 1:32, *KJV*).

Everything God requires of us is good for us. He instructs us in our relationship with material possessions because of the constant danger that things may possess us.

A steward manages something of value for its owner. He is to obey the owner's every instruction. Although a faithful steward protects his owner's property, he doesn't protect it from the owner. A steward is to be openhanded toward his master at all times. He is to give or spend with no reluctance when the master commands. Hands open to release are also open to receive and to worship.

Enrichment From the Church: The first-century church was challenged by the Holy Spirit to give everything to the church. The local church ministries were financed, and the gospel was carried abroad by this all-out giving. When Jerusalem was destroyed in A.D. 70, the Christians escaped because they owned nothing to hold them back. Then the Christians in other lands, who had been won through their giving, gave to them.

Enrichment From the Heart: Dear God, I open my hands to release everything I possess back to You. With open hands I praise You and serve You.

Stewardship   March, Week 2

Al Taylor

HANDLING FAMILY FINANCES

Scripture: Through wisdom a house is built, And by understanding it is established; By knowledge the rooms are filled with all precious and pleasant riches (Proverbs 24:3, 4).

Enrichment From the Word: Americans control approximately half of the world's wealth. With only 6 percent of the world's population, everybody in America should enjoy abundance. Of course, we know that is not the case.

Can we live in such a society and not be victimized by it? Absolutely! God's Word is not controlled by circumstances. We who believe the Word are to prove its power in our lives.

Our scripture for today reveals three ingredients necessary for our family finances: Wisdom builds our home, understanding establishes it, and knowledge prospers it. Wisdom is the ability to use knowledge and resources. It comes from fearing the Lord and obeying Him. Understanding is the ability to comprehend. It comes from meditating on God's truth and from spending time in His presence. Knowledge is the possession of truth. It comes from faithful study and practice of God's Word.

Enrichment From the Church: Church history reveals a definite pattern. Revival begins in an economically deprived group. As they learn to live by the Word of God, they are prospered. As each generation prospers, they begin to trust in their possessions and grow cold toward God and His Word. Decay and decline soon follow.

Enrichment From the Heart: Father, help me to establish my home and its finances on Your truth. May each member of my family learn to trust and obey You.

Outreach   March, Week 3

Ray H. Hughes

STRESSING OUTREACH ACTION

Scripture: And there accompanied [Paul]. . . . (Acts 20:4, *KJV*).

Enrichment From the Word: The average American is bombarded by hundreds of messages every day. Advertisers know that to attract the attention of potential buyers their messages must be bold and assertive. The response to this barrage of messages is often apathy and a willed ignoring of the communication. Outreach action, therefore, must not only be spoken but demonstrated as well.

That is one of the apparent reasons Paul chose team workers. He knew that outreach should not just be preached but practiced. Church leaders would do well to disciple younger ministers in outreach ministries.

Enrichment From the Church: For many years a missionary in China stressed the need for evangelistic witness to his new disciples. He preached and taught that Christians are to witness and multiply their faith. There was no response. He was ready to return home, discouraged and disappointed.

In prayer the finger of the Holy Spirit pointed out "And there accompanied [Paul]. . . ." (Acts 20:4). "That's it!" he shouted. "Paul was successful in stressing outreach action because he took others with him." The next Sunday the missionary announced that on a certain day he would travel to another village to preach. He instructed his pastor's council to pack a bag of rice and come along with him. The men accompanied him, learned evangelism by doing and became effective evangelists.

Enrichment From the Heart: Lord, help me to stress outreach action by showing others how it is done. Multiply effective witnessing through my example.

Outreach March, Week 3

Ray H. Hughes

DESIRING TO REACH OUT

Scripture: Brethren, my heart's desire and prayer to God for Israel is that they may be saved (Romans 10:1).

Enrichment From the Word: Paul expressed a deep desire of his heart. "'Out of the abundance of the heart the mouth speaks,'" was the truth spoken by Jesus in Matthew 12:34. It is possible, then, to measure the intensity of our heart's desire for souls by observing how often evangelism is in our conversation and lifestyle. All that is characterized in the nature of man by the term "heart" should be focused on that all-consuming desire to reach the lost. The desire of our heart will be expressed in the direction of our lives in everyday service and witness.

Enrichment From the Church: Nationwide surveys of a wide range of Evangelical churches have found a high degree of affection and love exhibited in churches that are growing. Respondents in those surveys said they were attracted to these churches because the people displayed a high degree of love, concern and care. Researchers called this factor the "Love Quotient." Let there be love for the lost and for one another in our congregations! Let there be tears of compassion. Let there be a "heart's desire" that others be saved.

Enrichment From the Heart: Lord, outreach to the lost is more than mental assent. Move me with compassion, and let there be a new desire in my heart to reach out.

Outreach March, Week 3

Ray H. Hughes

UNDERSTANDING THE SCRIPTURAL BASIS

Scripture: The Lord . . . is longsuffering toward us, not willing that any should perish but that all should come to repentance (2 Peter 3:9).

Enrichment From the Word: God wants the lost to be found. He wants outreach action.

God's Word portrays him as a patient God who does not want one single person to perish. Think of the most detestable, unregenerate person who may have committed a depraved act of sin. God wants that person to come to repentance. He does not want anyone to perish but all people everywhere to come to repentance. It is the will of God for all men to be saved. Since it is the will of God, we will answer to Him for our disobedience or obedience to His command to make disciples of all nations.

Enrichment From the Church: Our greatest enrichment comes from the model of the early church which began with 120 disciples (Acts 1:14, 15). Another 3,000 souls were added on the Day of Pentecost (Acts 2:41, 42). This number increased shortly to more than 5,000 (Acts 4:4), and then the increase becomes difficult to count. In Acts 5:14 the Scripture says that "multitudes" were added. Then a new process began—the process of multiplication. From the sixth chapter forward the Bible underscores the multiplication of disciples and of entire churches (Acts 6:1, 7; 9:31; 16:5; 21:20). The scriptural basis for outreach action concludes that God wants the lost to be found and discipled into responsible, reproducing congregations.

Enrichment From the Heart: Lord, help me not to be so confused about finding Your will when Your expressed will and desire is so explicitly stated in Your Word. Help me to obey Your Word.

Outreach March, Week 3

Ray H. Hughes

MAKING OUTREACH A PRAYER PRIORITY

Scripture: "Grant to Your servants that with all boldness they may speak Your word" (Acts 4:29).

Enrichment From the Word: Outreach for the early church was not a periodic revival campaign or an annual growth emphasis. It was their lifestyle. Regularly, on a daily basis, the Jewish tradition called for a visit to the Temple for prayer. The disciples incorporated this practice into their daily schedule. It was a natural and normal expression of their new life and power in the Holy Spirit.

Our outreach action must be a vital part of everyday life experiences. Evangelism should be the main agenda, with other activities of life revolving around it. Outreach should become a normal and regular daily expression. Therefore, it should be stressed from the pulpit, in training curriculum and literature, and in other activities. Let us pray for boldness to speak!

Enrichment From the Church: A local church in Korea had frequent and intensive prayer times scheduled into its services. On one occasion a visiting preacher noticed a small bell on the pulpit. After an extended time of prayer, the pastor lightly touched the bell and the prayer time gradually came to an end. At the close of the service the guest asked the host pastor about the meaning of the bell. "Our people love to pray for souls," responded the shepherd of this growing congregation. "If I didn't ring the bell, they would pray all day long!"

Prayer for outreach was stressed in that church, and the people had to be stopped from prayer for souls. Let our pulpits ring with a call to action!

Enrichment From the Heart: Call us to action, O harvesting God, until our lives are consumed with a desire to reach out for the lost.

Outreach March, Week 3

Ray H. Hughes

BUILDING FAITH TO REACH OUT

Scripture: Faith comes from hearing the message, and the message is heard through the word of Christ (Romans 10:17, NIV).

Enrichment From the Word: Faith springs from the soil seeded with the Word of God. Faith is the natural and normal response to the preaching of the truths of God.

Faith to reach the lost comes from hearing the Word of God. When God's people are taught and challenged from the biblical admonition to reach the world and when they see in the Scripture the heart of a God who desires all men to be saved, there will be a consequential response of faith that moves them to action. We build faith to reach out through proclaiming the Word of God. Only the Word can create faith; nothing else can, regardless of how important it may seem.

Enrichment From the Church: On May 30, 1792, young William Carey preached his now famous sermon from Isaiah 54:2, 3 in which he coined the familiar watchword, "Expect great things from God; attempt great things for God." The sermon had a profound effect upon his hearers. It resulted in the formation of a new missionary society which set off a chain reaction of 12 new missions organizations over the next 32 years. Since that time Carey has become known as the "Father of Modern Missions." The modern missionary movement to reach out to the world began with a sermon! Let us never give up on preaching and teaching God's desire from the Scriptures—that all men be saved.

Enrichment From the Heart: Let someone this week, O Lord, be inspired by me to reach out. Anoint me to preach and teach Your Word that builds faith and moves us to reach out to the lost.

Personal Witness　　　　　　　　**March, Week 4**

Leonard Albert

DEVELOPING A VISION FOR WITNESSING

Scripture: Knowing, therefore, the terror of the Lord, we persuade men (2 Corinthians 5:11).

Enrichment From the Word: Why did Paul believe he should persuade men? He uses the Greek word **phobos**, which is translated "terror," to describe the reason. This term refers to a reverential fear of God as the controlling motive of one's life in matters of a spiritual and moral nature. This is not a mere fear of God's power and righteous retribution but a wholesome dread of displeasing Him. Paul had this kind of reverent trust in God, and it influenced his disposition and attitude so that his entire new life was guided by trust in God through the indwelling of the Holy Spirit.

Enrichment From the Church: As a movement, the Church of God has always had a vision for witnessing. It is so refreshing to see this burden emphasized in the Project 2000 goal. Goal number five reads: "to motivate lay witness and ministry participation by all believers." The entire church—laity as well as clergy, women as well as men, youth as well as adults—must be mobilized to effectively witness for Christ. We have no higher priority.

Enrichment From the Heart: Today's scripture captivates my attention. Because I fear God, I want to be a witness for Him. What will I tell God at the judgment? What will count then—houses, land, worldly accomplishments, business, hectic time schedules, fervent activity? I persuade men because it is what really matters to God. Jesus came to seek and save that which was lost (Luke 19:10). He told us to share His message. When we stand before Him, nothing else will be more important.

Personal Witness   **March, Week 4**

Leonard Albert

TRAINING TO BE EFFECTIVE WITNESSES

Scripture: But he needed to go through Samaria (John 4:4).

Enrichment From the Word: Please take a moment to continue reading chapter 4 down to verse 30. The best training example for personal evangelism is Jesus Christ, the greatest soulwinner who ever lived. Notice in this passage a fivefold training outline.

   1. To be effective in witness one has to first get a person's attention. Jesus got the Samaritan woman's attention: "Give Me a drink" (v. 7).

   2. Arouse interest. Jesus said, "If you knew . . . who it is . . . you would have asked Him, and He would have given you living water" (v. 10).

   3. Create a desire. She wondered what "living water" was. She said, "Sir, give me this water, that I may not thirst, nor come here to draw" (v. 15). She was ready to taste of this living water.

   4. Deal with known sin. Jesus said, "Go, call your husband" (v. 16). Thus, He put His divine finger on her sin. This is conviction.

   5. Close with a commitment. After an encounter with Christ, she told others about her experience, "Come, see a Man who told me all things that I ever did. Could this be the Christ?" (v. 29).

Enrichment From the Church: After setting the example, Jesus told all called-out believers, the church, to "go into all the world." This is not the great suggestion but the Great Commission! It comes from our Commander in Chief, and it has never been changed or rescinded. Witnessing is an imperative from God. But to fulfill this task, we must be trained to witness.

Enrichment From the Heart: Thank God for Jesus who makes the gospel evangel come alive in the lives of others.

Personal Witness March, Week 4

Leonard Albert

SEEKING THE GUIDANCE OF THE HOLY SPIRIT

Scripture: Now an angel of the Lord spoke to Philip, saying, "Arise and go . . . " (Acts 8:26).

Enrichment From the Word: What a tremendous time those early Christians were having! Wherever they went, people were healed, saved and filled with the Holy Ghost. Can you imagine how it must have sounded to Philip when in the midst of this wonderful revival, the angel of the Lord said, "'Arise and go toward the south . . . to Gaza'"? The Bible explains Gaza was desert. Think of it! From the midst of revival to a barren desert! But that is what God told him to do. One of the first steps in learning how to become an effective witness is being open to the will of God for your life. Many times we feel impressed to say or do something for the Lord, but due to a lack of faith, or to doubt, we refrain from action. Philip simply did what God told him to do. Keep in mind the idea of being where God wants you to be. In this story it was a desert. It was not the best place to be as far as our natural senses tell us, but it was where God would do a miraculous work through Philip.

Enrichment From the Church: Twenty years ago Christ saved me, and I joined the Church of God. For the first two years of my new birth, I sincerely thought God wanted me to become a clergyman. I often tell people, "God really called me to preach, but when He heard me, He changed His mind." Well, really, God did call me to preach but as an "ordained layman." Let Him call you to a personal ministry today.

Enrichment From the Heart: Jesus, I ask You by the power of Your Holy Spirit, help me follow and always allow You to lead.

Personal Witness   **March, Week 4**

Leonard Albert

BEING SENSITIVE TO THE NEEDS OF PEOPLE

Scripture: The hearing ear and the seeing eye, The Lord has made both of them (Proverbs 20:12).

Enrichment From the Word: Wise Solomon said it clearly: Two ears. Two eyes. But we have a tendency to listen and not hear, to observe and not see the needs of others. God gave us two eyes and two ears but only one mouth. He wants us to use them in that same proportion.

Enrichment From the Church: Did you hear about the man who went to a psychiatrist and said, "Doc, my problem is that nobody listens to me." The doctor said, "Next, please!" Although humorous, that story reveals a basic problem in our society: People are hurting and have no one to help them. Have you ever practiced "listening evangelism"? We must be careful not to be so eager to share the good news that we forget to take time to listen patiently to others. The chief executive of a large corporation, a power person, began a board meeting with, "Now listen slowly!" Christ is the master example of this as over and over again He "listened slowly." As others talked, He peered deeply into the well of their soul, and it wasn't long before they became open to His message.

   St. Augustine once told a silent new student, "Speak, that I may know you." His secret? He listened. This takes caring, time, unselfishness and concentration. It means holding the other person in high esteem. It means allowing room for silence while the other person is thinking, trying to get the words straightened out. Wise is the listener who doesn't feel compelled to fill in all the blank spaces with useless verbiage.

Enrichment From the Heart: Lord, help me to be a "seeing eye" for the spiritually blind and a "hearing ear" for the spiritually deaf.

Personal Witness   **March, Week 4**

Leonard Albert

NURTURING YOUNG CONVERTS

Scripture: And the things that you have heard from me among many witnesses, commit these to faithful men who will be able to teach others also (2 Timothy 2:2).

Enrichment From the Word: Here is a wonderful plan for the nurture of new converts. Paul was writing to Timothy, his young son in the faith. He said "the things." This was in reference to Paul's teaching which, of course, is now a part of God's Word. The Scripture is the number one place for a new convert to begin his spiritual growth. The Word must be studied, meditated upon and applied to daily life. Paul then said "the things that you have heard from me." Here we see the interpersonal relationship between the discipler and the new convert. Next, he mentions commitment. God has given all believers a sacred trust: to share His Word with the world. Then Paul said "faithful men." The new convert must realize that God commits to faithfulness before He does to talent. It matters little how good we are at "doing" if we are not good at "being." Finally, Paul closes his admonition with the powerful word **others**. Is not this what it is all about . . . reaching **others**? Could not this be the one word for all of us to remember . . . others?

Enrichment From the Church: The best discipling center for any new believer is the local church. God has given ministry gifts to believers and placed them in the church in order for believers to minister to each other. The church is essential for the nurturing and growth process to take place.

Enrichment From the Heart: Without God we cannot. Without us He will not.

Prayer   April, Week 1

J. Herbert Walker

INTERCEDING TO GOD FOR OTHERS

Scripture: Far be it from me that I should sin against the Lord in ceasing to pray for you (1 Samuel 12:23).

Enrichment From the Word: Intercession is the primary work of Jesus in His exalted position at the right hand of God (Romans 8:34; Hebrews 7:25). Intercession is the work of the Holy Spirit (Romans 8:26, 27). Intercession was a main part of the work of the early church (Acts 2:42).

You and I are called to be partners with Christ and the Holy Spirit as intercessors for others. "I exhort first of all that supplications, prayers, intercessions, and giving of thanks be made for all men" (1 Timothy 2:1). "Praying always with all prayer and supplication in the Spirit" (Ephesians 6:18). "Pray for those who spitefully use you and persecute you" (Matthew 5:44). "Pray the Lord of the harvest to send out laborers into His harvest" (Matthew 9:38).

Enrichment From the Church: David Brainerd, missionary to Early American Indians, dropped to his knees to pray as hostile Indians aimed arrows at him. The Indians watched as a giant rattler approached him from behind, prepared to strike. As Brainerd prayed, however, the snake settled down and slipped away. Convinced that he was protected by a supernatural power, the Indians lowered their weapons and gathered around to listen to the good news he had come to tell.

"When Moses held up his hand . . . Israel prevailed; and when he let down his hand, Amalek prevailed. . . . Moses' hands became heavy. . . . And Aaron and Hur supported his hands . . . and his hands were steady until the going down of the sun. So Joshua defeated Amalek" (Exodus 17:11-13).

Enrichment From the Heart: Lord, let me not sin against You by failing to hold up the hands of my fellow workers by interceding for them.

Prayer　　　　　　　　　　　　　　　　　**April, Week 1**

J. Herbert Walker

BECOMING A PARTNER WITH GOD

Scripture: " 'Call to Me, and I will answer you, and show you great and mighty things, which you do not know' " (Jeremiah 33:3).

Enrichment From the Word: Daniel took Jeremiah's words to heart and began to call on the Lord. Though one of an ethnic minority, an exile in a foreign land, he "purposed in his heart that he would not defile himself" (Daniel 1:8). He set his heart to understand the things of God (10:12).

"Now while I was speaking, praying, and confessing my sin and the sin of my people Israel, and presenting my supplication before the Lord my God . . . yes, while I was speaking in prayer, the man Gabriel . . . reached me . . . and talked with me, and said. . . . 'I have come to tell you' " (Daniel 9:20-23).

Enrichment From the Church: Pavel Ignatov, a Christian leader in Bulgaria, told me in Sofia that the Holy Spirit revealed to him his impending arrest and exile for preaching before he received any word from the government officials. So he was prepared when they knocked on his door. Since his arrest and exile without a trial, both the general who arrested him and the judge who sentenced him have gone to meet their Maker, though only 55 and 49 years of age. Pray for the salvation of government officials in Bulgaria, for the safety of believers, for freedom to preach the gospel and for the official registration of the church.

Enrichment From the Heart: Lord, Your words invite us to be partners with You in prayer. You say, "Come, ask, seek, knock, listen, search, watch, hear, behold, call." Help me to call to You so that You can show me great and mighty things.

Prayer April, Week 1

J. Herbert Walker

DEVELOPING A RELATIONSHIP WITH GOD

Scripture: "Come now, and let us reason together," Says the Lord, "Though your sins are like scarlet, They shall be as white as snow; Though they are red like crimson, They shall be as wool" (Isaiah 1:18).

Enrichment From the Word: Love implies relationship and reasoning together. The great God of the universe created man in His image so they could have fellowship together.

Like other fathers, Father God wants His sons and daughters to be like Himself—loving, kind, good, holy, helping, healing, communicating, sharing.

God gives His children ears to hear, eyes to see, a mind to reason, a mouth to speak, freedom to choose and authority to rule over creation. But disobedience—sin—broke the fellowship. Now God invites us to restore the relationship, to be reconciled to Him.

How is this done? Through prayer!

Enrichment From the Church: Robert Schuler's book **The Be-Happy Attitudes** presents the beatitudes of the Sermon on the Mount as eight positive attitudes that can transform your life (Matthew 5:3-10). The first is the new-beginning attitude. It says, "I need help—I can't do it alone!" This attitude admits we need an ongoing relationship with God. The poor in spirit are the ones who admit, "I've got problems; I don't understand; I need peace; I need forgiveness; I need a friend; I need a Savior; I'm sorry; I need help!"

A right relationship with God gives us the help we need.

Enrichment From the Heart: Lord, I accept Your invitation. I come. Wash my sins as white as snow. Receive me in Your righteousness (Romans 3:23-25). Teach me to be more like You in desiring and cultivating loving relationships.

Prayer   **April, Week 1**

J. Herbert Walker

PRAISING GOD IN DIFFICULT TIMES

Scripture: By Him [Jesus Christ] let us continually offer the sacrifice of praise to God, that is, the fruit of our lips, giving thanks to His name (Hebrews 13:15).

Enrichment From the Word: This scripture speaks of offering the sacrifice of praise. This means praising God when things aren't going right, in the pain, through our tears, when we feel crushed.

Trouble comes to all—accidents, disease, financial reverses, death. We are victims of a sin-cursed world. Sometimes we bring trouble on ourselves by bad choices, bad habits, lack of information. The real issue is how we react to these hurtful circumstances of life.

Two important and popular seminar topics today are "Coping With Crisis" and "How to Handle Stress." A crisis crushes. But in crushing there is often refinement and purification. Bad things happen to good people. But more important than what happens to us is how we react to it. If our attitude is right, bad things can make us better rather than bitter.

Enrichment From the Church: Amy Carmichael's poem "No Scar?" asks, "Hast thou no scar?" The Lord was wounded, nailed to a tree, killed. Should not the servant be as the Master? She concludes by asking, "Can he have followed far, who has no wound nor scar?"

Stop and remember the difficult times of your life. What have they contributed to you today?

Enrichment From the Heart: Lord, I thank You that bad things can be turned into good with Your help. Out of my heartache I praise You. I choose to forgive and to let You help me pull out all bitter roots. Let me not waste my sorrow but turn it into a sacrifice of praise, a servant to serve You and others.

Prayer   **April, Week 1**

J. Herbert Walker

ENJOYING FELLOWSHIP WITH GOD

Scripture: Rejoice always, pray without ceasing, in everything give thanks; for this is the will of God in Christ Jesus for you (1 Thessalonians 5:16-18).

Enrichment From the Word: Enjoy. Rejoice. Be glad. Be cheerful, content, happy. Why? Because God has reconciled you. He is your friend, your present helper, your future eternal security. His Word is alive. His promises are sure. He is ultimate victory. Delight, exult, glory in your God. "Make a joyful shout to the Lord. . . . Enter into His gates with thanksgiving, And into His courts with praise. Be thankful to Him, and bless His name" (Psalm 100:1, 4).

The joy of the people of God rises above circumstances. Its source is in the character and nature of God. He is sovereign God, who works all things out for good according to His purposes—which is to make us like Christ (Romans 8:28-30).

Enrichment From the Church: Paul L. Walker, in **How to Keep Your Joy**, says, "In the biblical sense, joy then becomes a spiritual balance between expectations and achievements—the ability to approach problems objectively by accepting things as they are and working toward solutions and adjustments. Assuming this stance, joy is a sense of imperturbable gladness that sings when rejected, praises when persecuted, and stands when attacked. In this sense, joy is taking our crises in stride and utilizing our circumstances to bring glory to God."

Enrichment From the Heart: Dear Lord, thank You for the joy You give us; it is our strength. Thank You for praying that Your joy would be fulfilled in us. We praise You.

Worship   April, Week 2

J. D. Golden

WORSHIPPING WITH A CLAP OFFERING

Scripture: Oh, clap your hands, all you peoples! Shout to God with the voice of triumph! (Psalm 47:1).

Enrichment From the Word: The Hebrew word rendered here as "clap" is *taga*, which means "to slap your hands together and make a clatter." What a noisy word!

It is evident throughout Scripture, especially the Psalms, that we should praise God noisily. Why, even the noises of nature glorify God, as seen in Psalm 98:7, 8 and Isaiah 55:12. When we think of how wonderful our Lord has been and will continue to be to us, joy should well up within us. This joy can be expressed through a loud noise, even through clapping, as we worship the person of God. This pleases God! It pleases His heart for us to praise Him with all of our being.

What a gift we have been given—the ability to praise and exalt the Almighty!

Enrichment From the Church: When we hear someone speak eloquent words or sing a lovely song, we offer them appreciation by clapping our hands. What then shall we offer the One whose "faithfulness endures to all generations" (Psalm 119:90)?

I remember the time I visited a church in the Northeast where the people gave a thunderous clap offering to the God who had saved their souls. Such an expression was new to me, but I discovered that this was a normal way for these people to honor God. They made a joyful noise to their Lord.

Enrichment From the Heart: The next time we are in God's presence, let us remember to make a clatter of clapping our hands to the One who made us with His hands.

Worship   **April, Week 2**

J. D. Golden

WORSHIPPING WITH A FELLOWSHIP OFFERING

Scripture: I was glad when they said to me, "Let us go into the house of the Lord" (Psalm 122:1).

Enrichment From the Word: Coming together to worship God and have fellowship with one another produces unity in the body of Christ. "Behold, how good and how pleasant it is For brethren to dwell together in unity!" (Psalm 133:1). While fellowshipping together pleases God, it is costly: It costs time, effort and money. These are our sacrifice to God. However, the benefits we receive far outweigh the sacrifice we make.

Besides having fellowship with one another, we also enter into fellowship with the Father. Jesus said, "'Where two or three are gathered together in My name, I am there in the midst of them'" (Matthew 18:20).

Enrichment From the Church: A young Chicagoan named Claude had lost his job and was in the process of being evicted. Also, his wife had left him. He told me that something had urged him to go back to church just one more time, so he did. When he entered, the fellowship of the church was so rich and real that he broke down and confessed that he had written a suicide note. Then he had the brethren to pray for him. The following day three things happened: His former employer asked him to come back to work, a check came in the mail that covered all his bills, and his wife called asking to come back.

Enrichment From the Heart: Since we are created in God's image and God desires fellowship with us, it seems logical that we should desire fellowship with one another in His presence. Let us therefore worship our Father with a fellowship offering, joyously sacrificing our time and ourselves to fellowship with God and one another.

Worship

April, Week 2

J. D. Golden

WORSHIPPING WITH A LOVE OFFERING (NOT MONEY)

Scripture: Jesus answered and said to her, "O woman, great is your faith! Let it be to you as you desire" (Matthew 15:28).

Enrichment From the Word: Oh, how great was her faith indeed! Despite the circumstances—despite the thought that Jesus, a Jew, might not have anything to do with her and that the disciples had asked Jesus to "send her away, for she cries out after us" (v. 23)—this Canaanite woman persisted in calling out to Jesus on behalf of her demon-possessed daughter. She knew the only way for her daughter to be healed was for the One she recognized as the "Son of David" to heal her. Even after Jesus "answered her not a word," she bowed at His feet in worship, asking Him to heal her daughter.

What great love she offered to the Son of God! What great love she had for her daughter! Despite the circumstances, she offered Jesus her worship of love and believed on Him.

Enrichment From the Church: One time I asked a Haitian brother, "Do you love me?" This brother responded, "How can I answer this? I love you more than myself, and I love God more than you."

Enrichment From the Heart: In times of great trial, others may tell us to stop praying to and believing in God; they may tell us to just give up. But we have a choice. We can give up and walk away defeated, or we can fall on our knees harder than ever before and offer God our worship of love despite the storms raging around us. The Canaanite woman did the latter, and Jesus responded to her great faith by granting her soul desire—to see her daughter healed. Beloved, we too can see God work in our lives if we will love Him with all our heart, soul and mind.

Worship					April, Week 2

J. D. Golden

WORSHIPPING WITH A PRAISE OFFERING

Scripture: I will sing to the Lord as long as I live; I will sing praise to my God while I have my being (Psalm 104:33). My praise shall be of You in the great congregation; I will pay My vows before those who fear Him (Psalm 22:25). I will bless the Lord at all times; His praise shall continually be in my mouth (Psalm 34:1).

Enrichment From the Word: In these scriptures we see three basic types of praise: personal praise—"I will sing to the Lord as long as I live"; corporate praise—"praise . . . in the great congregation"; and perpetual praise—"His praise shall continually be in my mouth."

Whatever the circumstance of our praise, we know that God is enthroned in the praises of Israel (Psalm 22:3)—God dwells in the praises of His people. Knowing this, should we not praise Him when we are afraid, lonely, tempted, weak or scorned? If we are a people who thirst for God, should we not praise Him at all times? The psalmist declared, "I will bless the Lord at all times; His praise shall continually be in my mouth" (Psalm 34:1).

Enrichment From the Church: A Pentecostal girl brought her Catholic boyfriend to church with her. When they arrived, everyone was standing and praising the Lord with their hands raised. The boy had never seen anything like this in his life. He said to his girlfriend, "Honey, I think it is a holdup. Maybe we can get away before anyone sees us." While there will be some who will not understand why we Pentecostals praise God the way we do, we must realize that our sincere praise is pleasing to Him.

Enrichment From the Heart: Praising God continually—through difficult times as well as joyful times—will bring God closer to us. His presence will fill our lives—He will be all we need.

Worship — April, Week 2

J. D. Golden

WORSHIPPING WITH A FINANCIAL OFFERING

Scripture: Then King David said to Ornan, "No, but I will surely buy it for the full price, for I will not take what is yours for the Lord, nor offer burnt offerings with that which costs me nothing" (1 Chronicles 21:24).

Enrichment From the Word: In 1 Chronicles 21:18-30 we learn that God directed King David to build an altar to the Lord to atone for his sin of numbering Israel. He was told to build the altar "on the threshing floor of Ornan" (v. 18). When David came to Ornan, Ornan fell prostrate before him and offered his oxen, his threshing implements and his grain for the offering. But we see David's heart here: He could have taken the easy way out, accepting Ornan's offer without paying a cent to him. After all, David was king. But this was to be David's offering to his God, so he paid Ornan and then built the altar to God.

Enrichment From the Church: Our world is caught up in making financial investments such as CDs, IRAs, stocks and bonds. But what about investments that will have an effect on eternity? Are we supporting world missions? Are we pursuing those things that will further God's kingdom, or are we too caught up in "getting ahead" personally? Are we as concerned as we say we are about the poor in our world, our country and own town? Are we really doing our best to further the kingdom of God? Jesus said, " 'For where your treasure is, there your heart will be also' " (Matthew 6:21).

Enrichment From the Heart: What are we investing in? What do we treasure? What does the world say as it looks at our lifestyle? The answers to these questions will tell us where our heart is.

Self-Help   April, Week 3

Robert D. Crick

LEARNING TO DEAL WITH GUILT

Scripture: For godly sorrow produces repentance to salvation, not to be regretted; but the sorrow of the world produces death (2 Corinthians 7:10).

Enrichment From the Word: Paul's stinging rebuke in his first letter to the church in Corinth apparently had motivated the believers to repent and behave more like saints than carnal children. Although Paul regretted having to hurt them, he recognized that it was necessary in order for them to turn their hearts back to God.

Paul's discussion noted a difference between godly sorrow and worldly sorrow. Godly sorrow is that kind of sorrow, or guilt, that leads to real repentance, confession and reconciliation.

But there is another type of guilt that is destructive in nature: worldly sorrow. This guilt ultimately focuses on the self rather than on God. It may manifest itself in feelings of remorse, shame and self-condemnation over real or imagined actions. The person who experiences this type of guilt either does not respond in repentance or does not accept God's forgiveness.

Enrichment From the Church: Barbara's divorce two years ago had been a traumatic event. Although she had attempted to forgive her husband and repent of her own failings, she grew more and more depressed. Her church and pastor responded by continuing to demonstrate their love for her, and by emphasizing God's love and forgiving power. In time, Barbara was able to identify her feelings and express them openly. In doing so, several other church members bound by guilt feelings came forward and received assurance of their own forgiveness.

Enrichment From the Heart: "There is therefore now no condemnation to those who are in Christ Jesus, who do not walk according to the flesh, but according to the Spirit" (Romans 8:1).

Self-Help   **April, Week 3**

Robert D. Crick

LEARNING TO DEAL WITH BITTERNESS

Scripture: Pursue peace with all men, and holiness, without which no one will see the Lord: looking diligently lest anyone fall short of the grace of God; lest any root of bitterness springing up cause trouble, and by this many become defiled (Hebrews 12:14, 15).

Enrichment From the Word: The writer of Hebrews indicates that the one who harbors bitterness will not only be troubled himself but will also trouble others. The Scriptures are clear that if the record is to be set straight, God will do it in His own time and manner.

Enrichment From the Church: Marsha had tried to conceal her hurt when she overheard two ladies whispering about her 16-year-old daughter's unexpected pregnancy.

Her first thoughts were, *What right do they have to judge me or my daughter?* But Marsha remembered what the pastor had said that morning in the worship service: "You cannot make it through difficult times without God and without the church."

She took a deep breath and walked toward the women. "I need your help," she said. "I know you are concerned about my daughter's situation. I would like to ask you to help me by praying with me for her and for our family. We are all hurting very badly."

The two women, embarrassed by their cruelty, asked for Marsha's forgiveness. In time, they became close friends.

Enrichment From the Heart: Lord, help me not to harbor bitterness but to show kindness in every situation.

Self-Help — April, Week 3

Robert D. Crick

LEARNING TO DEAL WITH LUST

Scripture: I say then: Walk in the Spirit, and you shall not fulfill the lust of the flesh. For the flesh lusts against the Spirit, and the Spirit against the flesh; and these are contrary to one another, so that you do not do the things that you wish (Galatians 5:16, 17).

Enrichment From the Word: A healthy sexual relationship within marriage includes much more than the physical. It involves intimacy, communication and the giving of oneself to another. Lust is a specific desire for the body of another person, and it is apparent from the Scriptures that it does not refer to normal God-given sexual desires.

Paul understood the problems of lust and the passions of sexuality. He was aware that God's plan included sexual drives, and he occasionally mentioned methods of appropriately dealing with these needs. He contended that two things are important: first, a close, reflective walk with Christ; and second, good, confidential Christian friends who will allow us to talk about our deepest lusts and temptations.

Enrichment From the Church: How can we protect ourselves from the sin of lust? I would suggest the following: (1) Recognize that lust is a perversion of our God-given sexuality and that we can choose not to submit to its enticement; (2) maintain an attitude in our relationships that focuses on the value of others; (3) nurture the marriage relationship as holy; and (4) maintain a healthy self-image, which can only come through recognizing Christ as the redemptive, forgiving Lord.

Enrichment From the Heart: Lord, You understand my temptations and my inadequacies. Help me to walk in the Spirit and to remember that through You I have strength to overcome both.

Self-Help

April, Week 3

Robert D. Crick

LEARNING TO DEAL WITH JEALOUSY

Scripture: But when his brothers saw that their father loved him more than all his brothers, they hated him and could not speak peaceably to him (Genesis 37:4).

Enrichment From the Word: Joseph's brothers had a typical reaction to what they perceived as injustice: their father treated Joseph better than he treated them. Although some might feel they had cause to be angry over their father's behavior, their response to their anger is typical of what occurs in jealousy. First, there is a change in attitude toward others who may be completely innocent ("they hated him"). This is followed by a break in communication ("they could not speak peaceably to him"). Once the communication is severed, there is little chance for reconciliation. Jealousy has from the earliest of times destroyed individuals, families and even nations.

Enrichment From the Church: Bill was most unhappy. It was not that he wasn't likable; in fact, in his youth he was both popular and congenial. However, due to several crises, Bill began to struggle with jealousy. He was jealous of his brother, who had a better home and car than he; he was jealous of others who did not have to work as hard as he did; he was jealous of everyone who came near his wife.

But simply recognizing his tendency to be jealous did not cure the problem. He met with a Christian counselor for many weeks and talked about his feelings of low self-esteem. It was only when he began to really experience the love of Christ and recognize his own value that Bill began to let go of his jealousy.

Enrichment From the Heart: Lord, thank You for who I am in Christ. Thank You that You cared enough for me to give up Your treasures in heaven and sacrifice Your life for me.

Self-Help   April, Week 3

Robert D. Crick

LEARNING TO DEAL WITH REJECTION

Scripture: He is despised and rejected by men, A man of sorrows and acquainted with grief. And we hid, as it were, our faces from Him; He was despised, and we did not esteem Him (Isaiah 53:3).

Enrichment From the Word: Anyone who has ever experienced rejection is made keenly aware of how painful it can be. This prophecy of the rejection of Christ shows Him to have been "a man of sorrows and acquainted with grief." Surely He was undeserving of that title.

Enrichment From the Church: A friend recently shared the story of how his mother, who had been turned out of the church some 30 years ago, had her membership reinstated. The events leading to her exclusion were thus: Her husband, a small-business owner, had experienced severe financial difficulties. The woman's life was temporarily shattered. During the crisis she frequently missed church. During a church council, she along with several others were disfellowshipped from the local body. As the crisis subsided, she once again returned to church but for 30 years remained a nonmember. When she was asked why she remained faithful to this church, she replied, "I knew that God understood and would eventually take care of it."

Rejection can come from almost anywhere—even from those places and individuals we least expect, and whether or not we "deserve" it.

Enrichment From the Heart: Lord, help me to remember that You understand the pain of my rejection. Help me to look toward You and away from others.

Christian Growth — April, Week 4

Lance Colkmire

UNDERSTANDING THE NEED FOR CHRISTIAN GROWTH

Scripture: Do not be drunk with wine . . . but be filled with the Spirit (Ephesians 5:18).

Enrichment From the Word: "Keep on being filled with the Spirit" is the idea Paul was expressing. Instead of giving in to the natural desire to fill ourselves with carnal pleasures such as drinking, we are to become intoxicated with the Spirit, yielding ourselves to His influence. Galatians 5:16 puts it this way: "Walk in the Spirit, and you shall not fulfill the lust of the flesh."

There is no other route to Christian growth. If we continually cave in to temptation, works of the flesh such as hatred, impurity and idolatry will wreck us. But if we walk in the Spirit—giving ourselves to prayer, Scripture reading, obedience, and worship—the fruit of the Spirit will blossom from our maturing lives.

Enrichment From the Church: An Indian who was a new Christian came to his pastor with this dilemma: "Every day since I accepted Christ, a war has been fought inside me. From the time I get up until I go to bed, this big, black dog fights a big, white dog." The pastor asked, "Who wins?" "Whichever dog I feed the most," the Indian answered.

I know those dogs. As long as I feed my spiritual self, the white dog wins, I'm filled with the Spirit, and His fruit grows in me. But if I feed my sinful desires, the black dog rises up and my spiritual growth is hindered.

Enrichment From the Heart: The alternative to spiritual growth is spiritual stagnation, which leads to spiritual death.

Christian Growth   **April, Week 4**

Lance Colkmire

UNITING EFFORTS FOR SPIRITUAL GROWTH

Scripture: "These commandments that I give you today are to be upon your hearts. Impress them on your children" (Deuteronomy 6:6, 7, *NIV*).

Enrichment From the Word: In the Old Testament, children's church and graded Sunday school are not found. Instead, Hebrew children were participating members of the religious community at large. On the Sabbath and during the various annual festivals, children participated in religious activities with their respective families. Thus, children received their primary instruction from the family, but under the structure of the religious community.

Parents were commanded to love God with all their heart, memorize His law and diligently teach God's Word to their children. "The underlying assumption seems to be that as life is lived together, godly parents will explain their actions by pointing out the words of God that are guiding their responses. . . . Instruction is to infuse all of life" (Lawrence Richards, *A Theology of Children's Ministry*, Zondervan 1983, p. 24).

Enrichment From the Church: Too many parents rely on the church to provide all of their children's spiritual nurture, then blame the church when their kids turn away from God. What these parents don't realize is that, by default, they are already teaching their kids that their spiritual life is unimportant.

There must be a united effort between the church and home to win kids to Christ and disciple them.

Enrichment From the Heart: May the principles that my kids learn at church be lived out in our home.

Christian Growth April, Week 4

Lance Colkmire

GUIDING PRIMARIES IN SPIRITUAL GROWTH

Scripture: From childhood you have known the Holy Scriptures, which are able to make you wise for salvation through faith which is in Christ Jesus (2 Timothy 3:15).

Enrichment From the Word: Timothy's father was a pagan Greek, but his mother and grandmother were devout Jews who taught Timothy the Scriptures. While this godly training did not save Timothy, it did make him "wise for salvation"—it gave him the knowledge he needed to be saved. And Timothy acted on that knowledge by putting his faith in Christ, which is the way to salvation. The Apostle Paul wrote to Timothy, "I call to remembrance the genuine faith that is in you, which dwelt first in your grandmother Lois and your mother Eunice" (1:5).

Enrichment From the Church: Your spiritual responsibility as a parent or teacher of children is to prepare them to receive the gospel message by living a godly life before them and teaching them the truths they must know to be born again: (1) God loves me; (2) I am a sinner; (3) sin separates me from God; (4) Jesus took the punishment on the Cross for my sins; and (5) if I accept Jesus as my Savior and turn from my sins, I have eternal life. Don't worry about whether or not your child is old enough to be saved. There is no predetermined "age of accountability" when kids suddenly become aware of their need for a Savior. You must simply train your kids from infancy and leave the rest to God.

Enrichment From the Heart: Heavenly Father, help me teach my kids the basic truths of the gospel through word and deed. Enable me to make my children ripe for salvation, leading them to the brink of putting their faith in Jesus Christ.

Christian Growth   **April, Week 4**

Lance Colkmire

GUIDING JUNIORS IN SPIRITUAL GROWTH

Scripture: The Lord called Samuel (1 Samuel 3:4).

Enrichment From the Word: "The word of the Lord was rare" in Israel (v. 1). God was not speaking—because Eli the priest had allowed his sons to profane the tabernacle and the holy sacrifices. The nation desperately needed a new spiritual leader, and the Lord chose a boy named Samuel.

Why young Samuel? Consider three reasons: (1) Elkanah and Hannah, Samuel's parents, were devout followers of God. (2) Hannah dedicated Samuel, who was God's miraculous answer to her prayer for a child, to God. The name Samuel means "heard of God." (3) Hannah followed through on her dedicatory act by taking Samuel to the tabernacle to be reared in God's service.

Samuel was trained to serve the Lord, and when he was about 12 years old, "the Lord called Samuel." The boy answered, "'Speak, [Lord,] for Your servant hears'" (v. 10), and God spoke a word of prophecy to him. Best of all, "The Lord continued to appear at Shiloh, and there he revealed himself to Samuel through his word" (v. 21, *NIV*). Samuel became the spiritual leader of Israel.

Enrichment From the Church: Follow the example of Hannah on behalf of your children: Be a devout follower of God, dedicate your children to God through prayer and fasting, and disciple your kids (in your home and through the church) to live for Christ. Through these efforts, God will certainly speak to your children's tender hearts, and your children will likely respond, "Speak, Lord, Your servant is listening."

Enrichment From the Heart: If we do not win our kids to Christ before they become teens, we probably never will.

Christian Growth   **April, Week 4**

Lance Colkmire

GUIDING JUNIOR HIGHS IN CHRISTIAN GROWTH

Scripture: Jesus increased in wisdom and stature, and in favor with God and men (Luke 2:52).

Enrichment From the Word: Jesus would soon turn 13, when He would become an adult under Jewish law. Being human, Jesus surely battled the insecurity of leaving childhood while looking forward to the new privileges his next birthday would bring. As God's Son, Jesus was moving from dependence on earthly parents to total reliance on His Father, but Mary and Joseph didn't realize this. So when they finally found Jesus in the Temple after searching for Him three days, Mary cried, "'Son, why have You done this to us?'" (v. 48). Jesus replied, "'Did you not know that I must be about My Father's business?'" (v. 49). Twelve-year-old Jesus was not mistreating His parents; He was in the process of becoming the Redeemer.

After this event Jesus returned to Nazareth with His parents and continued living in obedience to them as He matured. Ever so slowly Mary would come to understand who her Son really was.

Enrichment From the Church: On the same day that your 14-year-old son writes an insightful essay on abortion, he also gets in trouble for throwing grapes in the cafeteria. Meanwhile your 13-year-old daughter doesn't want to be seen with you at the mall; but when she gets upset, she wants you to hold her.

Relax . . . your junior highs are normal. Even ups and downs in their spiritual lives are typical. However, you can help them grow spiritually by being an example of stability yourself, daily interceding on their behalf and loving them unconditionally.

Enrichment From the Heart: Lord, may my life preach.

Personal Devotions   **May, Week 1**

O. W. Polen

READING THE WORD DAILY

Scripture: It is written . . . (Matthew 4:4, 7, 10).

Enrichment From the Word: When tempted by Satan, Christ resisted by quoting God's Word. After each of three temptations, Christ defeated Satan with the words "It is written. . . ." Jesus cited to Satan the specific verse that was written. We, as Christians, through daily reading and memorizing the Word of God, can develop a reservoir of "Word power" with which to defeat Satan.

Enrichment From the Church: Reading the Word daily is a must for the Christian who would fortify himself to face life daily. Spiritual nourishment from the Word is necessary for spiritual growth just as food is essential for physical growth. I have always been impressed when visiting in a home to see the Word of God in a conspicuous place, indicating that it is read often.

One of the beautiful ways God speaks to His children is through His Word. How enriching it is to read the Bible and to suddenly sense, **God is speaking to me today in a special way through these particular words!** Throughout that day and perhaps for the next several days, the words the Holy Spirit so impressively called to our attention remained with us to comfort, to guide and to inspire.

Abraham Lincoln once said of the Bible, "Read this book for what reason you can accept, and take the rest by faith. You will live and die a better man." D. L. Moody said, "I know the Bible is inspired because it inspires me."

Enrichment From the Heart: Father, help me to hide Your Word in my heart. Help me to always use Your Word, the sword of the Spirit, to fight Satan.

Personal Devotions   **May, Week 1**

O. W. Polen

PRACTICING FELLOWSHIP WITH GOD (PRAYER)

Scripture: But you, beloved, building yourselves up on your most holy faith, praying in the Holy Spirit (Jude 20).

Enrichment From the Word: Just as reading the Word of God is necessary for the Christian to develop spiritual maturity and grow in the grace of the Lord Jesus Christ, so is praying. Prayer is not always easy, as any person who has served God for any length of time knows. To help us pray, even when it is not easy, and to help us maintain daily fellowship with God, the Holy Spirit is always present to assist us.

Enrichment From the Church: We must practice daily personal fellowship with God through prayer. We must also practice fellowship with God by praying with our brothers and sisters in Christ. For this reason we should take advantage of every opportunity to pray with others: in special prayer meetings, at church, or with small groups of three or four believers.

Christians sometimes come to the place in their daily living where burdens and situations are so heavy and complex that they don't know what to pray or how to pray. When our hearts are so heavy we can only cry and groan before God, it is a beautiful experience for the Holy Spirit to take control and pray through us.

There have been many times in my life when I couldn't pray and the Holy Spirit took over and prayed through me in tongues. I didn't know what I was saying. I did know, however, that victory came and the burden of my heart was lifted.

Enrichment From the Heart: Father, we are thankful for the Holy Spirit who is faithful to assist us in praying. Thank You also for the privilege we have to pray with our brothers and sisters in Christ.

Personal Devotions   **May, Week 1**

O. W. Polen

PRAYING IN THE HOLY SPIRIT

Scripture: Likewise the Spirit also helps in our weaknesses. For we do not know what we should pray for as we ought, but the Spirit Himself makes intercession for us with groanings which cannot be uttered (Romans 8:26).

Enrichment From the Word: To be speechless when you are to make a speech is terrifying. To be unable to pray when you desperately need to pray would be even more terrifying were it not for this encouraging fact: God has made provision to help us. He provides the assistance of the Holy Spirit to make intercession for us. I never fail to marvel at how beautifully God makes available the necessary provision to help us in every situation we face.

Enrichment From the Church: The body of Christ is made up of men and women who are brothers and sisters in the family of God. The Holy Spirit not only makes intercession for us when we ourselves can't pray, He also speaks to others in God's family at particular times, impressing them to pray for us. I have had individuals tell me they were inspired to pray for me and my family at a specific time. They didn't know why they were impressed at that particular time to pray; however, they proceeded to pray until the burden was lifted. Later, it was confirmed that the Spirit inspired them to pray at the time my family or I was facing a critical situation.

Enrichment From the Heart: Heavenly Father, thank You for the move of the Holy Spirit upon us and for the assurance that He does a supernatural work for us and within us. We, as Your children, could not survive spiritually without the wonderful benefit of "praying in the Holy Spirit," a treasured benefit You have provided.

Personal Devotions   May, Week 1

O. W. Polen

SUPPORTING THE CHURCH

Scripture: Praying always with all prayer and supplication in the Spirit, being watchful to this end with all perseverance and supplication for all the saints (Ephesians 6:18).

Enrichment From the Word: The Apostle Paul warns against the neglect of prayer. He admonishes us to be watchful. He also emphasizes that perseverance is especially needed to make prayer triumphant.

Further, he stresses the importance of prayer and supplication in the Spirit for "all the saints." This is one of the great purposes for which the people of God are gathered into the "one body"—the church. We uphold each other in prayer during times of spiritual warfare, sickness, death, tragedies, and so forth. We pray for God's servants in the gospel, for those who bear the burden and who are struggling in the heat of the battle.

Enrichment From the Church: There is nothing more beautiful on this earth than a congregation of people who support each other in prayer and who also support their leadership in prayer. This is a powerful church; it makes Satan tremble.

Many years ago an incident I shall never forget took place. A male church member shot another man in self-defense. He was charged with murder and tried in court. A number of members from the man's church attended the trial. When the jury went out to reach a verdict, the members gathered together for prayer. When the jury returned with its verdict, justice prevailed. The verdict was "Not guilty."

Enrichment From the Heart: Father, help me to support my pastor and his family, other church leaders and the members of my church with persevering prayer. And thank You for those who support my family and me in prayer.

Personal Devotions — May, Week 1

O. W. Polen

EXPECTING THE RETURN OF CHRIST

Scripture: Therefore you also be ready, for the Son of Man is coming at an hour when you do not expect Him (Matthew 24:44).

Enrichment From the Word: The warning given in this scripture may be used by the individual Christian for his own benefit. Being "ready" for the coming of the Lord is wise preparation. Every day in our personal devotions we should make a sincere, honest and personal check to see if we are ready should the Lord return that day. Our daily communion with God, through prayer and the reading of His Word, helps us reach and maintain a state of readiness. And when we are in a state of readiness for Christ's return, we will have no fear of His return—whenever it may be.

Enrichment From the Church: I vividly recall the fervent, stirring preaching I heard on the return of Christ when I was a teenager. It was so impressive and forceful that when I walked home from church at night I would look up at the sky, thinking, **He may come tonight.** Then I would try to imagine what His coming would be like.

The thought of His coming was not frightening; rather, it was exciting. I knew I was ready should the Lord come that night.

The thought of His coming and the certainty of it kept me in a state of readiness. We must be ready at all times.

Enrichment From the Heart: Lord, daily help me check my state of readiness for Your return. If at any time I am not ready, speak to me. Give me the courage and strength to do that which will make me ready.

Personal Organization   **May, Week 2**

Julian B. Robinson

ORGANIZING FOR TIME MANAGEMENT

Scripture: Redeeming the time, because the days are evil (Ephesians 5:16).

Enrichment From the Word: God expects us to use wisely His gifts. This seems to be the central meaning of Christ's parable of the talents in Matthew 25:14-30. The servant who was given one talent greatly disappointed his master because he buried his talent. How often is our Master disappointed in us for wasting one of His precious gifts to us—TIME?

We can best manage the time we are given by simply organizing it. God created all that is in six days and did so in an organized manner. Jesus organized His time: Throughout His three-and-a-half years of ministry, He wisely used His time as He ministered to the multitudes, the disciples, the sick and the lost; communed with His Father; dealt with the religious leaders; rested; and so forth. Christ did so much in such a short amount of time; and yet His days, like ours, consisted of only 1,440 minutes.

Enrichment From the Church: A few years ago I had the opportunity to visit London and toured the great Windsor Castle, one of the residences of the royal family. Materially, nothing has been spared, giving the estate an enchanting charm and awe. The worth of just this one mansion is astronomical. Yet, one of the last statements of Queen Elizabeth I was "All my possessions for a moment of time."

"I have only a minute, only sixty seconds in it. Forced upon me—can't refuse it. But it's up to me to use it. I must suffer if I lose it. Give account if I abuse it. Just a tiny little minute, but eternity is in it" (Anonymous).

Enrichment From the Heart: Lord, help me to redeem every moment, hour and day You give me by using my time wisely.

Personal Organization 　　　　　　　　　**May, Week 2**

Julian B. Robinson

KEEPING RECORDS

<u>Scripture:</u> And this is the record, that God hath given to us eternal life, and this life is in his Son (1 John 5:11, *KJV*).

Enrichment From the Word: From cover to cover the Bible puts much emphasis on keeping records. In the Old Testament we discover explicit records of kings, battles, numbering of the tribes of Israel, the building of the Temple, the Temple decor, Creation and much, much more. The New Testament also includes record keeping: "John bare record" that the Spirit descended like a dove and remained on Jesus (John 1:32, *KJV*); the crowd "bare record" that Jesus raised Lazarus (John 12:17, *KJV*); a witness "bare record" that Jesus' crucifixion fulfilled prophecy (John 19:35, *KJV*); and according to 1 John 5:7, "there are three that bear record in heaven, the Father, the Word, and the Holy Ghost" (*KJV*). In fact, the focus of the New Testament is the greatest of all records ever kept—the life of Jesus. Thank God, this record is kept today in the hearts of millions of believers.

Enrichment From the Church: Every month the Church of God International Offices receives thousands of pieces of mail containing the records of approximately 10,000 ministers and 5,700 churches from the United States and Canada. Since these records are vital to the church for reference and planning, they are filed on computer and microfilm for safekeeping.

You should keep records. Records will help you evaluate your present condition and prepare for what is to come. Many times records can save you money, especially if dealing with the IRS! Keep records—you will be glad you did!

Enrichment From the Heart: Can you remember when you were saved, sanctified, filled with the Spirit, healed, baptized, received into church membership? If you can't, you need to start keeping records.

Personal Organization May, Week 2

Julian B. Robinson

DEVELOPING A FOLLOW-THROUGH

Scripture: So he went down and dipped seven times in the Jordan, according to the saying of the man of God; and his flesh was restored like the flesh of a little child, and he was clean (2 Kings 5:14).

Enrichment From the Word: Naaman was a leper.

When Naaman learned about the prophet Elisha, he went to see him in hopes of being cured. Elisha sent a messenger with this word: "'Go and wash in the Jordan seven times . . . and you shall be clean'" (v. 10). Naaman was angry at Elisha because he preferred to wash in one of the beautiful rivers of Damascus. But after some prompting, Naaman obeyed and was cured. It was not pleasant; but had he not been willing to follow instructions, he would have surely died a leper.

Enrichment From the Church: On a football team, each player must follow through on his individual assignment for each play if the team's efforts are to be successful. The church is similar: Each member must follow through with his/her particular duties if the Kingdom work is to be advanced. The Word teaches that we are all members of one body though each of us has a different function. While some church jobs are not easy or pleasant, all are important. And each job requires follow-through. Your faithfulness will not only help the work of the church, it will also make you a better person. Just ask Naaman.

Enrichment From the Heart: Lord, just as You never leave anything unfinished, help me to follow through on my responsibilities and thus become more like You.

Personal Organization   **May, Week 2**

Julian B. Robinson

MAINTAINING A DAILY SCHEDULE

Scripture: He knelt down on his knees three times that day, and prayed and gave thanks before his God, as was his custom since early days (Daniel 6:10).

Enrichment From the Word: One of the prophet Daniel's greatest attributes was his ability to maintain a daily schedule of prayer. King Darius set 120 princes over all the affairs of the kingdom and placed over them three presidents, of which Daniel was first—so Daniel was a **very** busy man. Yet he prayed and gave thanks three times every day. Most likely he prayed in the evening, morning and noon as the psalmist David prayed. Daniel maintained this daily schedule even when, as a consequence, he would be put into the den of lions. How beautiful is the picture drawn by the words "He . . . prayed and gave thanks . . . as was his custom!" Regardless of what came his way, Daniel maintained his daily schedule.

Enrichment From the Church: The thought of a daily schedule brings back memories of the days I spent in boot camp with the United States Air Force. For nine weeks I followed the same schedule. Every hour was structured and filled with either exercises, marching, drills, class training, study or work. Only two hours each day were allowed for free time (mostly spent cleaning barracks or polishing boots). This disciplined routine allowed much to be accomplished in a given time period. Rain or shine, we maintained our schedule.

Enrichment From the Heart: Father, help me to develop a schedule that is best for me, and help me maintain it to bring more glory and praise to Your holy name.

Personal Organization May, Week 2

Julian B. Robinson

IMPROVING PERFORMANCE

Scripture: Therefore I remind you to stir up the gift of God which is in you through the laying on of my hands (2 Timothy 1:6).

Enrichment From the Word: On their first missionary journey Paul and Barnabas took John Mark with them. Later, left and John Mark returned to Jerusalem.

After about two years, Barnabas and Paul decided to visit the places where they had ministered, and Barnabas wanted John Mark to accompany them. Paul disagreed; thus Paul and Barnabas separated. Years later, however, the imprisoned Apostle Paul urged Timothy, "Get Mark and bring him with you, for he is useful to me for ministry" (2 Timothy 4:11). John Mark, though he had an unstable beginning, is remembered as an asset to the work of the early church because he improved his performance.

Enrichment From the Church: Webster defines **performance** as "the execution of an action; the fulfillment of a claim." But the real question is, How well do we perform? Here are four elements essential in improving performance: (1) Examine present conditions objectively. Are improvements needed? If so, in what specific areas? (2) Cultivate a genuine desire to improve. Do I really want to improve my performance and for what reason? (3) Practice and work hard. Am I willing to make the necessary sacrifices to improve? (4) Be patient. Improvement always takes time.

Enrichment From the Heart: In seeking to improve our performance, Colossians 3:17 should be our guide: "Whatever you do in work or deed, do all in the name of the Lord Jesus."

Self-Help

Mike Baker

May, Week 3

BUILDING POSITIVE RELATIONSHIPS

Scripture: Blessed is the man Who walks not in the counsel of the ungodly, Nor stands in the path of sinners, Nor sits in the seat of the scornful (Psalm 1:1).

Enrichment From the Word: Every day we rub shoulders with a wide circle of family, friends and acquaintances. Many of these relationships develop within the context of school and work, as well as in the church. Psalm 1 emphasizes the importance of relationships and interactions with others. It urges us to avoid negative associations and concentrate on building positive relationships. In doing so, we are blessed.

Enrichment From the Church: We all live in relationships. Some are positive, some negative. Common sense tells us that whoever we spend our time with will certainly affect our behavior.

I heard someone say, "Every town has a clank club." A clank club is a group of people who gather at local restaurants or homes to drink coffee, clank their spoons against their cups, and complain about the world's problems. Nothing positive will ever take place in their presence.

Jesus was very careful about the circle of friends He kept. He surrounded Himself with positive people.

If you really want to prosper, associate with those who really believe in getting things done.

Enrichment From the Heart: Associate yourself with individuals who are committed to building positive relationships. Forget the negative gobbles of flocking turkeys who never get off the ground, and soar with the positive high-flying eagles.

Self-Help   May, Week 3

Mike Baker

DEVELOPING COMMUNICATION SKILLS

Scripture: "Thus they shall know that I, the Lord their God, am with them, and that they, the house of Israel, are My people," says the Lord God (Ezekiel 34:30).

Enrichment From the Word: God has used so many diverse methods to communicate with man. He has spoken through His powerful hand in creation; He has revealed His will through dreams and visions; and He has spoken directly to man in his own language.

To the Israelites exiled in Babylon, God communicated His profound love for them and that under all circumstances He was still with them.

Enrichment From the Church: Human language is a gift from God. One of the divine blessings given to man at his creation was the power of speech—the ability to use and understand language. Our thoughts can be transmitted by means of written symbols, dots and dashes, recordings, and even smoke signals. A message recorded or written today can be preserved indefinitely and understood by future generations hundreds of years from now. While animals can make signs and sounds, their communication cannot compare with human language.

In *Effective Communication*, David Bishop divides human communication into three basic categories: intrapersonal communication (within one), interpersonal communication (one-to-one), and group communication (one-to-many). The most important communication skill we can develop is that of interpersonal communication with God.

Enrichment From the Heart: God speaks to us, we listen, and then we share His message with others. We have the responsibility to communicate the message of Christ in the most effective way with all mankind.

Self-Help   May, Week 3

Mike Baker

LEARNING TO RESPECT OTHERS

Scripture: Beloved, let us love one another, for love is of God; and everyone who loves is born of God and knows God (1 John 4:7).

Enrichment From the Word: Love is the language of God's kingdom. Love and respect for others will convince them that God is real. If we've failed to love others as we should, there is a way we can increase our love for our fellow Christians as well as for nonbelievers. First, we must allow God's love to flow through us. Second, we must accept and respect others as they are.

Enrichment From the Church: The traffic is moving along at a snail's pace. You're in a hurry to make an appointment. In front of you is someone who is traveling along leisurely. Your temper rises, "Get out of the way . . . don't you know how to drive?" Suddenly you kick your car into passing gear and away you go. Wow, you are now ahead 15 seconds. But where is your respect for yourself and the other driver?

If we have fellowship with God, we should love and respect one another. Non-Christians will not believe in Christ if Christians do not love each other. Do your friends or members of your family not believe in Christ because they see in you a spirit of disrespect toward others?

If we meet a fellow Christian who doesn't agree with us about everything, do we accept him anyway? Do we accept other Christians with different experiences from our own? Respect for others will promote the cause of Christ.

Enrichment From the Heart: Lord, help me this day to submit myself to loving and respecting other people. Let me honor all men, love fellow believers, and acknowledge Your sovereignty over all creation. In Jesus' name, Amen.

Self-Help   May, Week 3

Mike Baker

REMEMBERING THE LORD'S COMMAND

Scripture: Jesus said to him, " 'You shall love the Lord your God with all your heart, with all your soul, and with all your mind.' This is the first and great commandment" (Matthew 22:37, 38).

Enrichment From the Word: A Pharisee asked Jesus the tempting question, "Which is the great commandment in the law?" The Master put him to silence by citing the commandment to love God completely.

God wants us to love Him completely—heart, soul, mind and strength. He doesn't want lukewarmness in our relationship with Him. He realizes we can fall in love with many things that will leave us empty. That's why He instructs us to hear, remember and act on the command to love God above all.

Enrichment From the Church: Have you ever seen a person in love with yard sales? That's right! Every Saturday morning these individuals arise very early in order to be first to go from yard to yard finding bargains. They love the experience.

Others fall in love with fishing. They'll drive hundreds of miles to find the perfect lake where they can drop a line and wait in the hot sun for mindless fish to bite. The funny thing is, I love fishing, too!

These loves are not sinful in themselves, but they leave us empty and unfulfilled. God urges us to find satisfaction and fulfillment in loving Him.

Enrichment From the Heart: Love God with heart, soul, mind and strength. Clap your hands, sing, cry, laugh and even shout. If we never express our love to God, is it real? Express your love to God today!

Self-Help

May, Week 3

Mike Baker

DEPENDING ON THE HOLY SPIRIT

Scripture: Likewise the Spirit also helps in our weaknesses. For we do not know what we should pray for as we ought, but the Spirit Himself makes intercession for us with groanings which cannot be uttered (Romans 8:26).

Enrichment From the Word: When it is difficult to determine God's will, allow the Holy Spirit to pray through you. Have you ever experienced the Spirit praying through you? The Scripture says the Holy Spirit helps our weaknesses and makes intercession for us. Our dependence should be placed on the power of the Holy Spirit. This is why we need to pray and give the heavenly Dove a chance to work in our lives—especially when we feel like throwing in the towel.

Enrichment From the Church: Have you ever felt like giving up? I have! Sometimes we become so discouraged we can't even pray for ourselves. But don't give up. Don't become hardened to God. Depend on the Holy Spirit!

When we surrender to and depend on the Spirit of God, we can experience the Holy Spirit praying through us. It works! His intercession breaks through to the heart of God.

Enrichment From the Heart: When we reach the point where we need supernatural help to pray, the Holy Spirit will help us. It might happen through groans, tears or praise, but the Holy Spirit will help us reach God with our sincere prayers.

Christian Growth   **May, Week 4**

James E. Humbertson

GUIDING TEENS IN CHRISTIAN GROWTH

Scripture: Blessed are the undefiled in the way, Who walk in the law of the Lord! Blessed are those who keep His testimonies, Who seek Him with the whole heart! (Psalm 119:1, 2).

Enrichment From the Word: The psalmist declares there is happiness to those who are sincere and upright and who walk in the ways of the Lord. Double-mindedness was considered evil by the pious, since it revealed a divided heart—fearing God but worshiping other gods. The "undefiled" person is not stained by self-seeking motives or a spirit of hypocrisy. Rather he professes to walk in the law of the Lord, and he does. The psalmist also declares a blessedness to those who seek God with the "whole heart." Half-hearted service to God is accompanied by a miserable round of sinning and repenting, but the life spoken of in these verses is lived in the sunshine of the love of God and in the possession of a clear conscience void of offense.

Enrichment From the Church: Success in every sphere of action is attained by thoroughness, by concentrating one's forces and working "with the whole heart." Many teen lives have been wasted because peer pressures created divided interests, thereby destroying initiative and dissipating strengths. In no area of thought or action is thoroughness and singleness of thought more demanded than in one's relationship with God.

   The Apostle Paul said, "One thing I do . . . I press toward the goal for the prize of the upward call of God in Christ Jesus" (Philippians 3:13, 14). "One thing" is a worthy goal if the goal is a life fully committed to God. It requires doing it with the whole heart.

Enrichment From the Heart: Lord, grant that teenagers of this generation will make You the all-consuming goal of their lives.

Christian Growth — May, Week 4

James E. Humbertson

GUIDING SINGLES IN CHRISTIAN GROWTH

Scripture: Your word is a lamp to my feet And a light to my path (Psalm 119:105).

Enrichment From the Word: A study of the Word of God will help one understand what is of greater value than a science, an art or a language. Other books, however valuable, are unlike the Bible in one important way—they are not inspired by God; the Bible is. It alone is infallible and unerring.

The Bible can illuminate one's path. Without divine guidance, "it is not in man who walks to direct his own steps" (Jeremiah 10:23). Men go wrong, not from want of knowledge of the right but from an unwillingness to follow the right.

Enrichment From the Church: The streets of towns in many parts of the world are narrow, unlighted, ill-kept and terribly dark at night. Such streets often have large holes and soft muddy places or large loose stones; and if one is to choose his way safely, he must not only have a light, but he must hold it down at his feet so that his next footstep can be guided. This was the context in which the psalmist said God's Word "is a lamp to my feet." God's Word is not just a light for general use; it is something to hold close for the direction of each step in life that is taken.

Life is full of perils, pitfalls and stones of stumbling. But God's Word is relevant to all possible human experiences and dangers. It gives precise counsel, guiding conduct in every perplexing circumstance.

Enrichment From the Heart: Dear heavenly Father, remind us through the Spirit and through Your Word that You seek to guide our steps even in the darkest of nights. Too often we are prone to find man-made light or light a candle of our own.

Christian Growth   **May, Week 4**

James E. Humbertson

GUIDING YOUNG ADULTS IN CHRISTIAN GROWTH

Scripture: How can a young man keep his way pure? By living according to your word. I seek you with all my heart; do not let me stray from your commands (Psalm 119:9, 10, *NIV*).

Enrichment From the Word: In retrospect the psalmist looked over the past and reflected on what a help God's Word had been to him amid the perils and temptations of his early life. He had determined to be ruled by God's Word and now rejoiced that he had been victorious and unspotted from the sins of the world.

Experience is a precious school, and the lessons for the Christian are only gained fully when a life is ordered by God's infallible guide. The psalmist knew that the Word would help keep a young life pure.

Enrichment From the Church: Delbert and Mary Todd were members of a prestigious Midwest church. They were hardworking professional people with a promising future. But pressing demands of Delbert's job led to his missing church services and to neglect of his prayer life and Bible study. Soon there were temptations of infidelity, social drinking and the threat of divorce.

An alert pastor sensed the problem, and after hours of counseling and prayer, Delbert committed his life to the Lord, determined to keep his life pure. Within two weeks he was on a new job he applied for. There was an increase in salary, and he was surrounded by Christian workers.

Enrichment From the Heart: Lord, help all of us, especially young men and women, to keep You as our constant guide.

Christian Growth   May, Week 4

James E. Humbertson

GUIDING ADULTS IN CHRISTIAN GROWTH

Scripture: Teach me, O Lord, the way of Your statutes, And I shall keep it to the end. Give me understanding, and I shall keep Your law; Indeed, I shall observe it with my whole heart (Psalm 119:33, 34).

Enrichment From the Word: The psalmist who wrote these verses realized there were conditions he must meet and do since his well-being depended on his personal responsibility to the Word of God. He was aware there were commands from God he must learn. But he also knew he could not teach himself; God must teach him.

The knowledge he had motivated him to move in the direction of God, but soon he became ready to slow down or stop altogether his pursuit of understanding. God must help if he was to continue on. But with confidence that God would help, he determined to get away from any halfhearted effort in his relationship with God. Rather his prayer to God was that he would observe the law with his whole heart.

Enrichment From the Church: A church in London, England, regularly distributed Bibles to the poor of the city. A lady whose possessions had been destroyed in a fire, received one of the distributed Bibles. She sent a note to the church saying, "Thank you, and thank God, I now have a Bible. It was the guide of my youth, and it is the staff of my age. It wounded me and healed me. It showed me I was a sinner, and it led me to the Savior. It has given me comfort and understanding in life, and I know it will give me hope in death."

Enrichment From the Heart: Lord, teach me Your Word through the Holy Spirit's guidance. Give me determination to pursue with my whole heart a close, growing relationship with You.

Christian Growth   **May, Week 4**

James E. Humbertson

GUIDING SENIOR ADULTS IN CHRISTIAN GROWTH

Scripture: The righteous shall flourish like a palm tree, He shall grow like a cedar in Lebanon. Those who are planted in the house of the Lord Shall flourish in the courts of our God. They shall still bear fruit in old age; They shall be fresh and flourishing, To declare that the Lord is upright; He is my rock, and there is no unrighteousness in Him (Psalm 92:12-15).

Enrichment From the Word: "Fruit in old age." This is one of God's promises to His faithful people. Those advanced in years have the advantage of sharing the knowledge of a lifetime to help guide others. The disciplines of long life develop sanctity of character, patience, a heavenly-mindedness, but above all, the concern and desire to see others give their lives to Christ. The psalmist declared that the righteous will show forth God as their rock of stability in an unstable world. Their testimony will bear fruit since wisdom and understanding are gained through longevity. "Wisdom is with aged men, And with length of days, understanding" (Job 12:12).

Enrichment From the Church: Advancing in years does not mean productive service is over. At age 70 Billy Graham is still active in evangelism. Ronald Reagan became president of the United States at age 70. And at age 95 Herbert Lockyer delivered devotions at the Evangelical Press Association Convention. Many retired ministers are active in Kingdom service, and laymen by the hundreds are regularly involved in service to the Lord.

Enrichment From the Heart: Lord, grant to every senior Christian a desire to share the joys and experiences of a lifetime of service for You.

Discipleship   June, Week 1

Dorothy Jennings

UNDERSTANDING TRUE DISCIPLESHIP

Scripture: Then Jesus said to His disciples, "If anyone desires to come after Me, let him deny himself, and take up his cross, and follow Me" (Matthew 16:24).

Enrichment From the Word: The words Jesus used when He called disciples were, "Follow me." We must follow Jesus as sheep follow the shepherd, as servants serve their master, or as a soldier obeys his captain. We must make a deliberate choice to willingly come to Him, learn of Him and submit to His terms.

Jesus said, "Let him deny himself." These words are in direct opposition to sparing oneself. It is a hard lesson and one that goes against the flesh. But our Savior spared not Himself, and the servant is not greater than his Lord. We, then, are to take up our cross, designed for us by infinite wisdom, and follow with a lifestyle of holiness and obedience.

Enrichment From the Church: As followers of Christ we need the strength and encouragement of fellow believers. Within this community of trust one should be free to confess his faults, be prayed for and be healed. This is a vital and needed ministry for these days of adversity. In these times the prayers and mutual love of the saints will help steady our going and will lighten our load.

Enrichment From the Heart: I affirm my faith in words from the diary of Jim Elliot, one of five missionaries martyred by Auca Indians more than 25 years ago: "He is no fool who gives what he cannot keep to gain what he cannot lose."

Discipleship

Dorothy Jennings

COUNTING THE COST OF COMMITMENT

Scripture: Do you not know that your body is the temple of the Holy Spirit who is in you, whom you have from God, and you are not your own? For you were bought at a price; therefore glorify God in your body and in your spirit, which are God's (1 Corinthians 6:19, 20).

Enrichment From the Word: If the full impact of this scripture were realized, a revolution would take place in our lives. We are not our own to choose what we will or will not do. We are not proprietors of ourselves; therefore, we should live according to His will and for His glory. We are His.

What a price was paid to buy us back from the clutches of Satan! What a debt we owe! Yet, all we can give is ourselves in total commitment. Can we grasp the full meaning of the cost—Christ's dying in our stead? That changes our sentence of death to everlasting life!

Enrichment From the Church: Early in life I faced a crossroad. Everyone does sooner or later. Would Jesus be Lord of my life, my hopes, my dreams, my plans? That decision, a total commitment strengthened by my ties to the church, has lasted from my youth, through high school, marriage, raising a family. Now it sustains me in later years. Roosevelt Miller's song of commitment says it well:

> I will follow Thee, Dear Lord,
> I will follow Thee.

Enrichment From the Heart: I know that the peace and joy we receive here and the eternal rewards of the hereafter cannot be compared to any price we may pay.

Discipleship   June, Week 1

Martha S. Wong

BECOMING LIKE CHRIST

Scripture: For whom He foreknew, He also predestined to be conformed to the image of His Son, that He might be the firstborn among many brethren (Romans 8:29).

Enrichment From the Word: We cling to Romans 8:28— "And we know that all things work together for good to those who love God, to those who are the called according to His purpose"—often forgetting Romans 8:29, which explains the divine purpose of God's working: to conform us to the likeness of His Son! As Christ Jesus is the express image and glory of the Father (1 Corinthians 11:7), so are we to express Christ's glory and character to the world.

How can we be conformed? It is a work of cooperation between the saint and the Spirit. Removing all distractions or veils, we behold the glory of the Lord by looking into the mirror of His Word through prayer. In His presence we behold the splendor of His divine nature and the Spirit conforms us by transforming us into His likeness "from glory to glory," a step-by-step process into the ever-increasing splendor of Christ's character and glory! (See 2 Corinthians 3:18).

Enrichment From the Church: I have often observed the glory of God on Christians who are most like Christ. Though suffering great difficulties, they live with tremendous blessing and victory. Believing and obeying the Word, worshiping God, and cooperating with the Holy Spirit, they are transformed and conformed by His power. How gloriously they reflect Him!

Enrichment From the Heart: There is no splendor like that of Christ! I want to reflect the splendor of His "image" to my world.

Discipleship

June, Week 1

Martha S. Wong

PRACTICING CONSISTENCY

Scripture: They could find no charge or fault, because he was faithful (Daniel 6:4).

Enrichment From the Word: The prophet Daniel was one of the most consistently faithful individuals we have record of in Holy Scripture. His work was so exemplary, his spirit, knowledge and understanding so excellent, that God was able to shake empires and sway kings through his consistent life. A den of lions could not persuade Daniel to change his lifestyle!

Nathaniel Bartholomew, one of the Twelve, shared a similar trait. "Behold, an Israelite indeed, in whom is no guile [deceit]!" Christ exclaimed (John 1:47). What a compliment! Jesus did not make this statement about anyone else during His earthly ministry. Nathaniel was transparent in his motives and morals.

Enrichment From the Church: I read of an evangelist who once made a call on a pay telephone. After he gave the operator his name and told her the number he wanted, he deposited money in the slot, talked for a few minutes and hung up the receiver. When he did, all his coins were returned.

Calling the operator again he said, "I don't know if you are the person who took my call just now, but my coins came back."

"I know," she said. "I was in your audience tonight when you spoke on integrity, and I wondered if you practiced what you preached. So I flipped the lever and returned the coins."

The evangelist put the coins back in the box—but only after making an appointment to talk to the telephone operator in person. As a result of their meeting, she trusted the Lord as her Savior.

Enrichment From the Heart: Whatever the cost, whatever the inconvenience, whatever the results, O Lord, help me to "walk" my "talk."

Discipleship

June, Week 1

Martha S. Wong

BELIEVING CHRIST FOR MIRACLES

Scripture: Jesus said to him, "If you can believe, all things are possible to him who believes." Immediately the father of the child cried out and said with tears, "Lord, I believe; help my unbelief!" (Mark 9:23, 24).

Enrichment From the Word: Until the father of the child admitted and worked through his unbelief, he could not believe Jesus could or would deliver his son. Others did not believe in Jesus in spite of His many miracles. In Nazareth, Jesus was severely limited in working miracles. "He could do no mighty work there, except that He laid His hands on a few sick people and healed them. And He marveled because of their unbelief" (Mark 6:5, 6). Unbelief can sabotage your faith in Christ for miracles.

Enrichment From the Church: When a miracle is needed, it is imperative to find scripturally balanced believers in the church to pray with you. I have sought for a person who had complete confidence, faith and trust in God's power—one who believed God could and would do a mighty miracle. This person and I would then stand together in believing prayer according to Matthew 18:19, 20.

As my friend prayed with me, my focus changed from the need for a miracle to the God of miracles! Asking according to the will, plan, and purposes of God has brought miracles into my life! He has not granted every request; He is still a sovereign God. Nevertheless, all things, Jesus said, are possible to a believer.

Enrichment From the Heart: Am I limiting God's miracle-working power in my life or in my church because of unbelief? I cry out with tears, "Lord, I believe; help my unbelief!"

Nurture   **June, Week 2**

Daniel L. Black

REJOICING IN HOPE

Scripture: "Rejoicing in hope. . . . In hope of eternal life which God, who cannot lie, promised before time began" (Romans 12:12; Titus 1:2).

Enrichment From the Word: There is a familiar saying that goes, "While there is life, there is hope." Ordinarily this saying is taken to mean that right up to the point of death we can keep hoping that something good will happen. But for the Christian, hope does not end at death, just as his life does not end there. The Christian rejoices in the hope of eternal life. Hopes that are tied to the passing things of this life may give us joy for a while, but soon these hopes will perish. When earthly helpers fail and earthly comforts flee, we can rejoice in the hope of eternal life.

Enrichment From the Church: The setting was a meeting of a group of pastors from all denominations involved in clinical pastoral education. The man talking to the group was an ordained Lutheran minister and a well-known counseling psychologist. He was saying to us, "What you preachers have to offer people on Sunday morning is more powerful for helping people than anything we have in the field of psychology." He went on to speak of God and the hope of things eternal. He talked of how these realities are the only things which can give us real purpose and hope in life. Yes, the Christian hope of eternal life is a powerful help to people. It replaces sorrow and despair with rejoicing in hope.

Enrichment From the Heart: God our Father, fill us anew with the hope of the eternal life You have promised to us through our faith in Christ. Awaken our heart daily with an inward song of rejoicing in hope. Amen.

Nurture

Daniel L. Black

REJOICING IN PERSECUTION

Scripture: But rejoice to the extent that you partake of Christ's sufferings, that when His glory is revealed, you may also be glad with exceeding joy (1 Peter 4:13).

Enrichment From the Word: The scattered Christians to whom Peter wrote this Epistle were persecuted by pagan Gentiles who misunderstood the Christians and regarded them as atheists because they would not worship the pagan gods. In fact, the persecutions suffered by the early Christians were so constant and severe that some had become discouraged. Peter reminded the troubled believers that their sufferings for Christ should not be a cause of discouragement but a reason for rejoicing.

Peter spoke from experience. In the earliest days of the church, he had been beaten and threatened for testifying of Jesus Christ. But the Bible says he and the other apostles rejoiced "that they were counted worthy to suffer shame for His name" (Acts 5:41).

Enrichment From the Church: Church historians estimate that more people have died for their faith in Christ in the 20th century than in all previous centuries of the Christian era combined. In the modern world, unbelievers have many subtle and often explicit ways of opposing, discriminating against and mistreating Christians. While we should recognize that the unbelieving world is opposed to Christ and His people, let us never have a depressing persecution or martyr complex. Rather let us, as Christians should, rejoice that God counts us worthy to share the sufferings of Christ.

Enrichment From the Heart: Gracious Father, give to us the wisdom to understand and accept the fact that we are not cursed when we suffer for Christ but blessed. Cause us to rejoice in these sufferings, knowing that great is our reward in heaven. Amen.

Nurture June, Week 2

Daniel L. Black

REJOICING IN TRIALS

Scripture: My brethren, count it all joy when you fall into various trials, knowing that the testing of your faith produces patience. But let patience have its perfect work, that you may be perfect and complete, lacking nothing (James 1:2-4).

Enrichment From the Word: Trying experiences come to test the faith of every Christian. When this happens, "Count it all joy," said James. That is, to translate the words more literally, "Consider it a matter of rejoicing." But how can we do this? James went on to explain that God's purpose in allowing trials to come our way is to advance the development of our Christian character. With this divine goal in view, we can look past the trials of our faith and rejoice for the good that God aims to accomplish through our trials.

Enrichment From the Church: The Protestant reformer Martin Luther confessed that there were chiefly three things that had introduced him into a deeper spiritual life. These three things were meditation on the Word of God, persevering and earnest prayer, and trials he had suffered on account of the Word of God.

An untested faith becomes weak like a body without exercise. The trial that requires us to fight for our faith and struggle to be loyal to Christ can also cause us to grow strong in Christian character.

Enrichment From the Heart: God of all wisdom, we do not ask to have our faith tested; but when trials come, keep us faithful and cause us to rejoice in the remembrance that You are working for our good, even in times of trial. Amen.

Nurture   **June, Week 2**

Daniel L. Black

REJOICING IN VICTORY

Scripture: The Lord is my strength and my shield; My heart trusted in Him, and I am helped; Therefore my heart greatly rejoices, And with my song I will praise Him (Psalm 28:7).

Enrichment From the Word: The first half of this psalm is plaintive and entreating. But suddenly, at verse 6, it seems David must have received some divine assurance that his prayer was heard, and he began to rejoice, blessing and praising God for victory.

Do we rejoice over the many assurances of victory given to us in God's Word? As Christians, do we rejoice over the victory assured to us by the one great victory Christ won for us through His death and resurrection? Whatever may be our present circumstances, we can rejoice in our victory in Jesus Christ.

Enrichment From the Church: A black African pastor in Angola was bereaved of his wife. A large number of people came to the funeral. They all sat on the ground and began to wail, blending their voices in a dirge of despair. Suddenly, the pastor, who was standing by the coffin of his beloved wife, called out to the mourners, "Stop all this yelling and howling!" The shocked mourners fell silent. Then the pastor said to them, "This woman was a child of God. She has gone home to her Father. Today we are not crying, we are singing!" With that the pastor began to sing, and the mourners joined in—singing a hymn of praise to God, a song of Christ's victory.

Enrichment From the Heart: God of all grace, when we feel defeated, give us a new vision of the victory assured to us in Christ. Cause us to rejoice in the victory Christ has already won for us. Amen.

Nurture   **June, Week 2**

Daniel L. Black

REJOICING ALWAYS

Scripture: Rejoice in the Lord always. Again I will say, rejoice! (Philippians 4:4).

Enrichment From the Word: Joy in the Lord Jesus is not only the keynote of the Epistle to the Philippians, but it leaps out at us from the pages of the New Testament. Saint John Chrysostom said, "He who rejoices in the Lord, always rejoices, even in affliction."

Notice that the Christian's joy is *in the Lord*. The impossibility of rejoicing always—at all times and in all ways—disappears when we remember that we are to rejoice in the Lord.

Enrichment From the Church: Although he was not an ordained minister, the Welsh layman Billy Bray would work in the mines to earn enough money to go preaching. Then, when his wages were exhausted, he would return to the mines, earn more money and go preaching again. This joyful man, who continually praised the Lord out loud, led thousands to Christ. Billy Bray said of himself, "As I go along the street, I lift up one foot, and it seems to say, 'Amen!' I lift the other foot, and it seems to say, 'Glory!'" When someone chanced to meet Billy Bray as he went along singing, he would say, "Bless the Lord, I can sing. I can't sing as well as some, but my Father likes to hear me."

Enrichment From the Heart: God our Father, thank You for giving us joy in Your dear Son at all times. Fill us with the joy of believing and cause the world to see that the joy of the Lord is our strength. Amen.

The Holy Spirit   June, Week 3

Clyne W. Buxton

GROWING THE FRUIT OF THE SPIRIT— GOODNESS

Scripture: He was a good man, full of the Holy Spirit and of faith. And a great many people were added to the Lord (Acts 11:24).

Enrichment From the Word: "Goodness is that which is both upright and honorable as combined with and tempered by generosity," so stated Rubel Shelly in his *In Step With the Spirit*. That definition certainly applies to Barnabas (Acts 4).

Again, his goodness was demonstrated when he openly received Paul at Jerusalem after Paul's conversion, while others looked askance at the former persecutor. Later Barnabas was sent to stabilize the new church at Antioch of Syria (Acts 11). The brethren knew a good man like him would be a stabilizing force in a local church.

Enrichment From the Church: Good people in the local church are always at a premium. Those whose deportment is not just a facade or a pretense of goodness, who are genuinely committed to Christ and His service are invaluable. Some people may spend their time trying to make themselves appear good.

Others, meanwhile, demonstrate goodness by holy living, by preferring others before themselves, and by constantly putting forth an effort to help and encourage those about them. Like Barnabas, they demonstrate their goodness by their attitude and their actions.

Enrichment From the Heart: When my goodness is misunderstood, misused by others or rejected, that is when my motives for goodness are put to the test. If anger or retaliation rises up within me, my goodness is probably not Spirit-directed. Lord, help me to have the purest of motives as I work at practicing goodness as a fruit of the Spirit.

The Holy Spirit — June, Week 3

Clyne W. Buxton

GROWING THE FRUIT OF THE SPIRIT— FAITH (FAITHFULNESS)

Scripture: "Whoever can be trusted with very little can also be trusted with much, and whoever is dishonest with very little will also be dishonest with much" (Luke 16:10, 11, *NIV*).

Enrichment From the Word: Dependability is a quality that permeates everything the Christian does.

Paul discussed this spiritual fruit in 1 Corinthians 4:2 when he said, "Now it is required that those who have been given a trust must prove faithful" (*NIV*).

Our Lord constantly taught the importance of faithfulness. In the parable of the talents, for example, He told of the response to the faithfulness of each man. Each time the owner said, "'Well done, good and faithful servant; you were faithful over a few things, I will make you ruler over many things'" (Matthew 25:21).

Enrichment From the Church: On the office wall of Ray Kroc, founder of McDonald's restaurants, were the following words: "Nothing in the world can take the place of persistence. Talent will not; nothing is more common than unsuccessful men with great talent. Genius will not; unrewarded genius is almost a proverb. Education will not; the world is full of educated derelicts. Persistence and determination alone are omnipotent."

The Christian knows that persistence and determination are not omnipotent virtues, but the omnipotent Holy Spirit can give us those virtues.

Enrichment From the Heart: The Bible faithfully promises; "If we confess our sins, He is faithful and just to forgive us our sins and to cleanse us from all unrighteousness" (1 John 1:9).

The Holy Spirit — June, Week 3

Clyne W. Buxton

GROWING THE FRUIT OF THE SPIRIT— MEEKNESS (GENTLENESS)

Scripture: We were gentle among you, like a mother caring for her little children. We loved you so much that we were delighted to share with you not only the gospel of God but our lives as well, because you had become so dear to us (1 Thessalonians 2:7, 8, *NIV*).

Enrichment From the Word: Gentleness is one of the most valuable virtues of a believer. Brash, harsh words and actions will turn people from us, while a loving, tender demeanor will build up and encourage others. Paul said his approach to the Thessalonian believers was "like a mother caring for her little children." What a tender, graphic metaphor!

Christ was the epitome of gentleness. The world would have expected such a powerful figure to be stern and unapproachable. However, Christ knew that gentleness was a mark of true greatness. He said of Himself, "I am gentle and humble in heart" (Matthew 11:29, *NIV*). That is how we ought to be. Gentleness is a beautiful fruit of the Holy Spirit.

Enrichment From the Church: Church members need to study to be gentle toward each other instead of selfish and bitter. The Apostle Paul saw such a need in the church at Philippi, so he wrote, "Your attitude should be the same as that of Christ Jesus: Who, being in very nature God, did not consider equality with God something to be grasped, but made himself nothing, taking the very nature of a servant, being made in human likeness" (Philippians 2:5-7, *NIV*). Since we are the temple of the Holy Spirit, being a "gentleman" or "gentlewoman" should be our normal lifestyle.

Enrichment From the Heart: Lord, help us to be gentle and understanding toward people about us. Condemn us when we are abrasive and harsh. Let us cultivate gentleness.

The Holy Spirit   June, Week 3

Clyne W. Buxton

GROWING THE FRUIT OF THE SPIRIT—
TEMPERANCE (SELF-CONTROL)

Scripture: Like a city whose walls are broken down is a man who lacks self-control (Proverbs 25:28, *NIV*).

Enrichment From the Word: How graphic is the above reference! Without self-control, we are totally open to error. David's handling of his difficult situation with Saul is a glowing example of self-control (see 1 Samuel 26). David was fleeing for his life while Saul sought him with the help of thousands of soldiers. Saul had declared his intent to slay David.

But note David's self-control. Twice he had ample opportunity to kill Saul, but both times he refused to do so. Here is the account of his second opportunity: "David and Abishai came to the people by night; and there Saul lay sleeping within the camp, with his spear stuck in the ground by his head. And Abner and the people lay all around him. Then Abishai said to David, 'God has delivered your enemy into your hand this day. Now therefore, please, let me strike him at once with the spear, right to the earth; and I will not have to strike him a second time!' And David said to Abishai, 'Do not destroy him; for who can stretch out his hand against the Lord's anointed, and be guiltless? . . . the Lord shall strike him'" (1 Samuel 26:7-10).

Enrichment From the Church: The world does not always teach self-control. Instead, it says, "Eat, drink and be merry, for tomorrow we may die." The lack of self-discipline may cause a husband to abuse his wife or parents the children. Failure to restrain sexual desires may lead to adultery, and lack of control of the temper may lead to frightening consequences. Against that backdrop the Lord offers help in self-control.

Enrichment From the Heart: Lord, give me the fortitude to practice self-control in all areas of my life, including eating, recreation, conduct and spiritual matters.

The Holy Spirit   June, Week 3

Clyne W. Buxton

DISPLAYING THE FRUIT OF THE SPIRIT

Scripture: "The fruit of the Spirit is love, joy, peace, patience, kindness, goodness, faithfulness, gentleness and self-control. . . . Since we live by the Spirit, let us keep in step with the Spirit" (Galatians 5:22, 23, 25, *NIV*).

Enrichment From the Word: Paul's measure of spirituality.
  1. Love—the ability to reach beyond yourself.
  2. Joy—it demonstrates a sense of security.
  3. Peace—the result of living in serenity with God and others.
  4. Patience—the ability to live through difficulties and circumstances until God's will is revealed
  5. Kindness—enough interest in those about us to be involved.
  6. Goodness—honorable, upright living, conditioned with generosity.
  7. Faithfulness—complete dependability, reliability and loyalty.
  8. Gentleness—akin to kindness and goodness, this fruit has the additional quality of strength under divine control.
  9. Self-control—this fruit is all-important. Otherwise, we will enslave ourselves to drives and appetites which will ruin our testimony.

Enrichment From the Church: Being a Christian is not a pushover way of life. Instead, it is a difficult, demanding way to live. That is why we need the constant guidance of the Holy Spirit, for only the Spirit-filled life will yield the fruit of the Spirit. With self crucified we are given the power to walk with God, bearing the fruit of the Spirit as we go.

Enrichment From the Heart: Thank You, Lord, for showing me from Your Word that I can be a fruitful Christian, and in doing so I will be a truly spiritual follower.

Societal Relationships   **June, Week 4**

Douglas W. Slocumb

SERVING WITH AUTHORITY

Scripture: "As you know, the kings and great men of the earth lord it over the people; but among you it is different. Whoever wants to be great among you must be your servant. And whoever wants to be greatest of all must be the slave of all" (Mark 10:42-44, *TLB*).

Enrichment From the Word: James and John wanted the highest positions in Jesus' kingdom, but Jesus told them that true greatness came in serving others.

Most businesses, organizations and institutions in our world measure greatness by high personal achievement. Service is the way to please God and bring honor to His kingdom. Power, authority and trust are a vital part of leadership. Authority, according to John W. Gardener in the *Nature of Leadership*, is legitimized power, a mandate to exercise power in a certain way.

Our authority comes not from power but from our services to God and others. Our authority comes through the power of the Holy Spirit to do the work of building God's kingdom here on earth. He has chosen us, called us and entrusted to us the good news of His saving grace.

Enrichment From the Church: Mother Teresa is the best living example of this kind of leader with a lot of authority. She spends her life helping the powerless die with dignity; yet few people command more authority worldwide.

Enrichment From the Heart: Dear God, it is not always easy to be a servant; but through Your Holy Spirit help me to be one that brings glory to You and Your kingdom.

Societal Relationships June, Week 4

Douglas W. Slocumb

SERVING ONE ANOTHER IN LOVE

Scripture: "Love each other with brotherly affection and take delight in honoring each other" (Romans 12:10, *TLB*).

Enrichment From the Word: Love is the circulatory system of the spiritual body, which enables all the members to function in a healthy, harmonious way. This love must be an honest love—not a hypocritical or proud love, but one that is humble. Love is preferring one another and treating others as important as ourselves.

Paul reminds us that we must enter into the feeling of others. Christian fellowship should be more than a pat on the back or a handshake. It means sharing another's burdens and blessings so that we grow together and glorify the Father. Sharing ourselves with a humble attitude and having a willingness to share are the marks of a Christian who truly ministers to the Body. Our Lord ministered to the common man with love.

Enrichment From the Church: I will never forget how God helped me win a member's husband to God simply by showing love to him. I would often visit at his place of business and at his home. When he would attend church, as he was leaving, I would tell him that we were praying for him. His comment was always "I wish you wouldn't, for when you do, things get worse." When anyone in his family would become ill, we would visit. Through this love and caring it was not long until he gave his heart to God. Today he is a minister of the gospel.

Enrichment From the Heart: Lord, help me to truly be a part of the Christian community of faith (my church). May I be not just a spectator but a true fellow Christian sharing myself with others.

Societal Relationships   **June, Week 4**

Douglas W. Slocumb

RESPECTING THE ROLE OF WOMEN

Scripture: Some women went along, from whom he had cast out demons or whom he had healed; among them were Mary Magdalene (Jesus had cast out seven demons from her), Joanna, Chuza's wife (Chuza was King Herod's business manager and was in charge of his palace and domestic affairs), Susanna, and many others who were contributing from their private means to the support of Jesus and his disciples (Luke 8:2, 3, *TLB*).

Enrichment From the Word: Today there is much discussion concerning the role of women in the church. We must note that Jesus chose to let some of those He had helped travel along with Him and His disciples. These are the women that Christ had raised from degradation and servitude to fellowship and service. It is true that the Jewish culture would not let women learn from the rabbis, but here He was letting them travel with Him. Jesus was showing that all people are equal under God.

Throughout history women have played a vital role in ministry.

Even Paul reminds us to show proper respect to the women in the church in 1 Timothy 5:2. The church has always had women in places of honor and respect.

Enrichment From the Church: The church has been blessed with some great ladies who have been leaders. They have organized missions, pastored churches and helped the church financially as fund-raisers. But most importantly, they have helped through their prayers and devotion to God.

Enrichment From the Heart: Thank You, God, for our faithful women. We praise You, God, for what they have done to bring the gospel to us in teaching, preaching and in showing us how to be faithful servants of the Lord.

Societal Relationships June, Week 4

Douglas W. Slocumb

ACCEPTING THE RESPONSIBILITY OF MEN

Scripture: "Now look around among yourselves, dear brothers, and select seven men, wise and full of the Holy Spirit, who are well thought of by everyone; and we will put them in charge of this business" (Acts 6:3, *TLB*).

Enrichment From the Word: God has always chosen to use people to fulfill His ministry in the world. The scripture is clear that He has also called men for special responsibilities. Acts 6:3 lets us know that the administrative task was not taken lightly. They were to be men, wise, full of the Holy Spirit and well thought of by everyone. Jobs that require responsibility and dealing with people need leaders with these qualities.

Enrichment From the Church: Throughout its history the church has had men whom God has chosen to place in positions of leadership. Many of them have served as pastors, clerks or teachers on councils. It is important, therefore, that we respect leaders, for God has allowed us to place them in positions of responsibility. Our duty is to pray for them that they will accept their responsibility in service to God and to the building of His kingdom.

One such case brought to my memory is that of Michiko Teramoto, a lady pastor of one of our churches in Japan. She calls the men together and tells them of the problem and says, "Brethren, it is now your responsibility to say what we are to do about the problems." Here her role as a pastor and as a lady is respected. Also their role as administrators of the church is made clear. Through this the work gets done.

Enrichment From the Heart: Lord, help us today to remember to pray for all of our men who take care of Your business for the Kingdom. Thank You, Lord, for looking out for the welfare of the whole church and all Your children who work in it.

Societal Relationships　　　　　　**June, Week 4**

Douglas W. Slocumb

BEING WILLING TO ADJUST

Scripture: "Everything that has happened to me here has been a great boost in getting out the Good News concerning Christ. . . . (Philippians 1:12, 14, *TLB*).

Enrichment From the Word: Paul stated that even his imprisonment had brought glory and honor to Christ. He saw it as one more opportunity to spread the good news of Christ. The current circumstances were not as important as what he did with them. He turned a bad situation into a good one.

We may not be in prison, but we still have plenty of opportunities to be discouraged—times of indecision, financial problems, family conflicts, church conflicts or the loss of a job. How we act in each of these is very important. The way we react reflects what we believe and how we put it into practice.

Enrichment From the Church: When we have our difficulties, do we begin to grumble and complain, or do we seek God? Many times through my ministry I have had to go to Christ for His strength to face tomorrow. I was deeply concerned one day about one of my problems, and a fellow brother reminded me again that this is God's world and He is in control. "All things work together for good to those who love God, to those who are the called according to His purpose" (Romans 8:28).

When Joseph was sold into slavery, his brothers meant it for harm. He adjusted to the situation, and the Lord God worked it out for good.

Enrichment From the Heart: O Lord, may I know You today in such a way that I will always look for You in each situation. Help me to adjust, knowing that You are always in control.

Personal Devotions — July, Week 1

Delton Alford

STANDING FIRM IN THE FAITH

Scripture: "And the life which I now live in the flesh I live by faith in the Son of God, who loved me and gave Himself for me" (Galatians 2:20).

Enrichment From the Word: In this constantly changing world we need to be aware that our faith is rooted and grounded in God's Word and in Jesus, the Son of God. With all the new that God is doing through His people in every part of the world, it becomes increasingly important that we preserve the old so as to interpret the new.

Enrichment From the Church: The hymnist so beautifully expresses faith in Christ by proclaiming:

> "On Christ the solid Rock I stand;
> All other ground is sinking sand."

When all else seems to fail, when there seems to be no other place to go or even hide, we can know that our unshakable faith in Jesus, the Rock, will more than suffice. This is the evidence of things not seen, the substance of all that is hoped for.

When answers aren't enough . . . when directions aren't clear . . . when feelings and emotions are down and dark, faith in Jesus is the way. It's the only way through the darkness to light!

Enrichment From the Heart: In times of doubt and fear, to You, O Lord, I will sing:

> "Faith of our fathers! we will love
> Both friend and foe in all our strife,
> And preach thee, too, as love knows how
> By kindly words and virtuous life:
> Faith of our fathers, holy faith!
> We will be true to thee till death."
> — Frederick Faber

Personal Devotions July, Week 1

Delton Alford

SINGING AND MAKING MELODY TO THE LORD

Scripture: Be filled with the Spirit, speaking to one another in psalms and hymns and spiritual songs (Ephesians 5:18, 19).

Enrichment From the Word: The Apostle Paul is reminding us that music is an excellent form of communication. As spiritual persons he tells us we can share and speak with one another by singing various types of songs. He indicates we should sing psalms (scriptural songs) and hymns (songs of praise lifting up the name and deeds of God). He also calls us to sing spiritual songs—songs of testimony where we express the joys of the Christian life to believers and nonbelievers alike.

Paul also reminds us that in our singing we are to communicate directly to God by making melody in our heart.

Enrichment From the Church: There is no more healthy church than one that learns to express itself joyfully and powerfully by singing a wide variety of types and styles of music. In this way communication is established with all members of the Body, and this sharing of experiences promotes growth, health and spiritual renewal.

This same principle surely applies to the individual. To be balanced in our approach to God, we ought to use psalms and hymns and spiritual songs and express praise to Him. When we sing His Word, it doubtless gives Him pleasure. When we sing songs of praise, we lift Him up; and when we sing testimonies, we extoll His deeds and confirm them in our heart.

Let's begin to make melody in our heart and sing and minister to the Lord.

Enrichment From the Heart: As one of God's creations I earnestly seek to know Him and commune with Him. Through singing and making melody I open up the recesses of my heart and desire daily to praise, glorify and worship Him.

Personal Devotions   **July, Week 1**

Delton Alford

WALKING IN THE WILL OF GOD

Scripture: "In this manner, therefore, pray: Our Father in heaven, Hallowed be Your name. Your kingdom come. Your will be done On earth as it is in heaven" (Matthew 6:9, 10).

Enrichment From the Word: Christ is teaching us to pray daily, showing us that we should be concerned that God's will be done.

It is God's will that we live agreeably with one another and share in His blessings, love and divine care. It is His ultimate will that we become saved and brought into His presence for an eternity of praise, celebration and happiness. Until then, it is His will that we share the good news of salvation with all who have not yet heard or believed.

Enrichment From the Church: As members of the body of Christ and partakers in the life He gives, we can and should come to a personal knowledge of His will for us. How can we know and walk in His will? (1) He reveals His will in His Word. (2) We can know His will by the impressions and leading of the Holy Spirit. His Spirit will comfort and lead us daily. (3) We may sense His will for us by sharing ideas and concepts with other godly people. (4) We can take comfort that it is His will for us to use talents and abilities He has so graciously given us for His glory and pleasure. It is good and right to know His will, but even better to walk in it daily.

Enrichment From the Heart: O Lord, let me come to know Your will for my life and accept those things You show me. Give me the courage to believe and the desire to do. Through Your will let me walk in the light and build Your kingdom.

Personal Devotions   **July, Week 1**

Delton Alford

RENEWING THE MIND DAILY

Scripture: And do not be conformed to this world, but be transformed by the renewing of your mind (Romans 12:2).

Enrichment From the Word: Here the writer is clearly indicating that we are not to follow after the world but rather be a transforming agent in it. As a child of God we don't copy the world; rather, we reflect Jesus Christ.

What we think greatly influences how we feel and act. It is our thought process—our mind—that primarily controls our actions and reactions. Daily we need to renew our thoughts. Think of things good and true, positive and beautiful. In being renewed we can come to know His ways are best and that they do satisfy.

Enrichment From the Church: Computer technology reveals that when good data is inputted, good information is the output. When bad data is inputted, bad information is the output. So it is with our mind. When we put good in, good will come forth.

Nicky Cruz, the born-again gang leader, describes this phenomenon as "garbage in—garbage out." He once related that his life, even after being changed by salvation, was a continual struggle with bad thoughts and desires until he discovered his reading habits were still the same—same old thoughts, same old desires. He threw out the garbage—bad magazines, books and records—and began to concentrate on God. By his own admission, his mind, thoughts and life were instantly renewed.

Enrichment From the Heart: I will strive daily to think on the good things of the Lord. I will renew my life through the good things I allow to be entertained in my mind.

Personal Devotions   **July, Week 1**

Delton Alford

BELIEVING FOR THE BEST

Scripture: "With men it is impossible, but not with God; for with God all things are possible" (Mark 10:27).

Enrichment From the Word: Jesus clearly teaches us that our faith—our expectation, our belief—determines our attitude and our victory. The sick woman came to Him pressing through the crowd. She believed for the best; and contrary to the belief of others, she was healed. Her faith and expectation made her well. The blind man called to Jesus, and in spite of all odds his belief provided for healing.

When men say it's not possible, God says believe for the best! When circumstances seem darkest and defeat almost certain, we can hear Jesus say, "With God all things are possible." Let's believe for the best. Scripture reveals time and again that we can overcome. We are more than conquerors. Victory comes to us through the power of God. He is our strength; He is our source. It's only natural; let's believe for the best!

Enrichment From the Church: Expect the best, believe the best, and most often your dreams and hopes will occur. Studies confirm that we often speak circumstances into existence. When we tell our children they are bad, they often act that way. When we paint everything dark and bleak, it usually turns out to be so. When a sick patient believes the illness to be hopeless, death is not far away.

The church that believes for the best works to bring it about, and it happens. When we believe for the best and put our faith in God, we can expect positive results, and they will occur.

Enrichment From the Heart: Lord, because You have all power in heaven and earth and desire the best for Your children, in all times, in all places, I now place my faith in You and believe for the best!

Time Management — July, Week 2

O. Wayne Chambers

IMPROVING TIME MANAGEMENT

Scripture: So teach us to number our days, That we may gain a heart of wisdom (Psalm 90:12).

Enrichment From the Word: The message in this verse is clear. We need to value the time God has given to us. Time is to be wisely spent. We do not have enough time at our disposal to justify wasting a single hour. The psalmist Moses sends us to God for teaching about time. David gives similar instruction: "Teach me Your way, O Lord; I will walk in Your truth" (Psalm 86:11).

Richard Pigot in **Life of Man** wrote, "Improve time in time while the time thou dost have, for all time is no time when the time is past."

Enrichment From the Church: An Italian philosopher expressed in his motto that time was his estate—an estate, indeed, that will produce nothing without cultivation. Napoleon worked as many hours as the sun would let him and planned his great campaigns while his soldiers slept. Napoleon conquered all Europe because he utilized the time that the rest of the world was letting go to waste. Let us not waste our time but seek to number our days, every hour, not merely counting them but to consider each day as a special holiday time so that we may crowd every day with the best and worthiest things. Divine help is always available, on request.

Enrichment From the Heart: Just for today, Lord, keep me from wasting precious time. Just for today, teach me, guide me and use me so that I may gain a heart of wisdom. Help me to better manage the time You have given to me for good. Amen.

Time Management
O. Wayne Chambers

LISTING PRIORITIES

Scripture: Come now, you who say, "Today or tomorrow we will go to such and such a city, spend a year there, buy and sell, and make a profit"; whereas you do not know what will happen tomorrow. For what is your life? It is even a vapor that appears for a little time and then vanishes away (James 4:13, 14).

Enrichment From the Word: There is a rabbinic proverb that says, "Care not for the morrow, for you know not what a day may bring forth. Perhaps you may not find tomorrow." The future is not in the hand of men, and no man can arrogantly claim he has power to decide it. Therefore, in our allotted time, we must set priorities. We must make a difference between the urgent and the unimportant.

Enrichment From the Church: Let us ask, "Are we spending too much time on activities that are not really important? Are we overly concerned about what others expect from us?" Charlie Shedd recognized this problem when he said, "Our heavenly Father never gives us too much to do. Men will. We assign ourselves an overload, but never the Lord. He knows what He wants from each of us, and there is plenty of time in His day for things essential to His plan. We do Him a grave injustice when we fall into the habit of compulsive overwork. We sin when we pursue our selfish desires over His will."

Enrichment From the Heart: Our Father, who is in heaven, hallowed be Your name. Give us today a clear understanding that time is short. Help us to understand that You have called us to the "urgent" things of life. Give us the strength to say no to the non-important things of life and to make knowing You the highest priority of our life. Amen.

Time Management

July, Week 2

O. Wayne Chambers

PINPOINTING WEAKNESSES

Scripture: "For which of you, intending to build a tower, does not sit down first and count the cost, whether he has enough to finish it" (Luke 14:28).

Enrichment From the Word: Jesus in the written Word pinpoints the major weakness in achieving our goals in life—the failure to take time to count the cost. More than one time Jesus bids us, "Count the cost." Never take life lightly. Never fail to take time to count the cost. It takes time to pinpoint the weaknesses in anything we attempt to do.

In everything we do in life, Jesus warns us to take time to sit down and count the cost. Nothing brings reproach on the gospel like spiritual weaknesses and relapses which are the results of rushing into a decision.

Enrichment From the Church: In every sphere of life a person is called to count the cost. In the marriage ceremony, the minister usually says, "Marriage is not to be entered into lightly or inadvisedly, but thoughtfully, reverently and in the fear of God." When a person enters into a job contract, he should take time to count the costs, the strengths, the weaknesses. Unless we take time to count the cost, we will end up like a hapless painter who paints himself into a corner.

You can pinpoint your weaknesses in time management by sitting down to take a personal time inventory to find out where your time is actually spent.

Enrichment From the Heart:

> I would the precious time redeem,
> To spend and to be spent for Thee.
> Into thy blessed hands receive,
> And let me live to preach Thy Word
> My every sacred moment spend.
> —Charles Wesley

Time Management

O. Wayne Chambers

July, Week 2

REJECTING INTERRUPTIONS

Scripture: But He said to them, "Let us go into the next towns, that I may preach there also, because for this purpose I have come forth" (Mark 1:38).

Enrichment From the Word: Our Lord declared that nothing would be allowed to interrupt His mission on this earth. He came to be a preacher and a teacher. He came to show the way of peace, to proclaim deliverance to the captives and recovering of sight to the blind.

Jesus spent His time fulfilling His prophetical office. His mission was clear. He could have spent His time keeping up ceremonies, like Aaron. He might have ruled and reigned as a king, like David. But He would allow nothing to interrupt His purpose of proclaiming salvation.

Enrichment From the Church: We must reject interruptions that would hinder our spiritual development. Every person is given the same amount of time every day—86,400 seconds. Have you given thought as to why some people get so much accomplished while others accomplish so little? Someone has said, "Fifteen minutes a day devoted to one definite study will make one a master in a dozen years." James Hasting wrote, "One has to spend money to make money." Likewise, one must spend time to save time. Have you considered giving God a daily gift of uninterrupted time?

Enrichment From the Heart: Heavenly Father, forgive us for allowing so many interruptions in the time we have tried to set aside for You and others. We determine this day to reject all interruptions that would hinder us from our mission and purpose in life. Amen.

Time Management

O. Wayne Chambers

HANDLING EMERGENCIES

Scripture: Then a man of God came and spoke to the king of Israel, and said, "Thus says the Lord: 'Because the Syrians have said, "The Lord is God of the hills, but He is not God of the valleys," therefore I will deliver all this great multitude into your hand, and you shall know that I am the Lord'" (1 Kings 20:28).

Enrichment From the Word: The people of God were in the valley facing an enemy which had more soldiers, weapons, chariots, horses and physical strength than did Israel. The enemy thought Israel's God was a God of the hills because David their great leader had said, "I will lift up my eyes to the hills" (Psalm 121:1). But God is God of the hills and God of the valleys.

Enrichment From the Church: While attending a Church of God in Tarrant, Alabama, years ago, I heard an elderly saint testify, "Children, God does not always come to your rescue in a hurry, but He will always come in time." There have been times in my life when emergencies suddenly appeared on the scene and no one seemed to have the answer. But I have learned in times of emergencies to depend on God. I have learned that when storms of life suddenly appear, Christ gives us peace in the midst of sorrow, problems and anxiety. He is also Lord of the valleys.

Enrichment From the Heart: Thank You, Lord, for coming to us in emergencies. You fill heaven and earth. You are not limited to the hills; You are everywhere. We praise Your name for deliverance in the emergencies of life. Amen.

Communications　　　　　　　　　　**July, Week 3**

Bob Pace

TAKING THE GOOD NEWS TO SHUT-INS

Scripture: "Can a woman forget her nursing child, And not have compassion on the son of her womb? Surely they may forget, Yet I will not forget you. See, I have inscribed you on the palms of My hands; Your walls are continually before Me" (Isaiah 49:15, 16).

Enrichment From the Word: It is hard to believe that a mother could ever forget or neglect her newborn baby or not have compassion for him, but the Lord said it is possible. However, the Lord also said it is impossible for Him to ever forget us, no matter where we are. What a comfort!

God will never forget us or the suffering people among us. He will prompt our hearts to take His compassion, love and care to someone who might not be able to attend church.

Enrichment From the Church: Recently I visited a retired minister who had tears in his eyes as he shared his hurts. He said, "I can't preach anymore, and nobody wants me to come to their church. I'm just no good to anybody or for anything. The devil tells me nobody cares about me." I asked him how many people had been saved through his ministry, and he said several thousand. He also told me that about 200 men were preaching today because of his ministry. I pointed out to him that he is preaching more today and winning more people to the Lord than ever before. God is continuing to use the fruit of a shut-in to minister around the world.

Enrichment From the Heart: Take an encouraging word to someone who cannot leave home. Be thankful for your own good health, and show your thankfulness by visiting someone less fortunate.

Communications   **July, Week 3**

Bob Pace

TAKING THE GOOD NEWS TO INMATES

Scripture: Remember those in prison as if you were their fellow prisoners, and those who are mistreated as if you yourselves were suffering (Hebrews 13:3, *NIV*).

Enrichment From the Word: Our Lord was a prisoner and falsely tried. Knowing the pain and suffering of prisoners, He wants to show His love to them; but this can only be possible when we, His feet, His hands and His mouth, take His love to them.

When we see those in prison as if we were their "fellow prisoners," we will be motivated to become personally involved by taking the gospel to them. The gospel will heal, comfort, forgive and make whole—but first it must be shared!

Enrichment From the Church: I recall a young man in the Mississippi state prison named Jimmy Lee Gray. On September 2, 1983, he was executed for committing murder. Hear his words: "I never gave up on finding love! All my memories of my home life are of fighting and disharmony. I wanted so much for it to be different. I don't know if my mom loved me; I never believed she did. I just don't know. The love I longed for turned to hate and disrespect. I feel as though I am the most hated person that ever lived, besides Jesus, except I deserve the hate. It's hard to believe that Jesus could save a wretch like me, but I know He did."

While on death row, Jimmy Lee Gray was led to the Lord by a layman. "In Jesus I found love," Jimmy Lee said. "I found peace."

Enrichment From the Heart: There is hope for every individual, regardless of the sin. Instead of being judgmental, we should strive to show the love of God to those who need it most.

Communications   **July, Week 3**

Bob Pace

TAKING THE GOOD NEWS TO THE SICK

Scripture: Is anyone among you sick? Let him call for the elders of the church, and let them pray over him, anointing him with oil in the name of the Lord. And the prayer of faith will save the sick, and the Lord will raise him up. And if he has committed sins, he will be forgiven (James 5:14, 15).

Enrichment From the Word: What a powerful, personal invitation by our Lord that we can receive healing and forgiveness by asking our spiritual leaders to anoint us and pray for us! Prayer offered in simple obedience is powerful!

If you have sought God for healing but to no avail, today consider asking your church leaders to anoint and pray for you. Also, take a friend with you to visit someone who is sick—anoint and pray for that person. God will raise him up.

Enrichment From the Church: I have seen God perform miracles during my Christian walk. On one occasion we prayed for a teenage boy who had one leg that was about two inches shorter than the other. Within a few minutes the shorter leg grew before our eyes! The boy was made perfectly well.

The reason my home church was a place where healings took place is that the people would spend much time in prayer. And the God who healed them is the same today! He will heal you and those to whom you minister. Call on Him, and call on the elders of the church. Our Lord wants us to be well.

Enrichment From the Heart: Heavenly Father, let faith increase in the hearts of those who are sick today. In response to this request from one of Your sons, be favorable to my friends today by healing their sickness. Thank You for granting this request.

Communications July, Week 3

Bob Pace

TAKING THE GOOD NEWS TO THE SUFFERING

Scripture: I consider that the sufferings of this present time are not worthy to be compared with the glory which shall be revealed in us (Romans 8:18).

Enrichment From the Word: In this world we will have hardship, troubles and pain (John 16:33), but think about the time when we will be with our Lord forever. It will be worth it all!

In the meantime, however, we are encouraged to endure suffering with patience. When we suffer for doing right, we should not complain but be joyful that we are considered worthy to suffer for our Lord. Suffering is never easy, but by it we are made strong and can live overcoming lives.

Enrichment From the Church: I read a story about a man who was watching a butterfly trying to break its way out of its cocoon. As he watched the struggle, he decided to help the frail butterfly. With his fingernail he cut open the cocoon and let the butterfly go free. To his amazement, however, the butterfly never did fly. The man later discovered that for a butterfly to mature and become strong enough to fly, it *must* go through the struggle of breaking out of its cocoon. The strength gained from the struggle enables it to fly.

The message for us is that God could relieve us from all our struggles; but if He did, we would never become strong and mature.

Enrichment From the Heart: Consider struggles and suffering as a gift of God, who wants the very best for His children. In all things (even pain, suffering and struggles) give thanks to God. He loves you and wants you to be free and strong.

Communications   **July, Week 3**

Bob Pace

TAKING THE GOOD NEWS TO THE DYING

Scripture: "Do not be afraid; I am the First and the Last. I am He who lives, and was dead, and behold, I am alive forevermore. Amen. And I have the keys of Hades and of Death" (Revelation 1:17, 18).

Enrichment From the Word: Who do you know that has died and come to life again in his own power? Jesus is the only One that I know! He took the sting out of death and obtained the joys of a resurrected life. It is appointed to each of us to die, but thanks to our Lord and Savior, there is great joy beyond the grave. Jesus himself holds the keys of death, and in Him is life evermore.

Enrichment From the Church: My mother was very sick for the last several years of her life and suffered great pain. I remember when she went to the hospital for the last time. She told me, "Son, I want to be back home, but will you do me a favor? Take a small piece of paper, type this scripture on it, and bring it to me before the operation: 'The angel of the Lord encamps all around those who fear Him, And delivers them'" (Psalm 34:7).

That piece of paper, dotted with small spots of blood, is a reminder to me of the peace my mother had in our Lord as she faced death. That paper reminds me that even death is a victory for the Christian.

Enrichment From the Heart: You might not always know the right words to say to the terminally ill, but you can "be there," love them, and express to them what their life has meant to you and how their testimony will live on forever because of their faithfulness.

Outreach   **July, Week 4**

John D. Nichols

EXPECTING SINNERS TO BE SAVED

Scripture: The Lord is not slack concerning His promise, as some count slackness, but is longsuffering toward us, not willing that any should perish but that all should come to repentance (2 Peter 3:9).

Enrichment From the Word: There is no doubt that God cares. In fact, He cares enough for the souls of people that He was willing for His Son to suffer the shame and reproach of the Cross to redeem mankind. What more could He have done? Nothing more, for He made the supreme sacrifice. "God demonstrates His own love toward us, in that while we were still sinners, Christ died for us" (Romans 5:8).

Before an individual can be **LOST**, he must reject the Love of God, refuse the Offering for sins, resist the Spirit of God and neglect the Time that is given to accept the plan of salvation. We can expect souls to be saved because of the marvelous provision God has made.

Enrichment From the Church: We should expect all people to come to Christ because everyone needs a Savior. In a citywide meeting Billy Sunday, the famous evangelist, sent a letter to the mayor of the city and asked for the names of individuals the mayor knew who had a spiritual problem—people who especially needed divine help. How surprised the evangelist was when he received a city directory from the mayor!

Enrichment From the Heart: Father, enlarge our vision so our faith may increase—that we can believe You for a great harvest of souls. "'Whoever calls upon the name of the Lord shall be saved'" (Romans 10:13).

Outreach

John D. Nichols

EXPECTING CONVERTS TO JOIN THE CHURCH

Scripture: Then those who gladly received his word were baptized; and that day about three thousand souls were added to them. . . . And the Lord added to the church daily those who were being saved (Acts 2:41, 47).

Enrichment From the Word: Every born-again believer should become a church member. Church membership means more than surface fellowship. The true value of belonging is revealed in Ephesians 4:16: "Under his direction the whole body is fitted together perfectly, and each part in its own special way helps the other parts, so that the whole body is healthy and growing and full of love" (*TLB*).

We need each other, and there is no better way to receive the benefits of the body of Christ than to become a committed church member. It is right that we should expect people to become all they can become by receiving the full benefits of church membership.

Enrichment From the Church: In Jesus' parable the Good Samaritan did more than just doctor the wounds of the robbed and abused man; he then " 'brought him to an inn, and took care of him. On the next day, when he departed, he . . . gave . . . [money] to the innkeeper, and said to him, "Take care of him" ' " (Luke 10:34, 35). This is illustrative of the Lord's ministry to us. He lifts us up, heals our wounds and places us in the care of others in a church body.

Enrichment From the Heart: Thank You, Father, for the church. Help us to always appreciate the blessing of belonging!

Outreach   July, Week 4

John D. Nichols

EXPECTING SEEKERS TO BE FILLED WITH THE SPIRIT

Scripture: "If you then, being evil, know how to give good gifts to your children, how much more will your heavenly Father give the Holy Spirit to those who ask Him!" (Luke 11:13).

Enrichment From the Word: A Christian can never be what God intends for him to be until he is filled with the Spirit. It is a shame that so many think only of power when they think of being Spirit-filled, for there is so much more involved. The Holy Spirit is a guide, a teacher and a comforter. He brings Scripture to one's remembrance in time of need, He prays through the Spirit-filled person, He gives a heavenly language, and He empowers believers to witness.

While every aspect of Christian living is important, nothing affects the life of a Christian more than being filled with the Spirit and continually receiving a fresh infilling. **Now** would be a good time for all of us to experience His infilling.

Enrichment From the Church: During the time my father was pastoring a non-Pentecostal church in New Mexico, my mother received the baptism with the Holy Ghost. Her life was so dramatically changed that my father declared he would never preach again until he received the same experience. He did receive the baptism with the Holy Ghost and their ministry came alive!

Enrichment From the Heart: Father, help us to see that not only will we be blessed when we live a Spirit-filled life, but we will also impact the lives of others. "And do not be drunk with wine, in which is dissipation; but be filled with the Spirit" (Ephesians 5:18).

Outreach   July, Week 4

John D. Nichols

EXPECTING SUNDAY SCHOOL EFFECTIVENESS

Scripture: Then Jesus said to the twelve, "Do you also want to go away?" Then Simon Peter answered Him, "Lord, to whom shall we go? You have the words of eternal life" (John 6:67, 68).

Enrichment From the Word: Sunday school should speak loud and clear to all of us—it is a time set aside for looking into God's Word and listening to what He is saying. Some would respond, "But that's what I do during my personal devotions." True, but there is a difference: Sunday school is a time when we discuss the Word of God with others, which is very important to our Christian development.

Of course, Sunday school will be effective only if we place it high on our list of priorities: if we arrive on time, if we are faithful in our attendance, and if we are willing to receive and to share.

Enrichment From the Church: Moral courage without intelligence is dangerous; it leads to fanaticism. Intelligence without the moral courage to act upon it is worthless. True education should develop both intelligence and courage (Sidney Hook).

Enrichment From the Heart: Father, there is so much to learn. Teach us to pray; teach us to live and love; teach us to forgive. Help us to know there is a time to set aside the cares of daily living, sit at Your feet, and study Your eternal truths as Mary, the sister of Lazarus, did. "A wise man will hear and increase learning, And a man of understanding will attain wise counsel. . . . But fools despise wisdom and instruction" (Proverbs 1:5, 7).

Outreach

John D. Nichols

EXPECTING TITHES AND OFFERINGS TO INCREASE

Scripture: "Bring all the tithes into the storehouse, That there may be food in My house, And prove Me now in this," Says the Lord of hosts, "If I will not open for you the windows of heaven And pour out for you such blessing That there will not be room enough to receive it" (Malachi 3:10).

Enrichment From the Word: Success as a Christian will never come until a person addresses his attitude toward giving. Someone has said, "Tell me how a man makes his money and how he spends his money, and I will tell you what kind of man he is." When a person withholds his tithe and offerings, it reveals that he is unduly occupied with his own interests and has a heart that is ungrateful for the blessings of God.

Someone has said, "Lust is when you desire personal pleasure at someone else's expense. Love is when you desire another's pleasure at your expense." God loved, and God gave. Judge your dedication by what you give, not by what you receive.

Enrichment From the Church: John D. Rockefeller gave the following testimony: "I have tithed every dollar God has entrusted to me. And I want to say, if I had not tithed the first dollar I made, I would not have tithed the first million dollars I made. Tell your readers to train their children to tithe, and they will grow up to be faithful stewards of the Lord."

Enrichment From the Heart: Father, I do not want anything that I am not willing to share. If I am not willing to share what You place in my hands, then I do not deserve to receive what You give me.

Family Relationships   August, Week 1

Robert D. McCall

AVOIDING FAMILY CONFLICTS

Scripture: " 'Love the Lord your God and serve Him with all your heart and with all your soul. . . .' Lay up these words of mine in your heart and in your soul, and bind them as a sign on your hand, and they shall be as frontlets between your eyes. You shall teach them to your children, speaking of them when you sit in your house, when you walk by the way, when you lie down, and when you rise up" (Deuteronomy 11:13, 18, 19).

Enrichment From the Word: Moses, God's chosen leader of the children of Israel, told the people they were to diligently teach God's commandments to their children. They were to do this as a natural part of their daily life—while sitting, walking, lying down and rising up. We are to do no less with our families today. This will bring us closer to God, strengthen our family relationships and help us avoid family conflicts.

Enrichment From the Church: Within the church I have seen strong families with growing relationships and fragmented families with sour relationships. The strong families have open communication with God (a vertical relationship) and open communication with each other (horizontal relationships). This openness helps avoid family conflicts.

God created us to grow up in families and to form families of our own. Therefore, successful resolution of conflicts is essential to the growth of all family relationships: husband-wife, child-child and parent-child.

Enrichment From the Heart: Nothing destroys the bonding of family relationships faster than conflict. My prayer is, "Father, help me bring harmony to my family as I love You, keep Your commandments and teach them to my children through daily example."

Family Relationships
August, Week 1

Robert D. McCall

AVOIDING CONFLICTS BETWEEN HUSBAND AND WIFE

Scripture: Husbands, love your wives, just as Christ also loved the church and gave Himself for it (Ephesians 5:25).

Enrichment From the Word: Paul implied that responsibility for marital and family harmony begins with the husband and father. Husband, love your wife, and you will avoid conflict with her, with your children and between your children. Wife, submit to your husband (make the willful choice to be a part of every aspect of his life), as to the Lord, and you will be the bonding agent of family relationships that only a wife and mother can be.

Enrichment From the Church: God has given us a powerful longing for a meaningful relationship with another person; through marriage He has provided for the lifelong fulfillment of this longing. In the stages of marriage—from newlywed and childbearing years through empty-nest and grandparenting years—we learn to live with each other's differences and avoid extended conflict. One key to this learning process is making a deliberate effort to maintain open lines of communication. At times this is difficult, but it is well worth it because God still sees the happy union of husband and wife as "very good."

God has created us as men and women, each with strengths and weaknesses the other can balance. For His glory He has brought us together. "Therefore what God has joined together, let not man separate" (Mark 10:9). Conflict with our husband or spouse can be avoided and minimized through love and open communication.

Enrichment From the Heart: I once heard an older minister tell a group of husbands, "Rejoice with the wife of your youth" (Proverbs 5:18). Even today his words remind me of my marriage vow to "love, honor and cherish" my bride.

Family Relationships				August, Week 1

Robert D. McCall

AVOIDING CONFLICTS BETWEEN CHILDREN

Scripture: Now Israel loved Joseph more than all his children, because he was the son of his old age. Also he made him a tunic of many colors. But when his brothers saw that their father loved him more than all his brothers, they hated him and could not speak peaceably to him (Genesis 37:3, 4).

Enrichment From the Word: In this passage we see favoritism and jealousy as seeds of conflict between children. Jacob's expressions of favoritism toward Joseph provoked jealousy among his brothers. They could not speak peaceably to Joseph and plotted together against him. Despite the conflicts between Jacob's children brought about by favoritism and the resulting jealousy, God's plan was fulfilled for Joseph and his family. (Read Genesis 37—50 to see God's direction for Joseph's life.)

Enrichment From the Church: Jim and John (not their real names) are both faithfully serving the Lord today, yet they grew up with favoritism, jealousy and conflict. Jim was the father's favorite and John the mother's. The expressions of favoritism were not as open as those in Jacob's family nor was the jealousy so ruthless, yet conflict did result. Fortunately, enough development took place in Jim and John's family to bring about harmony between the boys as adults.

While conflict between children cannot be totally avoided, it can be minimized and the negative effects reduced. Parents must love, respect and encourage each child as an individual without showing favoritism. At the same time, each child must be taught to live as a vital part of the family unit.

Enrichment From the Heart: Father, help me to love my children as You love me. May I be able to say regarding my family what the psalmist said: "Behold, how good and how pleasant it is For brethren to dwell together in unity!" (Psalm 133:1).

Family Relationships August, Week 1

Robert D. McCall

AVOIDING CONFLICTS BETWEEN PARENT AND CHILD

Scripture: And you, fathers, do not provoke your children to wrath, but bring them up in the training and admonition of the Lord (Ephesians 6:4).

Enrichment From the Word: Scripture places great responsibility on the shoulders of parents, especially fathers, for the well-being and training of their children. This is clearly seen in Paul's admonition given above and in Proverbs 22:6, where the writer plainly said, "Train up a child in the way he should go, And when he is old he will not depart from it."

Enrichment From the Church: Think of the churches you know with a Family Life Center or those in the process of planning or building one. These churches know the importance of the family and the general home environment in their children's attitude and character formation. Achieving healthy families is a primary responsibility of parents, with help and support from the church.

One day I saw a church sign that read, "A good example has twice the value of good advice." If my children live with constant criticism, nagging and fear of punishment, they will learn to condemn, be apprehensive and be provoked to wrath. Paul admonished fathers not to exasperate their children to the point of defeat. Rather, fathers are to bring their children up in the Lord with encouragement, praise and security so they may learn confidence and acceptance with faith in the Lord and others.

Enrichment From the Heart: Lord, I ask for the wisdom to take a positive approach to avoiding conflict with my children through the life I live for You before them.

Family Relationships — August, Week 1

Robert D. McCall

MINIMIZING THE DIFFERENCES, MAXIMIZING THE AGREEMENTS

Scripture: "Now therefore, fear the Lord, serve Him in sincerity and in truth. . . . Serve the Lord! And if it seems evil to you to serve the Lord, choose for yourselves this day whom you will serve. . . . But as for me and my house, we will serve the Lord" (Joshua 24:14, 15).

Enrichment From the Word: Joshua knew there were divided religious loyalties among the tribes of Israel. In response to his challenge the people of Israel responded, "'We also will serve the Lord, for He is our God'" (24:18). Thus there was agreement between the aged leader Joshua and the people of Israel to trust in the Lord God. Differences were put away as the nation agreed to unite in serving God.

Enrichment From the Church: In *Building Stronger Families*, Royce Money encourages families to "keep on keeping on!" He pointed out: "Change takes a lot of time and effort. But the results of the effort are worth the price. I suppose the most common mistake newlyweds make is their gross underestimation of the amount of effort and time it takes to produce quality family relationships. When I got married, that certainly was true. Developing good relationships takes a lot of work and patience, and I don't know of any shortcuts. But I do know one thing—it is certainly worth the effort because it is hard to be happier than your family is. We grow together. You may lose a few battles along the way, but you can win the war" (p. 87).

Enrichment From the Heart: We can have a bold new vision for our family relationships! Through the power of the Holy Spirit, we can fulfill our responsibilities to each other and the Lord by building on our strengths and working on our weaknesses.

Societal Relationships   **August, Week 2**

Thomas Grassano

PROJECTING THE LOVE OF GOD

Scripture: And now abide faith, hope, love, these three; but the greatest of these is love (1 Corinthians 13:13).

Enrichment From the Word: It is remarkable that the three great doctrinal writers of the New Testament—Paul, John and Peter—all agreed that the highest of Christian graces is love. Gifts, however useful or attractive, fail; but greater than all gifts is love. In creation, God is love; in grace, God is love; in glory, God is love. Divine love "suffers long" and "endures all things." This is the very hope of man.

Enrichment From the Church: I remember when Mother and Dad became Christians. They were Italian immigrants. Back then there was a price to be paid for being a Christian. They were cast out by loved ones. Dad was injured when he fell off a truck, and my youngest brother broke his leg. They were both in the hospital, and there was no money and no food. On a Sunday morning Mother said to the children, "We are going to church, and there will be no food when we get back home." However, when we returned home, there was a large box full of groceries at the front door, with a note which said, "This morning we were praying, and the Holy Spirit spoke to us to bring these groceries. We feel it is the will of God." God had spoken, and food was supplied. This beautiful couple projected the love of Christ. Only when the Holy Spirit fills us to overflowing do we feel bound in love to all men.

Enrichment From the Heart: O, Lord, may I always be satisfied with You and refrain from sin. As I abide in You, may I bear the fruit of the Spirit, which is love, joy, and peace to Your honor and glory.

Societal Relationships	August, Week 2

Thomas Grassano

WINNING OVER AN ENEMY

Scripture: "But I say to you, love your enemies, bless those who curse you, do good to those who hate you, and pray for those who spitefully use you and persecute you" (Matthew 5:44).

Enrichment From the Word: Christianity is a religion of love. Holy love is its heart and soul. Christian love is to be displayed by honoring and esteeming others above ourselves. It is to be shown when discord arises by attending to the directions which the Lord Jesus has given for their removal. "If your brother sins against you, go and tell him his fault between you and him alone. If he hears you, you have gained your brother" (Matthew 18:15). Loving your enemy brings restoration of harmony and peace. It promotes the spiritual welfare of the Christian. Even sinners love those who love them. But we are to love our enemies. This is the true evidence of Christian love.

Enrichment From the Church: It is recorded that a Chinese emperor was apprised of enemies causing an insurrection in a distant province. He said to his officers, "Come follow me, and we shall quickly destroy them." He marched forward, and the rebels submitted. All thought he would destroy his captives, but he treated them with mildness and kindness. His first minister cried out and said, "Your royal word was given. Your enemies should be destroyed, and you have pardoned them and even caressed some of them." "I promised," replied the emperor, "to destroy my enemies. I have fulfilled my word; for you see, they are enemies no longer. I have made friends with them."

Enrichment From the Heart: Give us faith in Your love that never wearies nor faints. Fulfill in us the good pleasure of Your will and the work of faith with power.

Societal Relationships   **August, Week 2**

Thomas Grassano

TURNING THE OTHER CHEEK

Scripture: "To him who strikes you on the one cheek, offer the other also. And from him who takes away your cloak, do not withhold your tunic either" (Luke 6:29).

Enrichment From the Word: Every disciple of Jesus will find that the Christian life is truly a warfare. There are foes, fears and dangers that threaten the Christian. When he faces conflicts, the Christian has to endure and must join those in the Upper Room so that his assistance will come from above. Do not return blow for blow; bear the blow and act according to the Spirit. The letter of this rule is evident from our Lord's own procedure in circumstances of this kind. While standing accused before the Sanhedrin, Jesus was struck in the face, yet he did not react. He was meek and lowly in heart. Do as Jesus did. Leave the rest to the Lord, who says, "Vengeance is Mine, I will repay" (Romans 12:19).

Enrichment From the Church: There was a lad whose master would not permit him to hear a missionary preach. His master threatened to whip him to death if he did not give up going to hear the missionary; but in spite of the threat, he went three times, and after each time he received 25 lashes. His master mocked him with the question, "What can your Jesus do for you now?" The lad replied, "He strengthens me to bear all this." The second time he replied, "He helps me to believe in a future reward." When he was beaten the third time, ready to expire, the mocking question was once more answered as he responded with his last breath, "Jesus helps me to pray for you." What was possible to this lad is possible with every Christian.

Enrichment From the Heart: Help me, dear Lord, to walk in the footsteps of Your holy life. Teach me how to gain by giving and to find by losing according to Your Word.

Societal Relationships   August, Week 2

Thomas Grassano

RESISTING A SPIRIT OF RETALIATION

Scripture: That Christ may dwell in your hearts through faith; that you, being rooted and grounded in love, may be able to comprehend with all the saints what is the width and length and depth and height—to know the love of Christ which passes knowledge; that you may be filled with all the fullness of God (Ephesians 3:17-19).

Enrichment From the Word: The dimensions of the love of Christ are as broad as humanity, "for God so loved the world." True love is rooted in the heart. It is a spiritual affection toward Christ. Its fruits are left to men and are an imitation of Christ's example of resisting the spirit of retaliation. When there are people whom you cannot love, you must distinguish between love and emotion. Emotion will cause you to retaliate, but that's when you can be willing to be a channel of Christ's love.

Enrichment From the Church: While in the Caribbean, I was guest speaker at an island convention in Trinidad. Waiting for the afternoon service to begin, the evangelism director said, "Do you see those two men standing in the isle? The older man, who is a pastor, was preaching at his church one Sunday when the younger man walked to the pulpit and beat him and knocked him to the floor. The young man was a Hindu and was angry because the pastor was a converted Hindu. The pastor did not retaliate but got up and laid his hand on the young man and prayed, 'Satan, come out of this young man. Forgive him, Jesus, and save him.' The young man cried out for forgiveness, and he was saved, filled with the Spirit and called to preach the gospel."

Enrichment From the Heart: We thank You, O God, for the infinite love which You have given in Jesus Christ. Teach us to know more of You so that we can love more.

Societal Relationships　　　　　　　　August, Week 2

Thomas Grassano

SHARING HEAVENLY RICHES

Scripture: That in the ages to come He might show the exceeding riches of His grace in His kindness toward us in Christ Jesus (Ephesians 2:7).

Enrichment From the Word: Heaven and happiness are things everyone desires. Happiness is a condition we look forward to in the everlasting Kingdom of our Lord. Among all Christian duties, there are few that touch life in more points than the duty of sharing heavenly riches with the world. Those who study carefully the life of Jesus will be struck with this wonderful reverence for human life. He never despised any human being. He stood not as a king demanding attention, reverence and service but as One who wished to serve. Never did a poor ruined creature come into His presence that He did not see. Everyone was welcomed. We must put ourselves before men as Jesus did and share the benefits in order for Christ to show them the exceeding riches of His grace.

Enrichment From the Church: One day in a garment factory, Julia, an Italian immigrant who was recently converted, came to my mother and asked, "Do you know Jesus who loves you and died for your sins?" This was shocking. My mother had gone to church all of her life, attending Mass and praying to saints. She knew about Jesus Christ but did not know He loved her and died for her sins. She was invited to attend a church mission and there gave her heart to Jesus. Julia had shared the riches of heavenly blessings and led a soul to Jesus Christ.

Enrichment From the Heart: Teach us to abide in our daily calling. Help us not to get lost amid the perplexities of life. May we come to You, for "in Your presence is fullness of joy" (Psalm 16:11).

Prayer August, Week 3

Gary W. Sears

PRAYING IN ACCORDANCE WITH GOD'S WILL

Scripture: He went a little farther and fell on His face, and prayed, saying, "O My Father, if it is possible, let this cup pass from Me; nevertheless, not as I will, but as You will" (Matthew 26:39).

Enrichment From the Word: The burden was so heavy on the heart of Jesus that He could walk only a little farther and then collapse in prayerful agony. The pain of Calvary was being felt by Him before the cat-o'-nine-tails fell on His back or the first spike was driven into His hand.

Jesus' struggle was one of the will. Once His will was set to go to the Cross, the Crucifixion was the same as done. Once an issue is settled within us, it is as though the act has happened. Jesus settled the Calvary conflict in the Garden of Gethsemane on His knees. His example of taking the difficult issues of life to God in prayer is one each of us must learn to follow to be victorious in Christian living.

Enrichment From the Church: As a young man I was disciplined by an older minister in our church. "Knowing the will of God in all of life's choices," he said, "was not only required of me by God but necessary for a happy, fulfilled life."

The story was told to me of a young man who prayed selfishly, "Lord, have Your will, but give me Lil." This was not a prayer for God's will but his own. After a few short months of a stormy marriage, he was heard praying, "Lord, why did You answer my prayer?" Praying for God's will means removing all preconceived plans of our own and accepting His direction.

Enrichment From the Heart: Pray as He taught us! Our Father, Your will be done on earth as it is in heaven. Amen.

Prayer　　　　　　　　　　　　　　　　**August, Week 3**

Gary W. Sears

PRAYING FOR THE LOST

Scripture: For I could wish that I myself were accursed from Christ for my brethren, my kinsmen according to the flesh (Romans 9:3).

Enrichment From the Word: Paul's prayer for the salvation of his brethren shows the great concern he had for them in their lost condition. Israel had rejected Christ as Paul once had. His fear of their continued rejection brought him to pray that if their salvation could be assured by the forfeiture of his own, that would be considered.

Never have words been more forcefully spoken. The very thought of the man who wrote most of the New Testament being lost is inconceivable. We know that salvation is an individual experience and must be received as such. But to see Paul broken and pleading for the lost is an encouragement to us to pray for that lost friend or family member. Paul was willing to undergo the worst misery to see his loved ones saved, are you?

Enrichment From the Church: My personal salvation has often been attributed to the ministry of an evangelist who was preaching the night I accepted Christ. I'm sure that God used the man to speak to my need, resulting in my decision to follow Christ.

My father told me that my grandmother, who lived next door to us, would sit on the porch with me in her lap, praying for my salvation. I was a child, too young to know, but God heard her prayer. Hours of sacrifice and prayer will always pay in souls won to Christ.

Enrichment From the Heart: God, our sincere prayer is that we may share heaven with our loved ones and friends. "Win the Lost at Any Cost" is not only a song I sing but a prayer I pray! Amen.

Prayer   August, Week 3

Gary W. Sears

PRAYING FOR GOVERNMENT OFFICIALS

Scripture: Therefore, I exhort first of all that supplications, prayers, intercessions, and giving of thanks be made for all men (1 Timothy 2:1).

Enrichment From the Word: As the Christian movement grew, it was perceived to be more and more of a threat to the world's political leaders. The Roman Empire felt the strong influence of Christianity. Reaction to this influence was persecution. Paul's message and the church's growth were met head-on by the world with beatings, imprisonment and often death for the Christians. What was the church's stand in the face of such flagrant violations of its newfound freedom and rights?

Paul taught that prayer should be offered up to God "who desires all men to be saved" (1 Timothy 2:4). The prayer was to include "kings" and all government officials—"all who are in authority" (v. 2). The prayer list Paul used included the Roman soldiers and the emperor Nero. As your prayer list is compiled, do you plan to pray for your police department, local government officials and national leaders?

Enrichment From the Church: In this age where politics and religion have become mixed, the church must keep to a course distinct from that of the kingdoms of this world. However, there is one thing we can still use to make our greatest impact on government leaders. Prayer can change the heart of a president as well as that of a factory worker. Before we give our vote or support to any political leader, let us make sure we have sought God's direction. Praying for government leaders is a biblical requirement.

Enrichment From the Heart: At a time when any public prayer recited in a public school classroom will violate Supreme Court rulings, the silent prayer will still be heard by ears that know our deepest concern

Prayer   **August, Week 3**

Gary W. Sears

PRAYING FOR DAILY BREAD

Scripture: Give us this day our daily bread (Matthew 6:11).

Enrichment From the Word: The only request offered in the Lord's prayer for material needs is this one petition. The other six petitions have to do with spiritual realities. The word **bread** focuses the request on necessities, not luxuries, for life.

The word **daily** is derived from a Greek word meaning "sufficient for today." God supplies today what is sufficient for us today. Our request should be on a daily basis.

King David testified, "I have been young, and now am old; Yet I have not seen the righteous forsaken, Nor his descendants begging bread" (Psalm 37:25).

Enrichment From the Church: The Rev. P. H. McSwain tells a story of his early ministry which vividly portrays the promise of God's provision for daily bread. In those early years of ministry he was pastoring a small church, and the finances were not enough to pay the bills and supply food for the table.

He had gone out and returned home to be greeted by his wife who said, "Did you thank the delivery boy who brought us the groceries?" "What delivery boy?" was his response. "The one who just left," she said. After checking with the landlord who verified that no one had come up the steps to their apartment, they praised God for His providing angel. Did not the psalmist say, "Men ate angels' food; He sent them food to the full" (Psalm 78:25)?

Enrichment From the Heart: Today, Lord, we ask for the bread that will give us the strength to work in Your field. Amen.

Prayer   **August, Week 3**

Gary W. Sears

PRAYING TO AVOID TEMPTATION

Scripture: And do not lead us into temptation, But deliver us from the evil one (Matthew 6:13).

Enrichment From the Word: There is a world of difference between the words *temptation* and *testing*. Always, the word *temptation* refers to an allurement to do evil, while *testing* is intended to bring a response for one's good. Satan tempts us to do evil or respond negatively. Testings are permitted by God to increase our strength and encourage our growth toward maturity.

Jesus taught us to pray that we not be led by Satan into a temptation that will cause us to fall. We should, as Christians, pray against being tempted because it brings discomfort and trouble as well as danger of being overcome by sin.

Enrichment From the Church: The story is told of a young boy who got into his mother's fresh baked cake that was en route to a special party. When asked why he cut the cake, knowing it was for someone else, he replied, "It was too visible a temptation for me to resist." Often the temptations we fall prey to are those that are too visible for us to resist.

The closer we get to Jesus and the less distance there is between Him and us, the less room there will be for visible temptations to disrupt our Christian walk. Our prayer should be that our eyes will see Christ and that we will not be tempted to sin.

Enrichment From the Heart: Lord, do not let me be tempted and fall, but help me to accept every test as Your way of drawing me closer. Give me wisdom to know the difference between temptation and testing. Amen.

Church Growth August, Week 4

Bill F. Sheeks

UNDERSTANDING CHURCH GROWTH

Scripture: "And you shall be witnesses to Me in Jerusalem, and in all Judea and Samaria, and to the end of the earth" (Acts 1:8).

Enrichment From the Word: Jesus not only taught us that His church should grow, but He wanted us to understand how it was to grow. Christians first witness at home (Jerusalem). After we have clearly established a home base at our local church, we are to expand to regions around us (Judea). The gospel then must be taken to the underprivileged, the down-and-out, the poor, the outcasts (Samaria). Finally we must witness to the whole world—until every person alive has heard the gospel.

Enrichment From the Church: The Sumiton, Alabama, Church of God is located in a town with a population of 2,100. For 65 years the local church has labored to build a base to evangelize the community. The congregation now numbers over 600 weekly. They have expanded into the county and assisted with the organization of other local churches. Today, Walker County has 27 indigenous, self-supporting Church of God congregations. While growing locally and in the surrounding areas, Sumiton Church of God ministers weekly to 251 people in jails, nursing homes and other institutions of confinement. It averages giving in excess of $50,000 per year for world missions and on several occasions has financed a group of men to go outside the United States to build a church. They are taking the gospel to the ends of the earth.

Enrichment From the Heart: God, help me to understand that You have a specific plan in taking the gospel to the people of the world and that You wish to include me in that plan.

Church Growth August, Week 4

Bill F. Sheeks

SETTING CHURCH ATTENDANCE GOALS

Scripture: "Go into all the world and preach the gospel to every creature" (Mark 16:15).

Enrichment From the Word: The Great Commission as recorded by Mark sets a goal for the church—reaching every person on earth. The Commission was given to every Christian, layman and minister, to find where he fits in God's church to assist in propagating the gospel. This awesome responsibility is given to us by Christ himself. Regardless of the seemingly insurmountable obstacles that fall in the path of the church, the goal is still before us. We can make excuses until Jesus comes, but God still has set this goal for His followers to reach with the good news.

Enrichment From the Church: One very good stable church had averaged 200 in attendance for 30 years. An ambitious, optimistic pastor announced that on a certain Sunday, six months from the announced date, there would be 666 in attendance. The church worked, the pastor promoted, and the goal was realized. After that, the church gradually began to grow. The church had to be convinced they could do it. Once they reached the one-day goal of 666, they decided they could grow far beyond the 200 they had averaged for years. Today, the congregation averages 500 and is one of the most influential Pentecostal churches in the area.

Enrichment From the Heart: O, God, may we not settle for mediocrity. Don't allow us to be satisfied until we reach the goal of winning every person the church can for the Lord Jesus Christ. We want to use every spiritual talent and gift we possess to help accomplish this task.

Church Growth   August, Week 4

Bill F. Sheeks

DESIRING CHURCH GROWTH

Scripture: Brethren, my heart's desire and prayer to God for Israel is that they may be saved (Romans 10:1).

Enrichment From the Word: Paul was concerned about the salvation of sinners. He petitioned God to save men from temporary destruction and from the wrath to come. His desire was that they might be thoroughly convinced of their sinful condition, converted from their evil ways and brought into a relationship with Jesus Christ.

Many other scriptures in the New Testament speak of Paul's concern for the welfare of the people. He wanted Christians to be happy (Philippians 2:2) and to be healed (1 Corinthians 12:9). But his greatest desire was their salvation. He was very much aware that their need for Jesus Christ in their lives outweighed all other needs. The appeal was so intense that you could almost feel the compassion as he said, "My brothers, from the bottom of my heart I long and pray to God that Israel may be saved!" (Romans 10:1, *Phillips*).

Enrichment From the Church: Growth will not come to a church that does not desire an increase. The greatest growth does not come through biological or transfer growth, but by sinners being saved. For this to happen, there must be a sincere compassion for the lost to be saved. Like Paul, our heart's desire must be for the people of our city to be saved. This kind of intensive desire on the part of Christians will mobilize forces to witness for the Lord. The desire for church growth must stem from the right motive—sinners changed from a life of sin to a victorious life in Christ.

Enrichment From the Heart: The church that desires to win souls and will pay whatever price necessary to see that happen will be a growing church—qualitatively and quantitatively.

Church Growth   August, Week 4

Bill F. Sheeks

CANVASSING FOR CHURCH GROWTH

Scripture: " 'Go out quickly into the streets and lanes of the city, and bring in here the poor and the maimed and the lame and the blind. . . . Go out into the highways and hedges, and compel them to come in, that my house may be filled' " (Luke 14:21, 23).

Enrichment From the Word: The occasion referred to in Luke 14:15-24 is a banquet. Many people were invited but declined the invitation. The master who sent the invitation then told his servants, "Go—bring the poor, the maimed, the lame, the blind—whoever you can get to come. I want to fill my house for this feast."

The parable shows the kingdom of heaven as a feast because a banquet ritual symbolizes the rich variety and abundance of spiritual blessings provided by the Lord Jesus Christ. No matter the socioeconomic status of the person who receives Jesus, he will be abundantly blessed at this "feast." The church today must not stop with inviting. It must go where the people are and compel (constrain, urge) them to visit God's house.

Enrichment From the Church: The East Flatbush Church of God in New York City is amazing. It began in a storefront in 1970. In 1972, Peter Gayle became pastor and declared to the people that they must take the gospel to the streets. A care-and-share program was adopted. They took to the streets of New York, canvassing, inviting, praying, sharing, giving. After 16 years the East Flatbush congregation numbers 700 and has mothered nine other congregations! They have no plan to stop nor slow down.

Enrichment From the Heart: Lord, give us a concern that will send us to the streets witnessing for Jesus. Give us boldness and wisdom to win someone to Christ today.

Church Growth   **August, Week 4**

Bill F. Sheeks

PLANNING FOR CHURCH GROWTH

Scripture: Where there is no vision, the people perish (Proverbs 29:18, *KJV*).

Enrichment From the Word: A vision implies a thought process: planning, building, giving—action! People will perish unless someone has a vision to help them.

Church growth demands planning. Where there is no planning, there will be no church growth; and where there is no church growth, people will spiritually perish. So, real church growth starts with a vision—a vision that grips us and will not let go. This vision will drive us to our knees to talk to God about people and will drive us to the streets to talk to people about God. Many churches are failing to grow because no one there has a vision. It is not just a matter of another dead church. The problem is more serious. "Where there is no vision, the people perish."

Enrichment From the Church: I know a man who had a vision for a new church in a city. He felt he knew the very place where God wanted a church to locate. The cost of the land was astronomical. After much prayer was offered, the owner was approached, and he agreed to sell the land at a very modest price. The building was constructed by the pastor and his members—first, the sanctuary, then the educational building, then a fellowship hall and day-care wing. After a vision given to him by the Lord, this pastor planned every step of his venture. He mixed work with his faith, and God raised up a church that is reaching a city for God. This man did not plan to fail; he planned to succeed!

Enrichment From the Heart: God, may I always have my plans attuned to Your will. May I be a link in my church that causes it to grow, continuing to expand until You return.

Doctrine   September, Week 1

James D. Jenkins

BUILDING ON A SURE FOUNDATION

Scripture: As a wise master builder I have laid the foundation, and another builds on it. . . . For no other foundation can anyone lay than that which is laid, which is Jesus Christ (1 Corinthians 3:10, 11).

Enrichment From the Word: There is but one foundation: Jesus Christ. This same Jesus said, " 'The words that I speak to you are spirit, and they are life' " (John 6:63). If we stand on His Word, our foundation will be sure. It is an exclusive; no other is permitted. It is an offense to the Father for some to think this foundation has a substitute. All Christians are represented as living stones built upon Christ.

Enrichment From the Church: There are those who start with the proper foundation but try to build with improper materials. Some build with gold, silver and precious stones, while others use wood, hay and straw (1 Corinthians 3:12). If a Christian has true character, he will use the proper building materials. We must periodically examine the foundation. Check for ideas based on the sensual, the secular, the ambitious. Hopefully, we will find that our character is based on the Christian ideal—on His words, which are life.

We must strive to help one another use good building materials. The unity of no group—whether political, business or even family—can compare with that of members of the body of Christ who are "members one of another." Calvary is our bond; by His blood we are redeemed.

Enrichment From the Heart: Father, I am grateful that You are the judge of our temples. Help me to build properly on the true foundation. May the materials I use stand the test of judgment fire.

Doctrine   September, Week 1

James D. Jenkins

UNDERSTANDING THE DOCTRINE OF GOD

Scripture: What may be known of God is manifest in . . . [men], for God has shown it to them. For since the creation of the world His invisible attributes are clearly seen, being understood by the things that are made . . . so that they are without excuse (Romans 1:19, 20).

Enrichment From the Word: Writers in the Bible believe in God's existence; Scripture does not attempt to prove His existence. The knowledge of God is universal. Psalm 139 tells us of His omniscience, omnipotence and omnipresence. It shows that we cannot hide from His Spirit nor flee from His presence. We learn that God also knows us thoroughly and that we are never out of His sight. To those building on that sure foundation, these things are comforting. However, they serve as a warning to people who are not right in the sight of God. His Word tells us, "The way of the wicked is an abomination to the Lord, But He loves him who follows righteousness" (Proverbs 15:9). The approach to a holy God must be through the merits of Jesus Christ, His Son. We have no merit or righteousness of our own.

Enrichment From the Church: You cannot explain the history of the Jews and exclude references to God. You cannot talk about the church and omit God. "For by Him all things were created that are in heaven and that are on earth, visible and invisible, whether thrones or dominions or principalities or powers. All things were created through Him and for Him" (Colossians 1:16). We were made for Him. Let us give Him praise by believing on Him without question, as the writers of the Bible did.

Enrichment From the Heart: The doctrine of God can be summed up in three words: "God is love" (1 John 4:16).

Doctrine   September, Week 1

James D. Jenkins

UNDERSTANDING THE DOCTRINE OF CHRIST

Scripture: And the Word became flesh and dwelt among us, and we beheld His glory, the glory as of the only begotten of the Father, full of grace and truth (John 1:14).

Enrichment From the Word: Jesus, subject to the laws of human development, hungered, thirsted and became weary like an ordinary man. He was also Deity. Numerous references to Him contain the title "Son of God." We are sons by redemption; He is Son by nature. "'All should honor the Son just as they honor the Father. He who does not honor the Son does not honor the Father who sent Him'" (John 5:23). "In this is love, not that we loved God, but that He loved us and sent His Son to be the propitiation for our sins. Beloved, if God so loved us, we also ought to love one another" (1 John 4:10, 11). We cannot speak of Christ without speaking of love. Christ is omnipotent, omniscient and omnipresent.

Enrichment From the Church: Christians tell the story of Jesus, the plan of salvation, with fervor. These are the most important words which can be spoken. In Jesus' day, officers who were sent to bring Jesus to the chief priests failed in their task, reporting, "'No man ever spoke like this Man!'" (John 7:46). There was something different about Him—He was both God and man. There is something different about His name; it is the sweetest name I know.

Enrichment From the Heart: The Lord is my shepherd; I shall not want. Praise God, He is all I need or ever shall need!

Doctrine September, Week 1

James D. Jenkins

UNDERSTANDING THE DOCTRINE OF THE HOLY SPIRIT

Scripture: Do you not know that your body is the temple of the Holy Spirit who is in you, whom you have from God, and you are not your own? (1 Corinthians 6:19).

Enrichment From the Word: We are God's possession and His dwelling place. No longer our own, we are not to live as though we belong to ourselves. He wants our heart and our body. The believer is empowered for life and service by the Holy Spirit. Sin does not reign in a Spirit-filled life. The Holy Spirit in a life is the secret of victory over sin. In Galatians 5:22, 23, we learn that the Spirit yields a wonderful harvest. The fruit of the Spirit is "love, joy, peace, longsuffering, kindness, goodness, faithfulness, gentleness, self-control."

Enrichment From the Church: From Pentecost until the second advent of Christ is the Age of the Spirit. Many think of the Spirit as an agent rather than a person. He is called breath, wind, power. The symbols of oil, fire and water are used in Scripture. As John baptized Jesus, the Spirit descended like a dove, and a voice from heaven said, "'You are my beloved Son, in whom I am well pleased'" (Mark 1:10, 11). Jesus said, "'I will pray the Father, and He will give you another Helper, that He may abide with you forever'" (John 14:16). Only a person can take the place of another person. He is our guide and our teacher.

Enrichment From the Heart: We sing songs and worship Him in spirit and in truth. Christ did not leave us comfortless; we have the Spirit dwelling within us.

Doctrine				September, Week 1

James D. Jenkins

UNDERSTANDING THE DOCTRINE OF SALVATION

Scripture: Jesus answered and said to him, "Most assuredly, I say to you, unless one is born again, he cannot see the kingdom of God" (John 3:3).

Enrichment From the Word: The apostles placed great emphasis on the doctrine of repentance. Failure to heed God's call to repent means one will perish. God not only made complete provision for the removal of sin, guilt and spiritual death, but He has also provided righteousness and holiness, along with everything we need for growth in our spiritual life. In securing salvation for us, Christ was humiliated; in applying salvation to us, He was exalted. Man's sinful condition requires repentance; the holiness of God demands it.

Enrichment From the Church: We are instructed to go into all the world and preach the gospel. This is evidence that God still holds His claim on man, regardless of man's turning away. In addition to the preaching of the Word, God gives evidence of His existence through nature. We must confess our sins, forsake them and turn to God. The Prodigal Son not only realized his error and thought about the right thing to do, but he turned in the direction of home. Through salvation, we pass from death to life (1 John 3:14). Our faith must be based on God's Word, not on feelings.

Enrichment From the Heart: We might receive a gift from an acquaintance and wonder about the motive. God's gift to us is motivated by the purest love. Salvation is a gift. We need only to have faith in the truthfulness and integrity of the Giver. "For by grace you have been saved through faith, and that not of yourselves; it is the gift of God" (Ephesians 2:8).

Social Concerns   **September, Week 2**

B. J. Moffett

SHOWING CONCERN FOR THE NEEDY

Scripture: "The King will answer and say to them, 'Assuredly, I say to you, inasmuch as you did it to one of the least of these My brethren, you did it to Me'" (Matthew 25:40).

Enrichment From the Word: In Matthew 25:31-46 we find a plan of action for Christian service. Isn't it refreshing to know that God has clearly laid out what He expects of us? These verses exhort us to meet people at their felt needs and minister to them. Could our response to those in need be any simpler? Today, this concept of the gospel may be met with raised eyebrows, but whom do we seek to please—God or man?

Enrichment From the Church: With planning, the ministries of Matthew 25 can be set in motion in your church. The applications are limitless. Here are three suggestions:

1. A food pantry for needy members of your congregation and community could be stocked by bringing nonperishable food items to every service. (Clothing could be handled similarly.)

2. The Chamber of Commerce or another agency can provide you with the names of new families moving into your community. A welcome letter or perhaps a short visit in which a simple gift is given might open a stranger's door to your church.

3. Hospital, nursing home and shut-in visitation can be manned systematically if a calendar is kept, listing assignments. Seven teams of two, visiting one day a week for one month, completes the task. Rotate every second or third month, depending on the manpower available.

Enrichment From the Heart: Today, Father, I have read in Your Word what You expect of me. Please help me respond to Your commands by putting Your love in action in my home and community.

Social Concerns   **September, Week 2**

B. J. Moffett

LOVING THE UNBORN

Scripture: For you created my inmost being; you knit me together in my mother's womb. I praise you because I am fearfully and wonderfully made; your works are wonderful, I know that full well (Psalm 139:13, 14, *NIV*).

Enrichment From the Word: The psalmist made a statement for all mankind when he said, "I am fearfully and wonderfully made." He acknowledged God's participation in the creation of every person in his words "You knit me together in my mother's womb."

Those words, though written centuries ago, are as pertinent to our society as the headlines of any leading newspaper. Every unborn child is a spiritual being in creative process; every unborn child is already a wonderful work of God.

This is a song of comfort: How comforting it is to know that God knew us before we were born! This is a song of challenge: What role must we play in seeing that all of God's wonderful works are given life?

Enrichment From the Church: One of the greatest rewards of being involved in the benevolence ministries of the Church of God is seeing the potential in other human beings. This is especially true of our homes for unwed mothers. To be able to look beyond the circumstances of a birth and realize that a life is being saved not only for now but hopefully for eternity—that is loving the unborn.

Enrichment From the Heart: O Lord, I praise You for Your wonderful works, which include the creation of all people. Today I am comforted and challenged by Your Word. It is my prayer that I will be changed by it as well.

Social Concerns

B. J. Moffett

LOVING THE UNWED MOTHER-TO-BE

Scripture: Then Joseph her husband, being a just man, and not wanting to make her a public example, was minded to put her away secretly (Matthew 1:19).

Enrichment From the Word: Mary is no doubt the most famous unwed mother-to-be of all times. Not knowing the uniqueness of her dilemma—that she had conceived Jesus by the Holy Spirit—Joseph's initial response was to "put her away secretly." However, through divine intervention—an angel's appearance to Joseph in a dream—Mary was not abandoned. At the Lord's urging, Joseph married her and cared for her, and in due time she gave birth to the Son of God.

Enrichment From the Church: Few problems are solved by ignoring them, including "troubled" girls. To abandon the mother-to-be is to throw mother and child to the chaotic, pseudosolutions of our world.

The Church of God is responding to this need in our society. Two homes for unwed mothers currently operate under the jurisdiction of the Church of God benevolence ministries—Covenant Place in Sevierville, Tennessee, and Jireh House in Portland, Oregon.

As a church, we have chosen not to abandon these precious souls. Instead, we have chosen to help provide divine intervention for them. This is my dream.

Enrichment From the Heart: Lord, I am so thankful that You did not ignore me when I needed You. As I remember Your loving-kindness to me, rouse me from my dream state and prod me to watch over and care for those who so desperately need You. I pray that I will not allow anyone to feel abandoned by Your love. May the Holy Spirit guide me as I participate in Your divine intervention.

Social Concerns   September, Week 2

B. J. Moffett

LOVING THE HANDICAPPED

Scripture: Then the king said, "Is there not still someone of the house of Saul, to whom I may show the kindness of God?" And Ziba said to the king, "There is still a son of Jonathan who is lame in his feet" (2 Samuel 9:3).

Enrichment From the Word: Much had happened to David when he asked this question. As king of Israel he was not obligated to show kindness to Saul's family, but he chose to do so. When David learned that a son of his dear friend Jonathan was alive, David was no doubt even more anxious to express kindness.

It is important to note that David showed love and compassion to Mephibosheth because of who he was and not because he was handicapped. His actions were based on family ties, not pity or self-righteousness.

Enrichment From the Church: Just before we were appointed to our first pastorate, my wife and I discovered our boys had muscular dystrophy. Little did we know that God would use an elderly gentleman in that church to help prepare us for the hard days ahead with our sons.

This man was paralyzed from the waist down. It was my privilege every Sunday to drive to his home, physically pick him up, put him in my car and drive him to church. This man had very little in life. His home was just a shanty, but he taught me so much. He was content with who he was and what he had. I was honored some years later to preach this Christian gentleman's funeral to a packed church.

Enrichment From the Heart: Lord, in You all men find wholeness of heart and body. In You we can meet all people on the common ground of Your love. Help us to look past circumstances and physical conditions and minister to one another heart-to-heart.

Social Concerns September, Week 2

B. J. Moffett

LOVING THE AIDS VICTIM

Scripture: Then He put out His hand and touched him, saying, "I am willing; be cleansed." And immediately the leprosy left him (Luke 5:13).

Enrichment From the Word: Jesus was always doing the radical, the unexpected, wasn't He? He put mud in a blind man's eye, and He spoke with the Samaritan woman. He openly defended the adulteress, and He ate with sinners. Can you imagine the looks on the disciples' faces when Christ did these things? What do you suppose they thought when He reached out to the man with leprosy?

The striking words in this verse are "touched" and "willing." The leper asked for healing, and Jesus touched him and said, "I am willing." Jesus did not have to touch the leper to cleanse him; but what an impact His action must have made on the leper—not to mention the onlookers! Disregarding the thoughts and doubts of those around, Jesus ministered healing to this man, wasted by the most feared disease of the time, by touching him. The leper's heart and body were cleansed.

Enrichment From the Church: AIDS victims may well be compared to the lepers of times past, and the Christ who was willing to touch the "unclean" then is just as willing to do the same today. We must have this same selfless willingness in order to truly follow Christ. We must be willing to engage in radical living—living that says, "I am willing to reach out and touch you."

Enrichment From the Heart: I determine today to step out of my comfort zone. With God's help I will touch my world with the love of Christ. I can make a difference in my home, workplace, church and community.

Helping Others (Counseling)   September, Week 3

Esdras Betancourt

JOINING HANDS TO HELP OTHERS

Scripture: They came to Him, bringing a paralytic who was carried by four men (Mark 2:3).

Enrichment From the Word: Christ performed many works with the assistance of others. He could have performed them alone, but He has chosen to make us His coworkers.

One has to be impressed with the sympathy and faith of these four men who were so concerned about a paralyzed friend that they carried him to Jesus. They were not discouraged by the large crowd which kept them away from Jesus. They simply climbed atop the roof. After digging through it, they made an opening above Jesus and lowered the paralyzed man before Him. Jesus viewed the determined effort of the four as evidence of their faith in His healing power. Jesus healed the man and forgave him of his sins.

Enrichment From the Church: I pastored in East Harlem, New York—an area full of human misery. Many of the young men from the neighborhood had been sent to a state prison for crimes they had committed. Their relatives were poor and could not afford the cost of a bus trip to visit them, so several churches joined together to rent three buses to provide such a trip. Arrangement was made for a local church to receive the buses, feed the relatives and take them to meet their loved ones at the prison. This joining of hands by the churches brought Christ to many.

Enrichment From the Heart: While good works are not required to obtain salvation (which is wholly of grace), there is a reward for Christians who work for God. And since there are many too weak or too poor to reach Jesus by themselves, we must reach out.

Helping Others (Counseling)   September, Week 3

Esdras Betancourt

SETTING THE RIGHT EXAMPLE

Scripture: All who were sitting in the Sanhedrin looked intently at Stephen, and they saw that his face was like the face of an angel (Acts 6:15, *NIV*).

Enrichment From the Word: In the first scriptural reference to Stephen, he was called a man "of honest report" (Acts 6:3-5, *KJV*). This report was confirmed by the chain of events in his life. Besides serving the needy, Stephen became an eloquent speaker and teacher, a wonder-worker, and the church's first martyr. His life glitters like a diamond in the chronicles of the early church. He was a Christian full of the Holy Ghost, power, wisdom, grace and faith. He was so full of God that his interrogators "saw that his face was like the face of an angel." As they stoned Stephen he cried out, "'Lord, do not charge them with this sin'" (7:60).

Witnessing this event was a young man named Saul. The spectacle of Stephen's being stoned to death, yet not losing his faith or courage but abounding more and more in spiritual power, was likely one of the influences which finally changed Saul into the Apostle Paul.

Enrichment From the Church: Jesus was Stephen's example; Stephen became an example to Paul; and from Paul the Christian example has spread to men and women in every corner of the world. In fact, Paul's Christian life was so exemplary that he told the church at Corinth, "Imitate me, just as I also imitate Christ" (1 Corinthians 11:1).

Enrichment From the Heart: It was said of one person, "I saw her life, and I sought her Lord."

Helping Others (Counseling)   September, Week 3

Esdras Betancourt

BUILDING HOPE THROUGH LOVE

Scripture: "I have no man to put me into the pool when the water is stirred" (John 5:7).

Enrichment From the Word: "I have no one." A short phrase, but what a sad, lonely, hopeless feeling of desperation it conveys! Long ago friends had picked up this paralyzed man's pallet and carried him to Bethesda pool. Time and time again he watched the pool, waiting for the angel to stir the waters; but he was never able to get in first.

Then Jesus came. With resolution and love He threaded His way through the crowd of broken humanity and mass suffering to the most desperate case in the whole place. Jesus asked, "Do you want to be made well?" The man replied, "I have no one to help me." Then Jesus said, "Rise, take up your bed and walk." This man who had been paralyzed 38 years was healed immediately!

Enrichment From the Church: I pastored the campus church at the Spanish Institute of Ministry in Houston, Texas. After one evening service a youth from the church said to me, "I have a friend whose wife gave birth, and the doctor advised him to send for his priest because the baby is dying." The new father did not know a priest; I went instead. When I arrived at the maternity ward, I found the doctor examining the baby. The doctor explained, "The water bag broke in the mother's womb. He swallowed the water and poisoned himself. He will soon die." I gave the father the sad news and concluded by saying, "As long as there is life, there is hope." Then I prayed.

Three days later the perfectly healthy baby was sent home with his mother.

Enrichment From the Heart: Jesus offers new hope to all who are physically or spiritually paralyzed.

Helping Others (Counseling)   **September, Week 3**

Esdras Betancourt

RESTORING THE WAYWARD BELIEVER

Scripture: Jesus said to her, "Neither do I condemn you" (John 8:11).

Enrichment From the Word: This dramatic incident in which Jesus forgave a woman caught in the act of adultery was in keeping with Jesus' mission "to seek and to save" the lost (Luke 19:10). The story reveals the callousness of the scribes and Pharisees, who displayed no mercy when they exposed the woman's shame before Christ and the public. They also hoped to catch Christ in a declaration they could use against Him, but Jesus knew what was in their hearts. He said, "'He who is without sin among you, let him throw a stone at her first'" (John 8:7).

They all slipped away. Christ and the woman were left alone. He asked her, "'Woman, where are those accusers of yours? Has no one condemned you? . . . Neither do I condemn you; go and sin no more.'" (vv. 10, 11).

Enrichment From the Church: One evening my wife and I were washing clothes at a washateria when a sad-looking woman came in. My wife desired to witness to her. As they spoke, the woman confessed that she had recently committed adultery, and she felt that God would not forgive her. My wife explained that God would forgive her if she would repent. The woman confessed her sin to the Lord. Then she said, "God must have sent you to me tonight because I was planning to commit suicide." She handed me a loaded gun and asked me to dispose of it.

Enrichment From the Heart: The Pharisees wanted to destroy the woman caught in adultery, but Jesus wanted to restore her. Jesus could restore people because He first accepted them as they were.

Helping Others (Counseling)   September, Week 3

Esdras Betancourt

PROVOKING ONE ANOTHER TO GOOD WORKS

Scripture: For we are His workmanship, created in Christ Jesus for good works, which God prepared beforehand that we should walk in them (Ephesians 2:10).

Enrichment From the Word: The word *workmanship* denotes a work of art or a masterpiece. Believers are God's workmanship because they have been created in Jesus Christ. God's purpose for this creation has always been that believers would do good works. That is, believers are God's workmanship in whom and through when **He** performs good works. To be reborn "unto good works" is the miracle brought about by what the Bible calls conversion. A person is not a Christian unless his life is directed "for good works." "Faith without works is dead" (James 2:20).

Enrichment From the Church: In the early church we find ample examples to provoke us to good works. **Jesus** met the needs of Jew and Gentile, rich and poor, bond and free through His great love. **Paul,** who said he had become "all things to all men" (1 Corinthians 9:22), ministered to all races and classes. **The early church** had "no needy persons among them. For from time to time those who owned lands or houses sold them, brought the money from the sales and put it at the apostles' feet, and it was distributed to anyone as he had need" (Acts 4:34, 35, *NIV*).

Enrichment From the Heart: "There are Hands unseen working with our hands. There is a Will omnipotent emerging in our wills. . . . There is a strength untold directing our members. There is a Divine Craftsman repeating Himself in us. . . . We are ourselves workers together with Him, pledged to do our part, though always aware that without Him we can do nothing" (J. Stuart Holden).

Stewardship   September, Week 4

Gerald W. Redman

PRACTICING TOTAL STEWARDSHIP

Scripture: And this they did, not as we had hoped, but first gave themselves to the Lord, and then to us by the will of God (2 Corinthians 8:5).

Enrichment From the Word: Stewardship is more than a reference to giving monetarily or materially. God's invitation to all people is to give ourself. Oswald Chambers states in his book *My Utmost for His Highest*, "The only thing we own is our right to ourself." Yet, God cannot be a full partner in our spiritual relationship until all ownership is willingly given to Him.

A successful journey toward total stewardship will never be realized until some absolutes are settled. First, everyone is a steward. Second, there are only two kinds of stewards—profitable or unprofitable. Third, God must become our partner in all things. Fourth, as stewards we must realize He has entrusted us with certain areas of His property.

Enrichment From the Church: James Jackson and his two brothers had become very successful in real estate. However, their ventures in business had drawn them away from God, but James returned to the Lord. Through a series of events God asked him, "If I took everything, would you still love Me?" Then the Lord said, "If I took from you the ability I gave you to acquire, would you still love Me?" The result was, and still is, the Jackson brothers have been giving all—everything—literally to God. When asked why, they simply reply, "It belongs to Him."

Enrichment From the Heart: Lord, teach me to surrender all to You, most importantly, all of me.

Stewardship

Gerald W. Redman

September, Week 4

PRACTICING STEWARDSHIP OF TIME

Scripture: To everything there is a season, A time for every purpose under heaven: A time to be born, And a time to die; A time to plant, And a time to pluck what is planted . . . (Ecclesiastes 3:1-8).

Enrichment From the Word: Time is life lived or lost; opportunity realized or refused. Time is a divine entrustment. It is life's portfolio. It can't be saved. Once it is used, it cannot be retrieved. No matter the allotment, there are 60 seconds to each minute, 60 minutes to each hour, 24 hours to each day.

The only difference in time is the value placed on it. Time is always on duty. As stewards we must manage our time allotment. "The time is short" (1 Corinthians 7:29). Opportunity is narrowing down. Therefore, we must "[redeem] the time" (Ephesians 5:16) from the bondage of selfishness to the usefulness of service.

Enrichment From the Church: Bishop Ralph Cushman wrote a poem titled "The Secret." Following are the first and fifth stanzas:

> I met God in the morning
> When my day was at its best,
> And His presence came like sunrise,
> Like a glory in my breast.

> So I think I know the secret,
> Learned from many a troubled way:
> You must seek Him in the morning
> If you want Him through the day.

Enrichment From the Heart: Father, may I enter time with speed, attend to it diligently, guard it respectfully and use it methodically.

Stewardship **September, Week 4**

Gerald W. Redman

PRACTICING STEWARDSHIP OF TALENT

Scripture: "If anyone serves Me, him My Father will honor" (John 12:26).

Enrichment From the Word: Jesus addressed the use of talents emphatically in Matthew 25. He leaves no room for doubt regarding the use of talents.

Moses was asked, "What is that in your hand?" (Exodus 4:2).

Christians must first realize they have been called to salvation, then to separation and ultimately to service (Isaiah 1:18; 2 Corinthians 6:17; 1 Peter 4:10).

Christianity is designed for the complete use of the variety of each individual's talent(s). When this is realized, we meet the needs of our children in their simple faith, of the youth and adults with their complexities of problems and needs, and of the senior adult who has special insights for both extremes of the spectrum of life.

Have you ever stopped to think how many times small things were important to God? Not because they were small but because they were dedicated to Him; for instance, a rod, a ram's horn, an earthen pitcher, a shepherd's sling.

Jesus insists on separation, surrender and sacrifice.

Enrichment From the Church: A standard-bearer of a company of soldiers once advanced well ahead of his company as they were attacking an important enemy position. The captain called to him to bring the standard back to the company, to which the soldier replied, "Bring the company up to the standard."

Enrichment From the Heart: Father, it seems I have so little to offer. However, it isn't mine, it's Yours. Give me the courage to take it from the napkin where I've hidden it and bring it to You so You may help me to courageously use *Yours* for *them*.

Stewardship   September, Week 4

Gerald W. Redman

PRACTICING STEWARDSHIP OF MONEY

Scripture: "Where your treasure is, there your heart will be also" (Matthew 6:21).

Enrichment From the Word: Money! Is there a direct correlation between it and stewardship? Should the church say as much about money as it does? Yes!

Money is important. We will control it, or it will control us. Scripture frequently addresses the issue of money and possessions—not because of its evil but because of its relationship to our spirituality.

As stewards we are managers. It is required that we manage our money. The place to begin is to understand that all things (including money) come from God. Therefore, it is important to properly give God's hallowed share. "The tithe . . . is the Lord's" (Leviticus 27:30).

Enrichment From the Church: In his book *God's Miraculous Plan of Economy*, Jack Taylor lists and explains seven principles of giving:

1. God possesses and presides over all wealth in the world.
2. God wants His wealth in circulation.
3. God's wealth belongs to His children.
4. We are to properly appropriate God's wealth.
5. We are to give according to God's wealth.
6. It is rewarding to give God's way.
7. We must determine purposeful giving.

Enrichment From the Heart: O God, You've given me so much. Thank You. That portion of Your money which You have given to me, help me to use it as You would.

Stewardship **September, Week 4**

Gerald W. Redman

PRACTICING STEWARDSHIP OF LIFE

Scripture: And this they did, not as we had hoped, but first gave themselves to the Lord, and then to us by the will of God (2 Corinthians 8:5).

Enrichment From the Word: We end this series of devotions where we began. Our Father has given us a great endowment—life. When we seriously understand the responsibility and opportunity conscientious stewardship brings, then we will become good stewards of our lives.

True life stewardship will result in giving ourselves to others. This is the will of God. Remember this is what He did in giving His Son and what Jesus did in giving His life. Don't forget how many other personalities in Scripture filled their lives full of purposeful living for Christ.

Enrichment From the Church: In the book *Good Stewards*, J. E. Dillard tells a story of a peasant who met her King. The day came for the King to arrive. She decided she wouldn't join the crowd. Then her curiosity got the best of her, and she grabbed her black bonnet and her old bag and ran into the crowd. "He will not see me," she said. But just as the chariot approached her, it stopped. The King looked right through the crowd and into her face. She thrust her hand in her bag and took out a big copper coin, the only coin she had, and gave it to the King. The King smiled and said, "You can't afford to give all that gold to the King. Here, take it back." Awestricken, she took back the coin; and when she opened her hand, there was a piece of pure gold.

Enrichment From the Heart: Father, touch Your life in me. Turn it to meaningful substance. So when I give it back to You at the time of accounting, it will be all You expected.

Communications October, Week 1

Bennie Triplett

COMMUNICATING THE GOSPEL—RADIO

Scripture: So then faith comes by hearing, and hearing by the word of God. But I say, have they not heard? Yes indeed: "Their sound has gone out to all the earth, And their words to the ends of the world" (Romans 10:17, 18).

Enrichment From the Word: Can you imagine the bold new vision it took for the early church to believe, proclaim and act on the missionary passages of Romans 10? Such outreach is definitely possible in our time, especially with the means of mass communications. But you and I must have the same dynamic, daring, unhindered optimism that we can and will reach every individual with the gospel.

Enrichment From the Church: In 1958 the Church of God launched a department of media ministries by airing *Forward in Faith*, a 30-minute worship service, on six radio stations. Since that day hundreds of stations have beamed the gospel around the world each week through *Forward in Faith*. How has it happened? Involvement. The answer to world evangelism is the daring, enthusiastic, visionary, determined involvement of each individual in the body of Christ.

Enrichment From the Heart: Someone has said, "Radio is making a comeback." Not so! Radio has never gone away. Everywhere you go, there is radio! And I believe its influence will continue growing.

From my heart I believe media and electronics are last-day tools placed in the hands of the church to carry out the Great Commission. In reality, you and I are both receivers and transmitters. May we always be good stewards of that which He has placed in our hands.

Communications　　　　　　　　　October, Week 1

Bennie Triplett

COMMUNICATING THE GOSPEL—TELEVISION

Scripture: And . . . [Jesus] said to them, "Go into all the world and preach the gospel to every creature" (Mark 16:15).

Enrichment From the Word: "All the world!" "Every creature!" These two glaring headlines refuse to release their hold on the heartstrings of the followers of Jesus Christ. You and I are to go to every part of the world and proclaim the good news to everyone, everywhere. How, you ask, is it possible? How can we ever carry out this commission? When Moses asked God a similar question, God responded, "'What is that in your hand?'" (Exodus 4:2).

As Moses learned, even God's questions contain answers. An answer to the question of how we can get the gospel to our world is in our 20th-century hands—it's called television!

Enrichment From the Church: *Multimedia* will someday be a common description of ministry in almost every local church. Radio, television, video, VCRs, camcorders (and who knows what's next?) have a place in ministry. The church must never allow modern technology to be monopolized by satanic forces for satanic ends. Christians must seize every initiative and take advantage of every opportunity to communicate God's truth and love.

Enrichment From the Heart: Through a satellite dish the size of a teacup, videocassettes the size of two postage stamps and a television that a person can hold in his hand, people everywhere will be reachable. Converts can be won, and disciples can be made. Worship services may be held under a coconut palm, in a mountain hermit's cabin or on the veranda of a king's palace. By prayer, encouragement and financial support, you and I will help to reach "every creature" in "all the world."

Communications   **October, Week 1**

Bennie Triplett

COMMUNICATING THE GOSPEL—NEWSPAPER

Scripture: And the word of the Lord was being spread throughout all the region (Acts 13:49).

Enrichment From the Word: "How beautiful upon the mountains Are the feet of him who brings good news, Who proclaims peace, Who brings glad tidings of good things, Who proclaims salvation, Who says to Zion, 'Your God reigns!'" (Isaiah 52:7).

Enrichment From the Church: Nothing has demonstrated the power of the printed page more than the spread of Christianity. It is said, "The Reformation was cradled in the printing press, and established by no other instrument."

T. DeWitt Talmage said, "The newspaper is a great educator; there is no force compared with it. It is book, pulpit, platform, and forum, all in one." The newspaper is the people's university—half the readers of Christendom read little else.

In all my pastoral, administrative, evangelistic and missionary work, I have always used the local newspaper for the sake of the gospel. Every congregation ought to have a director of public relations or a press secretary to assist the pastor in keeping the ministries of the church before the public. I used to title this work "Keeping the Good News in the News."

Enrichment From the Heart: When I pastored in Nashville, Tennessee, the Lord impressed me to ask Morris Bradley to serve as director of public relations for the Meridian Street Church of God. I still stand in awe of what this professional Christian layman was able to accomplish for the glory of God through the local newspapers. Disraeli was right when he said, "The press is not only free, it is powerful."

Communications October, Week 1

Bennie Triplett

COMMUNICATING THE GOSPEL—TRACTS

<u>Scripture:</u> But these are written that you might believe that Jesus is the Christ, the Son of God, and that believing you may have life in His name (John 20:31).

Enrichment From the Word: Gospel tracts can be considered miniature Bibles or condensed Gospels. A tract is a simple way of amplifying the power of writing and reading. Over and over again Jesus asked people, "Have ye not read?" When the Lord sent a message of judgment to the people of Judah through Habakkuk the prophet, He told Habakkuk, "'Write the vision And make it plain on the tablets, That he may run who reads it'" (Habakkuk 2:2).

Enrichment From the Church: The Church of God has a great tract ministry, supervised and promoted by the Evangelism and Home Missions Department. Approximately 40 different tracts, specializing in the major areas of personal evangelism, have been produced; and millions of these tracts have been distributed.

Oswald J. Smith, former pastor of the great Peoples Church in Toronto, Canada, said, "More people are saved, for less money spent, through tracts than by any other method." Gospel tracts typically cost two or three cents each to produce, and some 20 people will read a single tract until it is worn out.

Enrichment From the Heart: Leonard Albert tells about a man on a passenger ship who was handed a gospel tract. Detesting anything that smacked of religion, he tore the pamphlet to pieces and flipped it over the side of the boat. Back in his cabin as he prepared to retire for the night, he noticed a small piece of torn paper attached to the lapel of his coat. Picking it off, he observed it was a remnant of the tract. Looking closer, he could read only one word on each side of the scrap. The first word was *God*; the second, *eternity*. The man was converted in his cabin that night.

Communications   October, Week 1

Bennie Triplett

COMMUNICATING THE GOSPEL—TELEPHONE

Scripture: A word fitly spoken is like apples of gold In settings of silver (Proverbs 25:11).

Enrichment From the Word: The term *fitly spoken* means "timely and appropriately spoken." Solomon wrote, "A man has joy by the answer of his mouth, And a word spoken in due season, how good it is!" (Proverbs 15:23). A wise man has fulfillment in his answers of wisdom, and a word spoken when needed is healthful and refreshing.

Enrichment From the Church: The telephone can be a wonderful instrument of ministry and evangelism: Sunday school teachers use it to contact absentees, music ministers use it to notify members of rehearsals, and pastors use it for countless reasons. When we think about the multiple purposes the telephone serves, we wonder how we ever got along without it.

Forward in Faith, the department of media ministries for the Church of God, has maintained a 24-hour prayer line—(615) 472-7414—for every day of the year for most of its history. Many local churches offer "Dial-A-Prayer." Some ministries have automatic, coded messages geared to the needs of a hurting community. Crises centers maintain telephone-alert vigils around the clock.

Enrichment From the Heart: It was about 3 o'clock in the morning. Sleepily I answered a ringing telephone. The caller was a young man whom Helen and I had been praying for since coming to Lawrenceville, Georgia, to pastor. After chatting briefly, Mike received Jesus Christ as his Savior over the telephone. He and his family became faithful members and workers in the local church.

Parenting   October, Week 2

Junus Fulbright

HELPING YOUR CHILDREN WITH SCHOOL

Scripture: Where there is no revelation, the people cast off restraint (Proverbs 29:18).

Enrichment From the Word: A child can study better when he can study with a purpose. The case of Daniel demonstrates this. After Israel lost in a war with Babylon, Daniel was given an unusual opportunity: he was placed in a special school to make him an adviser to the king. He was chosen because his family had taken great pains to provide him with an excellent education and a foundation in the Word of God. Upon receiving the appointment, Daniel realized he could serve his people, Israel, better if he could become the best adviser the king had. Daniel had a purpose!

Enrichment From the Church: Children's church, Sunday school and the ministry of the Word can impress upon a child a feeling and a concept of his purpose in life. As a parent you can help your child to do well in school by:

1. Teaching him/her to be observant by sharing your interests in the world around you—nature, mechanics, music, and so forth.
2. Recognizing and complimenting his learning.
3. Becoming involved with the PTO. Your child will appreciate your personal concern about his school life. PTO is a public demonstration that you care and want to be positively involved in his school situation.
4. Securing assistance for your child if help is needed. If he is weak in an area, tutors are available to provide more personalized help.

Enrichment From the Heart: Dear Lord, please give us the vision, the compassion and the determination to impart a sense of purpose to our children. Amen.

Parenting October, Week 2

Junus Fulbright

HELPING YOUR CHILDREN WITH ADJUSTMENTS

Scripture: Trust in the Lord with all your heart, And lean not on your own understanding; In all your ways acknowledge Him, And He shall direct your paths (Proverbs 3:5, 6).

Enrichment From the Word: Congratulations! You are a parent. Now you have the opportunity to experience the step-by-step progress your children will make to mature and fulfilling lives. This dynamic process of change and adjustments will be heartwarming and heartbreaking. The challenge of change triggers fear of the unknown. Yet, God's Word declares, "Fear not, for I am with you" (Isaiah 4:10). What a "success warranty" is found in our text. Impress these three things upon your children.

Enrichment From the Church: Negative reaction to change can be devastating. Many youth are hurting because of a move to another town, a new school, the death of a parent, a broken home, and/or other life-shocking changes. The values they have been taught by their parents may be challenged by the immense pressures of peers, the power of the media, school and friends.

A good strong church youth group can reinforce Christian morality. A Christian youth group allows a teen to discuss problems with other teens and see how they dealt with the problem and found a solution. Biblical principles shared in the youth group help young people to make right decisions.

Enrichment From the Heart: Dear Lord, help us not to fear change, since it is only indicative of a dynamic life. Help us, as parents, to lead our children into really trusting You. We know this is the only way to Christian growth and maturity. Amen.

Parenting   October, Week 2

Junus Fulbright

HELPING YOUR CHILDREN WITH THEIR FRIENDS

Scripture: For it is not an enemy who reproaches me; Then I could bear it. Nor is it one who hates me who has magnified himself against me; Then I could hide from him. But it was you, a man my equal, My companion and my acquaintance. We took sweet counsel together, And walked to the house of God in the throng (Psalm 55:12-14).

Enrichment From the Word: Once again David was running for his life. This time he had lost his kingdom, his family and his possessions to a rebellious son.

It was the darkest day of his career!

Yet the person he feared the most was not Absalom, or even another giant—it was his close friend and adviser, Ahithophel.

On occasion, things do not go well between our children and their friends. Sometimes, like David, it is because they have befriended the wrong people. More often, however, it is because of the normal conflicts that arise in adolescent relationships.

Enrichment From the Church: To help our children avoid some of the bumps and bruises of life, we would do well to assist them in picking the right friends. Naturally, the primary criteria for a person being a "right friend" (a best friend) would be that he know Christ as his personal Savior. "Do not be unequally yoked together with unbelievers" (2 Corinthians 6:14).

Next, we should teach our children some basic principles of getting along, such as being a friend, being a Christian influence, being slow to argue and learning to share.

Enrichment From the Heart: Dear Lord, help us to impress upon our children that a true friend is priceless and is, therefore, worth an endless commitment of love and respect. For surely "there is a friend who sticks closer than a brother" (Proverbs 18:24).

Parenting   **October, Week 2**

Junus Fulbright

HELPING YOUR CHILDREN WITH MONEY MANAGEMENT

Scripture: Honor the Lord with your possessions, And with the firstfruits of all your increase; So your barns will be filled with plenty, And your vats will overflow with new wine (Proverbs 3:9, 10).

Enrichment From the Word: The first thing our children need to learn about money management is to give back to the Lord that which is His. This can be done by providing them with two banks. One is for their allowances, birthday money and other income, and the other is for their tithes. Children who learn to tithe when they are young will continue to do so when they get older and will reap the benefits of God's blessings for doing so.

Enrichment From the Church: If children see that we care more about things than people, they will often become cynical and unbelieving.

Once our children understand the proper place for money in their lives, they need to be taught how to save and to manage it properly.

Some time ago, a child saw a big wad of dollar bills in his father's wallet.

"My," he said, "Daddy, you're rich!"

Upon hearing that, his father pulled the money out of his wallet. He separated it into a half dozen little piles, then explained how each pile would be spent for upcoming bills and weekly needs. That object lesson made a lasting impression on that child and went far to teach him fiscal responsibility.

Enrichment From the Heart: Lord, as parents, help us to be good examples of faithful stewardship in handling money. Let our lives demonstrate that money is not an end in itself, but to be used to glorify God and for the needs of mankind. Amen.

Parenting October, Week 2

Junus Fulbright

LETTING YOUR CHILDREN GROW UP

Scripture: When I was a child, I spoke as a child, I understood as a child, I thought as a child; but when I became a man, I put away childish things (1 Corinthians 13:11).

Enrichment From the Word: Perhaps the most critical years of a young person's life are between the ages of 8 and 18. This is aptly called the "Decade of Decision." It is a decade when a child will form values, be influenced the most by those outside his family, find outlets for energy and experience the most intense peer pressure.

It will be much easier on parents to loosen their hold and then eventually let the young person go as he grows up if a proper foundation has been laid. This involves living the example before him and indoctrinating him in the Word of God.

Enrichment From the Church: What an exciting time to be alive! The church is challenging young people to grow spiritually and emotionally into meaningful discipleship. Opportunities for ministry are available in the local church in youth groups and youth ministries, tract distribution, YWEA involvement and STEP (Summer Training and Evangelism Partners). Through youth camps, lock-ins, retreats, youth prayer meetings and a host of other activities, children and teens are enabled to discover their gifts and to realize the ministry God has for them.

Enrichment From the Heart: Dear Lord, we want our children to grow up into the men and women You want them to be. Yet in our hearts, we will always remember them as the tender babies and children they were. Thank You for that time when You bound them to us. We will always cherish all those intense moments of love as we give them back to You. Amen.

Involvement   **October, Week 3**

R. Lamar Vest

BELIEVING GOD FOR A BOLD NEW VISION

Scripture: "Enlarge the place of your tent, And let them stretch out the curtains of your habitations; Do not spare; Lengthen your cords, And strengthen your stakes" (Isaiah 54:2).

Enrichment From the Word: A key event in the celebration of 200 years of modern Protestant missions occurred on May 30, 1792. On this day young William Carey preached from Isaiah 54:2. In his message he declared, "Expect great things from God; attempt great things for God." He believed God for a bold new vision that launched the modern missionary movement and changed the course of the church. He was not content to hold back. The challenge of this passage is to enlarge, stretch, lengthen, strengthen. Church history was forged by pioneers with a vision that was both bold and new.

Enrichment From the Church: Esther 4:14 says, "Yet who knows whether you have come to the kingdom for such a time as this?" In the book *Azusa Street and Beyond*, this is called the "Mordecai-Esther Factor." It is a sense of destiny characteristic of Pentecostal pioneers. Our forefathers had no doubt God had raised them up with a new anointing for a new day. They believed God for a bold new vision.

A first-semester Bible college student looked over his schedule. "'Church History 101,'" he read. "I didn't come here to *study* church history; I came to *make* church history!" Scoff at the arrogance and triumphal attitude of the young preacher if you like, but that is the stuff from which a bold new vision emerges. The future of the Church of God will be forged by those who face tough times with a bold new vision from God.

Enrichment From the Heart: O God, deliver me from timid preoccupation. Come, shake the world through me!

Involvement   October, Week 3

R. Lamar Vest

DEVELOPING A TEAM SPIRIT

Scripture: But Peter, standing up with the eleven. . . . (Acts 2:14).

Enrichment From the Word: When Peter stood up, he felt the presence of 11 brothers standing behind him and around him. They were together in a team spirit. They understood the importance and beauty of brethren dwelling and working together in harmony (Psalm 133). This same team spirit caused six men to go with Peter to the house of Cornelius in a new Spirit-led adventure of preaching to the Gentiles (Acts 11:12). The team spirit was evident in the first commissioning of cross-cultural missionaries from a local church in Antioch (Acts 13).

Paul was one of those commissioned. He learned to appreciate the value of a network of supporting friendships in the work of the Lord. Teamwork became his ministry lifestyle as he planted churches across the Mediterranean world (Acts 20:4). Every letter he wrote to fledgling churches was written in a team spirit. Every action of the New Testament church in polity, worship, evangelism, fellowship and nurture was developed out of the soil of teamwork. A biblical church is a church with a team spirit.

Enrichment From the Church: A spate of current business and economics articles contrast American and Japanese business and management practices. The verdict: Japanese productivity is higher because it is based on "group consciousness," an agressive "team spirit." Pentecostals knew this long before the days of modern industry and technology. New Testament church leaders, however, realized it before our Pentecostal forefathers. "Robinson Crusoe" Christianity will not survive our trying times. Today's church must be a team, or it will cease to be a church.

Enrichment From the Heart: Father, Son and Holy Spirit, inspire me to be interdependent with my brothers and sisters.

Involvement   October, Week 3

R. Lamar Vest

DEVELOPING A SPIRIT OF ACTION

Scripture: "Why are we sitting here until we die?" (2 Kings 7:3).

Enrichment From the Word: A spirit of action is needed in our move toward a bold new vision for God's work. Four lepers in the 2 Kings text knew their days were numbered. It was only a matter of time until they would die. But they shook themselves into action. Their action caused them to live and abound.

A squadron of American soldiers, outnumbered and surrounded during one of the Korean War battles, faced certain death. It seemed they would be overrun and defeated. The general called them to action, saying, "Men, we are surrounded, but don't let one get away." The soldiers rallied, took the offensive and drove off the enemy while saving their own lives.

Enrichment From the Church: Too many congregations are affected with "remnantitis." They are satisfied to sit where they are until they die. Look at every thriving and growing church. They have a spirit of action. There is no resignation or retreat; there is advance. The spirit of a bold new vision has replaced lethargy and spiritual laziness. A spirit of action has been nurtured and developed. In modern Hebrew there is no expression for the command "Forward march!" Instead, Israeli military commanders give the shout, "Follow me!" A spirit of action is often a solitary act. But positive, active leadership moves believers into action.

Enrichment From the Heart: "Take my life and let it be Consecrated, Lord, to Thee; Take my hands and let them move At the impulse of Thy love, At the impulse of Thy love."

Involvement　　　　　　　　　　**October, Week 3**

R. Lamar Vest

DEVELOPING A SPIRIT OF ADVENTURE

Scripture: It has always been my ambition to preach the gospel where Christ was not known, so that I would not be building on someone else's foundation. . . . There is no more place for me to work in these regions . . . I plan to . . . go . . . to Spain (Romans 15: 20, 23, 24, *NIV*).

Enrichment From the Word: In the eastern and northern circle of the Mediterranean world, Paul had run out of room. He wanted to go west toward Spain. Spain was uncharted territory for Kingdom work. It represented a new frontier. Paul knew that the antidote for drudgery and boredom was the constant challenge of doing something new for the Lord or finding a new dimension of God's abounding love and grace. Christian living and service for Paul was an adventure because it was inexhaustible.

Enrichment From the Church: The lead character in a modern drama pleads to be delivered from "this depressing regularity." Regularity and boredom seem to plague our times and characterize much of the rituals of some local churches. For many, "Churchianity" has become "precisely predictable."

Fresh life is being breathed into the Church of God. Ministries are developing in new areas. Entirely new segments of the population are being reached. The laity are exciting the church in adventure of ministry. Where there is adventure, there is life and hope for a new generation. Let's give the next generation the seed of the gospel and watch it grow in new soil. There's no adventure in a potted plant.

Enrichment From the Heart: A prayer of repentance I offer, O Lord, for all the times I prematurely predicted Your work and what You would do. Surprise me with Your power. Grant to me the spirit of adventure.

Involvement   October, Week 3

R. Lamar Vest

DEVELOPING A SPIRIT OF DETERMINATION

Scripture: As the time approached for him to be taken up to heaven, Jesus resolutely set out for Jerusalem (Luke 9:51, *NIV*).

Enrichment From the Word: A battle raged when Jesus "set His face to go to Jerusalem." He resolutely started for that great city for the last time before His atoning death. The consequences of what would happen there involved the eternal souls of mankind.

The skies darkened. Torrents of rain turned the road into a sea of mud. Discouraged and tired, Kaiser Wilhelm's lieutenants suggested that the army be halted until morning. "March forward," was the reply. "Herr Kaiser," complained his subordinates, "we cannot move forward. Don't you see the mud?" "I don't see mud because I don't look down. March forward!" thundered the commander.

"Never give up!" warned Sir Winston Churchill a generation later. In the face of impending attack, Churchill marshaled the British empire and marched it to war. For Winston Churchill and Kaiser Wilhelm, the spirit of determination was indispensable to national survival.

Enrichment From the Church: Early Pentecostal saints testified, "I'm saved, sanctified and filled with the Holy Ghost. I'm determined to make heaven my home." Let their example stir us to a bold new vision. We must prepare for one final battle for the souls of men. The last decade of the 20th century will polarize the forces of darkness against the people of light. The weak and indifferent will not stand.

Shake yourself, Brother! Stir yourself, Sister! Let there be a new spirit of determination for Christ and His work!

Enrichment From the Heart: Most powerful God, drive the shaft of determination deep into my being until I set my face to resolutely finish my course and please my God!

Self-Help   **October, Week 4**

Paul Conn

DISPLAYING AN ATTITUDE OF JOY

Scripture: Be joyful in hope, patient in affliction, faithful in prayer (Romans 12:12, *NIV*).

Enrichment From the Word: Paul knew what it meant to be assailed by all types of difficulties. He was attacked in every imaginable manner throughout his walk with the Lord. Both physically and emotionally, he faced enemies in the world as well as those within the church who did not understand him. We can listen to him when he talks about being joyful in times of trial. Notice he doesn't tell us to be happy or carefree, but to be joyful. Joy is an attitude, a mind-set, a mental and emotional discipline that can exist even in the face of trouble.

Enrichment From the Church: Several years ago I learned that a friend of mine, who pastored a small church, had suffered a fire which had totally destroyed his parsonage. All the belongings of his family had been lost, including those many irreplaceable personal items that hold memories of a lifetime. I called my friend to console him, knowing he was financially devastated by the loss and expecting him to be emotionally wiped out as well. To my surprise, he was as cheerful and upbeat as if he were describing a trivial incident of little importance. It was not a posture; it was real. "Hey, man," he said, "don't waste any tears on us. God has given us joy in all this. I can't explain it, but I feel as good as if it were someone else's house. Tell everybody I'm doing fine!"

Enrichment From the Heart: Somehow, God is able to give us a joyful heart even when things are otherwise going terribly. He did it for the Apostle Paul; He did it for my pastor friend; and He will do it for me if I lean on Him.

Self-Help   October, Week 4

Paul Conn

MAKING A DECISION TO BE CHEERFUL

Scripture: He who is of a merry heart has a continual feast (Proverbs 15:15).

Enrichment From the Word: Cheerfulness comes from an internal source and can be transported with us wherever we go, in whatever conditions we find ourselves. Cheerfulness comes from the heart; it does not come from external circumstances. The person who maintains an internal cheerfulness will "feast" constantly on that attitude, not having to depend on others to supply it.

Ernest Hemingway, in *A Moveable Feast*, described the friendship and camaraderie of the community of American expatriates in Paris in the 1920s. Their pleasure was in one another, he says, not in any particular circumstance of time or place, so they carried it with them wherever they went; it was a "moveable feast." The writer of the Proverbs has a similar, though much more spiritually elevated, thought in mind when he refers to one's cheerfulness as "a continual feast." It is something we take with us wherever we go!

Enrichment From the Church: The fellowship of the church is often also a "moveable feast." One of the characteristics of a close-knit church family is the emotional environment which it creates for its members, whether they meet in a church building, in a foreign land, in a home or in a hotel convention hall. There is an *esprit de corps*, an environment of cheerful goodwill, which seems to travel wherever the family of God goes.

Enrichment From the Heart: Lord, help me to have the kind of cheerful heart that is transportable. Help me to carry with me, wherever I go, an attitude of cheerfulness that I can share with others in the family of God.

Self-Help   October, Week 4

Paul Conn

SHOWING A SPIRIT OF ENTHUSIASM

Scripture: Whatever you do, do it heartily, as to the Lord and not to men (Colossians 3:23).

Enrichment From the Word: For the Christian believer, there is little difference between the sacred and the secular, when it comes to one's work. If a thing is worthy of being done by God's children, it is worthy of a conscientious, workmanlike effort. The Apostle Paul is telling us that God is not glorified by laziness or inattentiveness to duty, even if the matter at hand is a secular occupation. The New Testament is replete with this message: Give honest value, a day's work for a day's pay, whether laying bricks or driving a truck or preaching a sermon. Particularly in doing the work of the church, Paul says, we are working for God and not for man; therefore we should do it with 100 percent effort and enthusiasm.

Enrichment From the Church: There is a slogan from motivational literature: "Wherever you are, *be* there!" This means focus on the matter at hand, whatever it is. Give it your full attention and energy. If you are playing golf, don't play with half your mind back at the office; if you are at the office, don't waste energy fantasizing being on the golf course. Wherever you are, be there! Do one thing at a time, then do it with all your heart. If this is true for the unbeliever, it is doubly so for the Christian. There is no such thing as a part-time Christian; wherever we are and whatever we are doing, we ought to be able to do it "as unto God."

Enrichment From the Heart: If I cannot ask You to bless me as I do it, Lord, should I be doing it at all?

Self-Help   October, Week 4

Paul Conn

CREATING A POSITIVE ATTITUDE ABOUT LIFE

Scripture: Whatever things are true, whatever things are noble, whatever things are just, whatever things are pure, whatever things are lovely, whatever things are of good report, if there is any virtue and if there is anything praiseworthy—meditate on these things" (Philippians 4:8).

Enrichment From the Word: This scripture tells us how to think. This suggests that the way we think is subject to a certain amount of control; we are able to "program" the material that comprises our normal thought life. Naturally, this control is not absolute. Our brains are not hermetically sealed chambers which we can monitor and manage with total success. But there are several scriptures which, like this one, challenge us to exercise care in the kinds of thoughts on which we dwell.

A familiar axiom is that "we cannot keep birds from flying overhead, but we can keep them from building nests in our hair!" And so it is with our thoughts; the negative ideas—those which are *un*true, *un*pure, *un*lovely—might well occur to us, but we can guard against letting them linger.

Enrichment From the Church: A sainted old sister in the local church of my childhood, Grandma Bryant, testified frequently and always had the same message for the church: "It's agonna take a clean people to go when Jesus comes!" she reminded us. She was so highly respected that the congregation always listened. She delivered her message in various words, but the theme was always the same: clean thinking, clean living, a clean people.

Enrichment From the Heart: God is a positive God, and He wants His people to be positive people.

Self-Help

Paul Conn

PRESCRIBING THE MEDICINE OF LAUGHTER

Scripture: When the Lord brought back the captivity of Zion, We were like those who dream. Then our mouth was filled with laughter, And our tongue with singing. Then they said among the nations, "The Lord has done great things for them" (Psalm 126:1, 2).

Enrichment From the Word: Have you ever considered that laughter is biblical? Here in the Psalms is a song which describes laughter—not just joy or happiness, but outright laughter—as a result of the blessings of God. When Jehovah brought the Israelites out of captivity, they literally laughed in celebration as they praised their great God.

Enrichment From the Church: Norman Cousins, former editor of the prestigious *Saturday Review*, is one of the most respected thinkers of our generation. He certainly is not one to make false or frivolous claims about the "power of positive thinking." His book *The Anatomy of an Illness* tells of his recovery from a life-threatening disease and attributes much of his remarkable comeback to the therapeutic value of simple laughter. He approached laughter as seriously as if it were a type of drug prescribed by his physician. Using books of humor and classic films by the great masters of comedy (Abbott and Costello, Laurel and Hardy, the Marx Brothers), he exposed himself to a regular regimen of laughter which, he believes, helped save his life. He makes a convincing case that laughter is quite literally the best medicine.

Enrichment From the Heart: I affirm that laughter, God-given, is as natural and can be as sacred as tears. Piety is not always expressed in tears and the *sotto voce* whispers of the confessional but also in the loud, full-throated laughter of those whom God has blessed.

Church Growth   **November, Week 1**

W. C. Ratchford Sr.

PLANNING A STRATEGY FOR CHURCH GROWTH

Scripture: Go, stand in the temple and speak to the people all the words of this life (Acts 5:20).

Enrichment From the Word: It wasn't the first time Peter and the apostles had been imprisoned, and it wouldn't be the last. Their continued involvement in a growing church would keep them before those officials who would like to somehow ignore them.

This time, however, the angel of freedom had more than the apostles' release on his mind. His words to them, as recorded here, were a directive to take action—go, stand, speak. In the angel's words lies the basis for a sound church growth strategy.

We have, through years of experience, got the "going" and "standing" part of the strategy down to a science. However, these aspects are of little value if we do not speak the words of this life. What life? A life made new by Christ, a life released from sin's prison, a life filled with God's peace and presence. Eternal life!

Enrichment From the Church: When I was state overseer of Nebraska, the Lord awakened me one night and gave me the formula for the success of the early church: (1) They were right (conviction); (2) they were willing to share (concern); (3) and they kept on going (commitment).

Implementing an almost 2,000-year-old strategy may not be in vogue today; but what "vogue" is, is not our concern—responding to God's Word is! The strategy for church growth is established and proven. Our task is to make it workable today.

Enrichment From the Heart: Lord, I know that it is Your will for Your church to grow. I commit myself to respond to Your word. May the Holy Spirit guide me as I go, stand and speak the words of this life. Amen.

Church Growth — November, Week 1

W. C. Ratchford Sr.

TRAINING WORKERS FOR CHURCH GROWTH

Scripture: Then Barnabas departed for Tarsus to seek Saul. And when he had found him, he brought him to Antioch. So it was that for a whole year they assembled with the church and taught a great many people. And the disciples were first called Christians in Antioch (Acts 11:25, 26).

Enrichment From the Word: Wouldn't you like to know exactly what caused the word *Christian* to be coined? Although it may have been coined by unbelievers out of a spirit of mockery, something in the believers' behavior and attitude caused this new name to emerge. Since believers were both Jews and Greeks, the new term *Christian* encompassed both. Perhaps the outstanding leadership of Barnabas and Saul in Antioch merited a name change, or it could be attributed to the church's year of training—year of growth. They were rightly called disciples, correctly labeled Christlike.

Training for church growth in Antioch produced a thriving, stable congregation. Today, training can produce the same results in our churches and communities.

Enrichment From the Church: Perhaps bringing a well-known teaching team to your church for a year might be considered radical today, but short-term training sessions using innovative methods and approaches can be successful. Home Bible studies, pastoral care groups, women's circles, men's fellowships and breakfast prayer meetings all provide opportunities for church growth training. Training produces disciples, "and the disciples were . . . called Christians."

Enrichment From the Heart: Dear Lord, I realize that to truly be Your disciple, I must be trained in Your Word and be willing to respond to its call. Then and only then can I be a disciple—Christlike. Amen.

Church Growth   November, Week 1

W. C. Ratchford Sr.

BUILDING A PROSPECT LIST FOR CHURCH GROWTH

Scripture: Philip found Nathanael and said to him, "We have found Him of whom Moses in the law, and also the prophets, wrote—Jesus of Nazareth, the son of Joseph" (John 1:45).

Enrichment From the Word: In the preceding verses Jesus had been calling His disciples. In verse 43 the Bible says, "[Jesus] found Philip and said to him, 'Follow me.'" Philip, an enthusiastic new convert, set out to bring his friend Nathanael to Christ.

It is interesting to note that Philip did not lose his conversion zeal. According to early Christian tradition, after the ascension of Christ, Philip became a missionary in Asia Minor. The historian Eusebius said Philip was a "great light of Asia."

Nathanael and many others were saved because Philip told them of Christ. Many who were perhaps unlikely prospects for the church at the time received the message of salvation proclaimed by Philip.

Enrichment From the Church: Often a prospect list can start in a most unusual place, a Sunday school enrollment book for instance. Such was the case at a church in the Piedmont area of South Carolina. Several young adult couples brought their children to Sunday school every Sunday. They even attended an adult class themselves, then headed home before the worship hour. These people, though technically in the church, were spiritually out of the church—they weren't saved.

Beginning with prayerful attention to these people, entire families were won to Christ. Their experiences resulted in more prospects and more converts.

Enrichment From the Heart: We must be careful and not overlook the obvious when we consider prospects for the church. Our prospect list should start in our own home and church, then encompass our community.

Church Growth · November, Week 1

W. C. Ratchford Sr.

PARTICIPATING IN CHURCH GROWTH

Scripture: Now the multitude of those who believed were of one heart and one soul. . . . And with great power the apostles gave witness to the resurrection of the Lord Jesus. And great grace was upon them all (Acts 4:32, 33).

Enrichment From the Word: Something always happened to the people in the early church when they responded to God—something glorious, miraculous, phenomenal! Evidence of this is scattered all through the Book of Acts. When the early Christians joined together in God's movement, they experienced His power and miracle-working presence.

The passage in Acts 4:32, 33 specifically notes three things that happened to believers as they joined together as the church: (1) They became unified; (2) they witnessed with great power; and (3) God's great grace rested upon them. There are always benefits when we participate in Kingdom work.

Enrichment From the Church: An Air Force sergeant, Charles Wright, attended the church I pastored in Amarillo, Texas. Through his efforts we brought to the church busloads of young airmen in basic training. Scores of the men were converted. It was wonderful to know that they had an opportunity to hear and respond to the gospel before they were transferred overseas. Excitement over these new converts sparked spiritual and numerical growth in the church.

Enrichment From the Heart: Lord, I trust as I commit myself to participate in the growth of Your church, that I will become unified with my brothers and sisters in Christ, that I will witness with great power, and that most of all Your grace, Your great grace, will rest upon me. Amen.

Church Growth   November, Week 1

W. C. *Ratchford Sr.*

PRAISING GOD FOR CHURCH GROWTH

Scripture: Therefore by Him let us continually offer the sacrifice of praise to God, that is, the fruit of our lips, giving thanks to His name (Hebrews 13:15).

Enrichment From the Word: A discussion of praise and church growth could easily deteriorate into a "Which came first, the chicken or the egg?" issue. Scripture says in Acts 2:46, 47 that early Christians praised God and "the Lord added to the church daily." Praise occurs before church growth!

The Bible also tells that angels rejoice whenever lost men come to God. Praise occurs after church growth! Perhaps a scripture like Hebrews 13:15 bears out the answer to the dilemma: "Let us *continually* offer the sacrifice of praise."

Praise is a unique thing. It is multifaceted. The psalmist said praise builds a throne for God. Praise brings us into God's presence; it glorifies God, testifies to His power. Praise draws men to Christ.

Enrichment From the Church: Four-year-old Megan Johnson was singing a chorus she had heard in church. It was one the congregation often sang, "We Bring a Sacrifice of Praise." But Megan had the words a little mixed up. Her version was something like "We bring a sack of prizes!" Was she really so far from the essence of the song?

"Oh, give thanks to the Lord, Call upon His name; Make known His deeds among the peoples. Sing to Him, sing psalms to Him; Talk of all His wondrous works" (Psalm 105:1, 2).

Enrichment From the Heart: O worthy God, today I offer a sacrifice of praise to You so I might experience Your holy presence, give testimony to Your infinite power and draw others to You. Amen.

Personal Witness — November, Week 2

Christopher Moree

MAINTAINING PERSONAL INTEGRITY

Scripture: Then Zacchaeus stood and said to the Lord, "Look, Lord, I give half of my goods to the poor; and if I have taken anything from anyone by false accusation, I restore fourfold" (Luke 19:8)

Enrichment From the Word: Zacchaeus, whose name meant "pure" or "innocent," likely was a publican who collected taxes for the Roman government from the district of Jericho.

Publicans were considered extortioners. The people who despised them and ostracized them from society. However, after contact with Jesus, Zacchaeus was ready to restore integrity to his life. He promised to give half of his goods to the poor and make fourfold restitution, a courage which comes only with new birth

Enrichment From the Church: Two of my parishioners were business competitors. Unbeknownst to each other they both offered bids on an important contract. The man who lost the bid openly accused the other of being dishonest. Hurt by this false charge, the man who won the bid offered the other an apology along with all the profits made from the contract. The other man refused the generous offer and later left the church. The generous parishioner continued as a respected member of the church and business community until his death many years later.

Enrichment From the Heart: A daily encounter with Jesus will help us maintain personal integrity. The power of His presence will drive out the evil from our lives and maintain the good.

Personal Witness   **November, Week 2**

Christopher Moree

MAINTAINING MORAL CONVICTIONS

Scripture: "There is no one greater in this house than I, nor has he kept back anything from me but you, because you are his wife. How then can I do this great wickedness, and sin against God?" (Genesis 39:9).

Enrichment From the Word: Joseph, a favored young man, is shamefully sold by his own brothers into slavery. In Egypt he is bought by Potiphar, captain of Pharaoh's guard, and has been made overseer of his household. He seems on top of the world, and all he has to do to stay there is compromise his moral convictions.

Joseph is assaulted with a great temptation. The tempter is his master's wife whom it is his place to obey and his interest to oblige. Opportunity favors the temptation. His business requires him to be, without any suspicion, where she is. Yet, by the grace of God and his moral convictions, Joseph overcomes the temptation. He flees from its presence as one escaping for his life, realizing that it is far better to lose his coat than his convictions.

Enrichment From the Church: In the fourth century A.D., a brilliant young scholar who was far from God took up Paul's Epistles and read, "Let us walk properly, as in the day, not in revelry and drunkenness, not in licentiousness and lewdness, not in strife and envy. But put on the Lord Jesus Christ, and make no provision for the flesh, to fulfill its lusts" (Romans 13:13, 14). This prodigal learned the secret for acquiring and maintaining moral convictions, the miracle of inward renewal. The church had found a mighty advocate—the great Augustine.

Enrichment From the Heart: Maintaining his moral convictions got Joseph thrown into prison, but even there God was with him. Eventually he rose to become prime minister of Egypt without having compromised his moral convictions.

Personal Witness   November, Week 2

Christopher Moree

MAINTAINING SCRIPTURAL VALUES

Scripture: Your word I have hidden in my heart, That I might not sin against You (Psalm 119:11).

Enrichment From the Word: The Word of God is sacred, inspired and infallible. It is "profitable for doctrine, for reproof, for correction, for instruction in righteousness, that the man of God may be complete, thoroughly equipped for every good work" (2 Timothy 3:16, 17).

God gave us His Word to reveal Himself to us and show us how to live. No other authoritative guide has been given or revealed. Through the centuries many desperate souls have taken refuge in the Scriptures, finding confidence for life and for eternity. The psalmist sought for the most appropriate place to store this great treasure. If he put it only in his head, knowing it only intellectually, his memory might fail him. But if he hid it in his heart, it would be ready to him whenever he had occasion to use it. There it would be able to influence his every decision and keep him from sinning against God.

Enrichment From the Church: Situational ethics dominates modern society, including much of the religious world. Bishop Pike of the Episcopal Church, before his untimely death some years ago in the Holy Land, wrote a notorious article for a popular magazine in which he outlined three situations in which a person could justifiably violate the biblical ban on adultery. In his eagerness to provide excuses for those wishing to violate scriptural values, he failed to recognize that God has absolutes and that those absolutes are clearly stated in God's Holy Word.

Enrichment From the Heart: God's Word is a treasure of great price. It is worth acquiring and storing in the safest place—in our heart. We should acquire a little of this treasure each day so the values of our life will remain those of the Scriptures.

Personal Witness
Christopher Moree

MAINTAINING BIBLICAL COURAGE

Scripture: Daniel said to the king, "O king, live forever! My God sent His angel and shut the lions' mouths, so that they have not hurt me, because I was found innocent before Him; and also, O king, I have done no wrong before you" (Daniel 6:21, 22).

Enrichment From the Word: King Darius, seeing in Daniel extraordinary wisdom, strength and courage, made him his right hand. Daniel's enemies could find no fault in him except in his religious exercises, which he continued performing in the face of danger. Many good men would have thought it prudent to omit public prayer for the forbidden 30 days; but the aged Daniel, who had so many eyes upon him, acted courageously. He defied the law enacted against him by his enemies and came into conflict with the king. Because the law had to be obeyed, the king unwillingly had Daniel cast into the den of lions. Daniel went courageously, trusting God completely.

What about us? We must always take heed lest under pretense of discretion we be found guilty of cowardice in the cause of Christ. We must follow Daniel.

Enrichment From the Church: Jesus portrays true courage. It is the heroic Christ on the Cross who draws us to Himself. Think of Him as He won the penitent thief. Here, probably, was a youth who had been captivated by some bold and daring spirit among the insurrectionist bands who robbed the rich for the benefit of the poor. Now the man saw a leader of courage and magnanimity who could inspire his moral respect, largehearted as well as brave, and he surrendered to Christ.

Enrichment From the Heart: The story of Daniel in the lions' den, which has emboldened countless millions in their service to God, reminds us that God can defy nature to assist His children in time of need.

Personal Witness — November, Week 2

Christopher Moree

MAINTAINING ETHICAL COMMITMENT

Scripture: Daniel purposed in his heart that he would not defile himself with the portion of the king's delicacies, nor with the wine which he drank; therefore he requested of the chief of the eunuchs that he might not defile himself (Daniel 1:8).

Enrichment From the Word: Daniel and his three companions were among those taken from Judah by Nebuchadnezzar to be trained in Babylon for employment and preferential treatment. The procedures described in Daniel 1, including the name changes, were only the beginnings of the process which would turn these young men, reared in the ethical system of Judaism, into Chaldean princes.

Uprooted from their homeland, separated from the Temple and settled in a strange land controlled by pagans, these young men would seem to be easy targets for the Babylonian colonial system. Yet Daniel and his fellows stood firm in their commitment to the values instilled in them from childhood. After three years in Babylon they were examined by the king. These poor, young, captive Jews were found to be wiser and "ten times better than all the magicians and astrologers" in Babylon (v. 20).

Enrichment From the Church: When you do something for Christ and the church which you know will cause you to be misunderstood, opposed, criticized and disliked, that is ethical commitment—commitment to a set of moral principles or values. When you speak out against some custom which you consider wrong and sinful (when you could be thought of as a "good fellow" by remaining silent), that is ethical commitment.

Enrichment From the Heart: The example of Daniel, Shadrach, Meshach and Abed-Nego flies through the centuries to remind young men and women that it is short-sighted to abandon eternal Christian values for the passing values of modern society.

Outreach November, Week 3

Hector Camacho

REAPING THE HARVEST FOR THE GLORY OF GOD

Scripture: To Him who is able to keep you from stumbling, And to present you faultless Before the presence of His glory with exceeding joy, To God our Savior, Who alone is wise, Be glory and majesty, Dominion and power, Both now and forever. Amen (Jude 24, 25).

Enrichment From the Word: Jude, in his brief letter, emphasizes the need to "contend earnestly for the faith which was once for all delivered to the saints"(v. 3). He also makes us aware of false teachers; he shows how easy it is to fall into apostasy. At the end, he calls us to keep ourselves in the love of God. The message is that we have a personal obligation to persevere in the faith.

Alluding to our responsibility to others, he says, "On some have compassion, making a distinction; but others save with fear, pulling them out of the fire"(vv. 22, 23). All of this assures us that one day we will stand in the presence of His majesty, bringing those who have been won to His glory.

Enrichment From the Church: As Christians we exist to care for one another. Salvation is more than simply believing in God at a given moment; it means staying faithful. The Lord of the harvest, Jesus Christ, has commissioned us to preach the gospel. We must help others stand in the presence of the glory of the Lord.

This must not be done for the sake of numbers, denominational goals or personal prestige. It must be done exclusively to the glory of God.

Enrichment From the Heart: "Not unto us, O Lord, not unto us, But to Your name give glory, Because of Your mercy, And because of Your truth" (Psalm 115:1).

Outreach   **November, Week 3**

Hector Camacho

REAPING THE HARVEST AMONG THE POOR

Scripture: "The Spirit of the Lord is upon Me, Because He has anointed Me to preach the gospel to the poor" (Luke 4:18).

Enrichment From the Word: Two kinds of poor are mentioned in the Scriptures: those who have no material resources and "the poor in spirit." For both there are promises and blessings. To those with no means and no power, the gospel is preached that they may be saved and transformed. To the "poor in spirit," the Kingdom is promised. The wealthy person can be "poor in spirit" if he or she acknowledges humbly the lordship of Jesus Christ. God loves and cares for the poor. He summons us to share our means with the less fortunate. Let us give them the Word and, when possible, the **things** they need.

Enrichment From the Church: Christianity began in a manger. Jesus himself never had material possessions. When the Pentecostal fires blazed anew at the end of the 19th century, it started primarily among humble country peasants and poor city dwellers. Today, because of a phenomenon known as "redemption and lift," many of the descendants of those "poor folks" have become upper middle class, educated and wealthy. But we should never forget that the gospel must still be preached to the poor (Matthew 11:5). They too must be incorporated into the body of Christ: His church. "For your sakes He became poor, that you through His poverty might become rich" (2 Corinthians 8:9).

Enrichment From the Heart: Lord, help me realize how fortunate I am to have found You in my youth, when I had nothing. Help me to accept the fact that everything I have belongs to You. Help me to share it with others.

Outreach — November, Week 3

Hector Camacho

REAPING THE HARVEST AMONG THE HISPANICS

Scripture: "God, who made the world and everything in it, since He is Lord of heaven and earth. . . . He has made from one blood every nation of men to dwell on all the face of the earth" (Acts 17:24, 26).

Enrichment From the Word: Long before the natural sciences posed the theory of a common ancestor for humanity, **Homo erectus**, the Bible had the answer. We all come from Adam. Whether black, white, Hispanic or Oriental, we all share a common ancestry in the first created being.

There were nine million Hispanics in America in 1970, according to the U.S. Census; 14 million in 1980. *Time* magazine says there are 23 million now, with a projected 35 million by the year 2000. What a challenge! To each Hispanic we are debtors. Paul writes, "I am a debtor both to Greeks and to barbarians" (Romans 1:14).

Enrichment From the Church: Guillermo Cook, noted Latin American theologian, writes: "To perceive the specific moment when a given people . . . or a person are open to receive the message from God is a vital part of an in-depth reflection on the implications for evangelism. It would be of little value to have revolutionary concepts and excellent methods if resources are spent year after year in sterile ground. It could happen that because of our prejudices (social or religious), we would end up being insensitive to the voice of God calling us to follow Him (and to preach) in the most unusual circumstances."

Enrichment From the Heart: Dear Lord, You brought Hispanics to America many years ago. For centuries, they have given us their music, art, food, cities and values; now, help us give to them the Bread of Life: Jesus, the Christ!

Outreach   November, Week 3

Hector Camacho

REAPING THE HARVEST AMONG THE INDIANS

Scripture: "'I have certainly seen the oppression of my people ... I have heard their groaning and have come down to deliver them'" (Acts 7:34).

Enrichment From the Word: The Bible teaches implicitly that all men are created equal. But in the application of these "inalienable" truths, minority groups have often been ignored. The story of the Indian in the white man's America is one of sharpest contrasts: brotherhood and hate, missionary devotion and senseless plundering, noble sacrifice and base betrayal. Yet, there have been men who proved that the Indian could be dealt with fairly and could deal fairly in return. Some have also proved that the command to go, baptize and preach has not been forgotten and will not be ignored.

Enrichment From the Church: The first Bible to be printed in America was on behalf of the Indians: John Eliot's famous Indian Bible. As early as 1646, Eliot began preaching to the Indian of Massachusetts; a decade later he founded a church. In the 18th century, missionary activity was renewed because of a mighty revival which swept over the colonies.

David Brainerd preached with "saintly devotion" to the tribes of New York and New Jersey from 1745-47. He was stopped by death from tuberculosis at age 29. Of the approximately 500,000 Indians now living in the United States, less than half testify that they are Christians. Disenchanted and betrayed, many are given to heavy drinking. Uprooted and dehumanized, yet they await the healing Word of God.

Enrichment From the Heart: Lord, forgive this nation for the rapacity of greedy men, who act more as wolves than as brothers to their fellowman! Help me share the gospel with native Americans.

Outreach   November, Week 3

Hector Camacho

REAPING THE HARVEST AMONG BLACKS

Scripture: Then Miriam and Aaron spoke against Moses because of the Ethiopian woman whom he had married (Numbers 12:1).

Enrichment From the Word: The woman from Ethiopia was black. Evidently, Miriam was not too pleased with Moses for having married Zipporah, a Cushite. Even Aaron was persuaded to talk about her. Miriam became infected for seven days with leprosy. Thus, Jehovah showed how displeased He was with bigotry and racism. Resisting these ugly evils, we are to share the good news with black men and women, feeling compassion and respect for the despised children of Cush. Through Christ, they become children of God.

Enrichment From the Church: An understanding of the black revolution, of the black man's rage, can only come from a knowledge of his violent past. To understand the gospel of Jesus Christ, and its implication for the black revolution, we must examine black history.

Before the Civil War, Negro slaves who became Christians found themselves in the same churches with Caucasians, but segregated. They were, as the saying went, "separate but equal." We know today that, unfortunately, they were not equal. To truly evangelize blacks, non-blacks must do so from a perspective of caring concern and love. Nearly 30 million blacks are waiting for Jesus to save and heal them. They deserve the best, and the best is Christ.

Enrichment From the Heart: Heavenly Father, help me to love people, not because of the color of their skin but because of Your love for humanity. Help me to share Christ and myself with my black brothers and sisters, for Jesus is truly "the Man for others."

Social Concerns   November, Week 4

Paul Duncan

CARING FOR THE UNDERPRIVILEGED

Scripture: "Thus says the Lord of hosts: 'Execute true justice, Show mercy and compassion Everyone to his brother. Do not oppress the widow or the fatherless, The alien or the poor'" (Zechariah 7:9, 10).

Enrichment From the Word: God wants His people to reach out to the underprivileged. God's Word admonishes the Christian community to help the poor and to provide for widows and the fatherless. The Bible does not call for "lip service" but for love that results in tangible service. Caring for the less fortunate is, in fact, one way we demonstrate that we know the Lord. Concerning the king of Judah, the Lord said, "'He defended the cause of the poor and needy, and so all went well. Is that not what it means to know me?'" (Jeremiah 22:16, *NIV*).

Enrichment From the Church: The New Testament church and the postapostolic church clearly understood their responsibility to care for the underprivileged. They established homes for orphans and abandoned children, they provided shelter for the elderly and disabled, and assisted stranded travelers and the unemployed.

The Church of God began caring for homeless children as early as 1920. Recently, the church established Covenant Place, a maternity home for unmarried, pregnant young women, and Crowley Center, a program for physically and sexually abused children. The Department of Benevolences is also committed to developing a residential program for widows, retired ministers and returned missionaries.

Enrichment From the Heart: "It would be possible to do any and all of these programs [serving the underprivileged] and lose our soul and the soul or heart of our church. Without *love*, it profits us nothing" (Steve Land).

Social Concerns   November, Week 4

Paul Duncan

DEFINING THE ROLE OF THE CHURCH

Scripture: "You are the salt of the earth. . . . You are the light of the world" (Matthew 5:13, 14).

Enrichment From the Word: The best example of the true church is found in the Book of Acts. The early church adhered to the confession of truth, practiced the fellowship of public family worship and demonstrated its faith through works of self-denying love. In Acts the church is pictured as the family of God, centered on Christ and empowered by the Holy Spirit. God expects no less of the body of Christ today. We are called to be salt, light and leaven in our world.

Enrichment From the Church: What should the church be doing in these last days before the return of Christ? What is the role of church administrators? Pastors? The laity? It is vital that we understand what the Bible says in regard to the mission of the church.

The church has been guilty at times of overemphasizing one aspect of its mission to the exclusion of the other. At times we have sought to win the sinner with little regard for his physical and social needs. At other times we have focused on social issues and overlooked spiritual needs. The truth is that the role of the church is to do both evangelism and social ministry.

Enrichment From the Heart: Lord, help me to be salt, light and leaven to my neighbor. Help me to show forth Your love to my brothers and sisters in Christ as a testimony to them and the world that You died for us, rose from the dead and are living with us.

Social Concerns   **November, Week 4**

Paul Duncan

HONORING SENIOR ADULTS

Scripture: " 'Rise in the presence of the aged, show respect for the elderly and revere your God. I am the Lord' " (Leviticus 19:32, *NIV*).

Enrichment From the Word: Throughout the Old and New Testament, we are admonished to show honor and respect to the elderly. What a difference in the prevailing attitude of our society toward older people, who are often seen as liabilities and burdens or else ignored all together. Senior adults are frequently made to feel useless and unwanted. Scripture, on the other hand, views old age as a reward for honoring our parents—" 'Honor your father and mother,' which is the first commandment with promise: 'that it may be well with you and you may live long on the earth' " (Ephesians 6:2, 3).

Enrichment From the Church: I fondly remember "testimony time" in the church of my youth. When silver-haired, mature Christians would tell about the goodness and faithfulness of God, I was reminded that my Lord could be counted on to be with me in all situations. Their testimonies were not just "hype," but expressions of their true convictions based on years of trusting in His promises. These senior adults had a perspective of history not available to the young. Their words of wisdom and prayers were invaluable treasures to me and the entire church.

Enrichment From the Heart: One true test of any civilization is how it treats its elderly people. How much more true is this of the church! As the body of Christ, we must honor our senior adults and give them every opportunity for meaningful involvement.

Social Concerns November, Week 4

Paul Duncan

FIGHTING DRUG DEPENDENCY

Scripture: Do you not know that you are the temple of God and that the Spirit of God dwells in you? If anyone defiles the temple of God, God will destroy him. For the temple of God is holy, which temple you are (1 Corinthians 3:16, 17).

Enrichment From the Word: Scripture tells us that we are fearfully and wonderfully made by our Creator. Not only did He create us, but His Spirit lives in us if we have been redeemed. Since our body is God's temple, we should not harm it through drug abuse. While many of today's drugs were not available in biblical times, the values and principles taught by Scripture clearly prohibit the misuse of drugs.

Enrichment From the Church: Among adults in this country, alcoholism is the third leading health problem, second only to cancer and heart disease. Among our youth, however, no disease produces the mortality figures that the abuse of alcohol and other chemical substances produces. Drug dependency accounts for more than half of all suicides in the United States annually. The suicide rate among drug users is almost 60 times higher than the rate among nondependent individuals.

The most effective treatment programs for drug dependency are those which present Christ as the complete cure. Programs such as Peniel, a Church of God ministry in Pennsylvania, and Teen Challenge recognize that the vacuum the addict is trying to fill with drugs can only be filled by commitment to Jesus Christ.

Enrichment From the Heart: If we are filled with God's Spirit, we have no need for illicit drugs and alcohol.

Social Concerns   **November, Week 4**

Paul Duncan

REACHING THE INNER CITY

Scripture: When . . . [Jesus] saw the multitudes, He was moved with compassion for them, because they were weary and scattered, like sheep having no shepherd. Then He said to His disciples, "The harvest truly is plentiful, but the laborers are few" (Matthew 9:36, 37).

Enrichment From the Word: During His earthly ministry, Jesus was involved with people: teaching, healing, delivering and loving them. He went wherever people were—the wilderness, small towns and villages, the cities—to love and accept the minorities, the outcasts, the poor and the oppressed—those whom the religious leaders of His day ignored and despised.

Enrichment From the Church: Man seems to be both attracted to the city and repulsed by it. The city provides culture, excitement and adventure. On the other hand, it is ugly, cold, indifferent and dangerous. Many people choose to live in the city while others are trapped in its slums and barrios. All too often the inner city has been abandoned by an upwardly mobile church seeking the good life in the suburbs.

From a cultural standpoint, we might feel more comfortable elsewhere, but the city needs us. The church has the good news that gives meaning and purpose to life.

Enrichment From the Heart: Lord, if You were here in the flesh, You would go where the people are—to the city. Yet, I do not like cities. I guess I'm afraid of them. I don't like their unfriendly, cynical ways or their overcrowdedness. I hate their open display of drugs, pornography and prostitution. But Lord, since You loved the city enough to weep over it and to die for its people, help me not to abandon those trapped in the inner city. Instead, help me to see the city as You see it—with love.

Doctrine   December, Week 1

L. Grant McClung Jr.

DISPLAYING POSITIVE FAITH

Scripture: In everything give thanks; for this is the will of God in Christ Jesus for you (1 Thessalonians 5:18).

Enrichment From the Word: Paul's heart of thanksgiving overflowed to his friends at Thessalonica. The words of this text were not empty words for him. He had suffered much persecution and had, at times, been very uncomfortable with trying situations. But this praise of thanksgiving still comes forth because Paul knew God wanted him to spread the gospel of Jesus Christ to a sinful world.

Stephen was a man "full of faith and power." Although his words caused him to be stoned to death, his final prayer was, "Lord, lay not this sin to their charge" (Acts 7:60, *KJV*). These words of love were prayed for those who were stoning him.

Stephen was following the example of Jesus, who prayed for those who brutally nailed Him to the Cross. They had mocked His name, laughed at Him, even spit on Him. Jesus prayed, "Father, forgive them, for they know not what they do" (Luke 23:34, *KJV*). Where are better examples of love and true dedication to service?

Enrichment From the Church: Because of our positive proclamation of Christ's love for the world, the Church of God has grown to be a prominent worldwide Pentecostal denomination. Now, more than any other time in its history, the church must stand together and display a positive statement of faith to all people. We must continue to follow Christ's example of love and service.

Enrichment From the Heart: Lord, help me to serve You by making a positive statement of Your love to everyone I meet. May my life be an example of positive faith so that others will want to follow Your Son, too!

Doctrine   December, Week 1

L. Grant McClung Jr.

STANDING FIRM IN THE LORD

Scripture: Therefore, my beloved brethren, be steadfast, immovable, always abounding in the work of the Lord, knowing that your labor is not in vain in the Lord (1 Corinthians 15:58).

Enrichment From the Word: It is important for the Christian to stand firm in the midst of struggle. Problems and situations can cause even the most dedicated servants to stumble. They frustrate and hinder the work of a Christian. David was a man whose heart was "perfect with God," yet he did not guard himself against moral failure. Jonah was afraid to preach to the Ninevites and went "from the presence of the Lord" (Jonah 1:3). Peter, one of the Twelve, denied Christ. He had fooled himself into thinking he would always stand firm.

These biblical characters failed the Lord. But they also made things right and came back to serve the Lord. David fought and won victory in battle. Jonah was spared from the depths of the sea and preached mightily with great results. Peter was restored, and on the Day of Pentecost he saw 3,000 souls added to the church. These men realized their mistakes. They repented and allowed God to overcome their problems.

Enrichment From the Church: We stumble, we sometimes fall. But we don't have to be defeated. We can learn from these who have gone on before. We must allow Christ to stand firm in us. As Christians we must realize that it is not a person, but the Savior, who brings people to the saving knowledge of Jesus Christ.

Enrichment From the Heart: God, help me to stand. I will trust not in myself but totally in You.

Doctrine   **December, Week 1**

L. Grant McClung Jr.

SEEKING PERSONAL FULFILLMENT

Scripture: Delight yourself also in the Lord, And He shall give you the desires of your heart. Commit your way to the Lord, Trust also in Him, And He shall bring it to pass (Psalm 37: 4, 5).

Enrichment From the Word: The Lord Jesus Christ himself is a lesson in personal fulfillment. His life had purpose and meaning. Sent to earth with a commission to fulfill, He knew His life and ministry were ordained of God. He knew His death and resurrection would be the most significant event in the history of the world. Christ was pleased to do the will of His Father who sent Him.

Paul also serves as a great example. Before conversion, he was bound in a frustrated life of works. He tried to earn his own righteousness. In Christ, however, he learned to be content in whatever state he found himself. He learned that fulfillment does not come from things you do. He found real fulfillment in Christ.

Enrichment From the Church: There are many dedicated servants of God in the fellowship of the Church of God. In all types of ministry, in every kind of special assignment, Christian workers find special fulfillment in their service to Christ. They could have many opportunities in the world, they could do many things other than what they are doing, but the satisfaction of serving Christ has transformed their view. The fulfilled Christ lives in them, and they are fulfilled. Fulfilled people make a fulfilling church.

Enrichment From the Heart: I am so glad I am not searching the world for something to fulfill my life. I am fulfilled in Christ and His service.

Doctrine　　　　　　　　　　　　　**December, Week 1**

L. Grant McClung Jr.

EMBRACING THE GLOBAL COMMISSION OF CHRIST

Scripture: "Go therefore and make disciples of all the nations, baptizing them in the name of the Father and of the Son and of the Holy Spirit, teaching them to observe all things that I have commanded you; and lo, I am with you always, even to the end of the age" (Matthew 28:19, 20).

Enrichment From the Word: Our greatest responsibility as Christians is to promote the name of Jesus. Christ told us to go and make disciples; He told us to be His witnesses; He told us to pray for laborers; and He told us to study the Word of God.

Believers must be involved if the church would move toward its mission. The church's mission and duty is to promote the Kingdom of God and to go into all the world. It is necessary for us in the church to heed our Lord's command and bind together to see the world come to know Christ as Savior.

Enrichment From the Church: A pastor in the United States says the best way to enhance growth is to support missions. In every situation where his congregation has undertaken a building program, he says, they first built a church, a parsonage, a convention center or some other project for an overseas church. He testified that this personal involvement and unselfish commitment always helped tremendously when initiating home projects for his own people. He affirms that it is not enough for the local church to simply take care of its own. His and the congregation's concern for others in need sparks new commitment at home!

Enrichment From the Heart: Here I am, O mighty God. I surrender my will to Your glorious will. Embrace me as I embrace Your global cause.

Doctrine   **December, Week 1**

L. Grant McClung Jr.

BELIEVING ALL OF GOD'S PROMISES

Scripture: [Abraham] did not waver at the promise of God through unbelief, but was strengthened in faith, giving glory to God, and being fully convinced that what He had promised He was able to perform (Romans 4:20, 21).

Enrichment From the Word: Doubt is something every Christian must deal with and learn to reverse. Faith, the opposite of doubt, must be a part of every Christian's life. God's promises are meant to be believed.

If Abraham had not believed in God's words, he would not have become the father of a great nation. If Noah had not believed and built the ark, he and his family would have perished. Because Daniel was committed to prayer and faith in God, he escaped the lion's den. Had the three Hebrew children not been strong enough to bow only to God in faith, they would not have been visited by the Fourth Man in the fire. Had Job not believed his Redeemer lived, he would never have regained his health and abundant life. Because Gideon believed and obeyed the Lord's command, his army was victorious in battle.

Enrichment From the Church. Today's church is no different from yesterday's. Today's Christians are made of the same stuff early saints were made of. It took enthusiastic, complete, committed, unwavering faith for the early church to overcome and multiply; it will take the same kind of faith for us. Christians must believe that God has the power to do what He has promised He will do.

Enrichment From the Heart: Lord, I believe with my heart and soul. Help any remaining unbelief that may be lingering inside!

Helping Others (Counseling)   December, Week 2

Donald M. Walker

COUNSELING THE DISCOURAGED

Scripture: "Let not your heart be troubled" (John 14:1).

Enrichment From the Word: Jesus spoke to His disciples about departure . . . death . . . satanic attack . . . betrayal . . . falling away. This accumulation of statements by Jesus greatly perplexed and discouraged the disciples.

To settle the emotions of the disciples, Jesus gave them counsel to not let their hearts be troubled. This was His message of hope and encouragement to them.

Jesus Christ is acquainted with all our secret undiscovered sorrows and with the wound that bleeds inwardly. He knows how we are affected by affliction, and He is cognizant of all the troubles we face. He knows better than we do when we are in danger of being overwhelmed by adversity or discouragement.

Enrichment From the Church: Discouragement can arise from a sense of failure or inadequacy caused even by seemingly insignificant factors in one's life. This can lead to guilt, inactivity, grumbling, complaining and worrying so that one feels as though there is no hope or way of escape.

The Bible gives us counsel that hope in God's mercy and steadfast love provides deliverance from discouragement.

God's everlasting Word will uphold us if we simply relinquish our discouragement to Him. The safety and security offered by such a complete reliance on Him will quiet our hearts in the most desperate hour of perplexity, discouragement and uncertainty.

Enrichment From the Heart: We must never allow our attitude toward God to be dictated by our circumstances.

Helping Others (Counseling) December, Week 2

Donald M. Walker

COUNSELING THE LUKEWARM AND UNRESPONSIVE

Scripture: "So then, because you are lukewarm, and neither cold nor hot . . ." (Revelation 3:16).

Enrichment From the Word: Lukewarm . . . neither hot nor cold . . . wretched . . . poor . . . blind . . . naked . . . NAUSEATING was the description Christ used to describe the church at Laodicea.

This condition resulted from their being content with their material wealth and unaware of their spiritual poverty.

The dangers of lukewarmness and unresponsiveness are just as prevalent today as they were in the church of Laodicea. We need to recognize that lukewarmness is a sin against God. Lukewarmness or indifference in our relationship with God is a form of worldliness. Christ would not have us to be neutral in our spiritual life but either hot or cold.

Enrichment From the Church: One of the many causes of inconsistency and lukewarmness in our spiritual experience is that of self-conceitedness or self-delusion.

In His counsel, the Lord urged the Laodiceans to buy gold tried in the fire, that they might be truly rich. They were urged to wear white clothes symbolic of righteousness which would cover their nakedness, and they were urged to put salve on their eyes which would give them spiritual sight.

The Lord Jesus Christ always gives the best counsel and is today admonishing His people to be conscious of their spiritual needs. Christ calls us to be inspired with fresh zeal and vigor and to be more than conquerors through Him.

Enrichment From the Heart: If Christianity is worth anything, it is worth everything. Complacency and indifference are inexcusable.

Helping Others (Counseling) — December, Week 2

Donald M. Walker

COUNSELING THE COMPLACENT AND SATISFIED

Scripture: " ' "Take your ease; eat, drink, and be merry" ' " (Luke 12:19).

Enrichment From the Word: The disciples of Jesus needed to learn the lesson that satisfaction in life comes from more than the possession of material things.

To explain His message and give a warning regarding becoming complacent and satisfied, Jesus told the parable about the rich fool. The fool's attitude was that he would have an easy life because he had every material possession he could possibly want or need. Consequently, he took no thought of the condition of his spiritual life.

If we treasure things, our heart will be drawn away from God and our spiritual vision clouded.

Enrichment From the Church: We must be on guard against falling victim to the illusion that what is happening on this earth materially is all that matters. The illusion of materialism can cause us to become complacent in the spiritual matters of life.

The error of complacency and self-satisfaction is that we take no care to be rich toward God—rich in faith, rich in good works, and rich in fruits of righteousness and spiritual gifts.

Complacency can make us destitute of everything that can enrich our soul, make us rich toward God and rich for eternity.

Enrichment From the Heart: We must resist the constant temptation to develop our life around material things. Let us throw off complacency and experience a growth relationship with Jesus Christ.

Helping Others (Counseling)   December, Week 2

Donald M. Walker

COUNSELING THE COLD AND UNCARING

Scripture: No one cares for my soul (Psalm 142:4).

Enrichment From the Word: There issued from the lips of the psalmist David this plaintive cry: "No man cares for my soul."

To be uncaring and cold toward others in need is the tragedy of man's inhumanity to man. It is the deadly undoing of a human soul.

It is an indictment of the most serious nature when those who profess to be the people of God can be truthfully charged with lack of compassion and care for a soul in desperate need.

The comfort of David was that God knew his case. God was his refuge; God would deliver him.

Enrichment From the Church: There is no power so powerful in all the world as the power of love. To break out of the doldrums of coldness and insensitivity, one must become active in personal witness, testimony and love toward others. Reach out for lost sinners! Reach out for young people who are coasting the downward road! Reach out for people whose toil is rigorous and their lot in life hard! Reach out for professionals who are sidestepping God, the soul and eternity! Reach out to brothers and sisters in Christ who are in need!

Our prayer should be "O Lord, enlarge my heart with Your love." Out of the heart spring the issues of life, and the highest achievement in life is to rescue a soul in need.

Enrichment From the Heart: To intercede for others and care for them by the authority of Christ is one of the great privileges of the Christian. Loving intercession will put an end to coldness and carelessness toward others.

Helping Others (Counseling)   December, Week 2

Donald M. Walker

COUNSELING THE UNFORGIVING AND STUBBORN

Scripture: "Lord, how often shall my brother sin against me, and I forgive him? Up to seven times?" (Matthew 18:21).

Enrichment From the Word: To reinforce His message of forgiveness, the Lord Jesus told the parable of the unforgiving servant (Matthew 18:23-25).

Jesus taught that our forgiveness of others ought to be in direct proportion to the amount we have been forgiven by God. As children of God we have had all our sins forgiven by faith in Jesus Christ. Consequently, we ought to be willing to forgive others, no matter how many times we are offended.

Unlimited forgiveness must characterize the true disciple of the Lord Jesus Christ, not a retaliatory listing of others' offenses in an attitude of stubbornness and limited forgiveness.

Enrichment From the Church: The Bible makes it very clear that for us to be the kind of person Christ would have us to be, we must forgive (Ephesians 4:32; Colossians 3:13).

By being stubborn and unforgiving we injure ourselves by not allowing the proper relationships to develop with other people. A lack of forgiveness may lead to far more harm for the unforgiving person than does the harm done by the offender.

To the inquiry of Peter, Jesus responded that not only was forgiving seven times insufficient, but that one should be forgiven "seventy times seven."

If we are going to be in the center of God's will, forgiveness of others is essential for our spiritual and mental well-being.

Enrichment From the Heart: When we know we have been forgiven and in turn we have forgiven others from whom we may have experienced wrong, we can give praise and rejoice in the truth that truly God is doing a new thing.

Nurture   December, Week 3

C. C. Pratt

ACCEPTING GOD'S PROMISES FOR LONELINESS

Scripture: We are hard pressed on every side, yet not crushed; we are perplexed, but not in despair; persecuted, but not forsaken; struck down, but not destroyed (2 Corinthians 4:8, 9).

Enrichment From the Word: The Apostle Paul testified of his personal spiritual experience of God's faithfulness in times of loneliness. Paul's words "but not forsaken" fortify our Christian hope. What he had learned about God's faithfulness through times of the stress of earthly sorrow and the passing of years he shared with others through his writings. He had God's presence and support through all his trials. He was never forsaken nor abandoned by the Lord. He knew by blessed experience the truth of the promise, "'I will never leave you nor forsake you'" (Hebrews 13:5).

When Joshua became the leader of Israel, God said to him, "'Be strong and of good courage; do not be afraid, nor be dismayed, for the Lord your God is with you wherever you go'" (Joshua 1:9).

Enrichment From the Church: As Christians we are saved by the grace of Christ and sent into the world to serve Him with this promise: "'I am with you always, even to the end of the age'" (Matthew 28:20). My greatest comfort in life is to know that in my deepest trials, Christ is with me. One may feel lonely in the midst of a crowd, but every Christian should know that he or she is never really alone. What a comfort to know that when I feel lonely, He will give the assurance of His presence!

Enrichment From the Heart: Lord, we know that according to Your promise You are always with us. Give us this day a mind and heart alert and sensitive to Your presence so we will know You are with us. Amen.

Nurture   December, Week 3

C. C. Pratt

ACCEPTING GOD'S PROMISES FOR WORRY

Scripture: "Let not your heart be troubled; you believe in God, believe also in Me" (John 14:1).

Enrichment From the Word: Jesus said to His disciples, " 'Little children, I shall be with you a little while longer. You will seek Me; and as I said to the Jews, "Where I am going, you cannot come." ' " (John 13:33).

Jesus explained He was going to His Father's house to prepare a place for all who believe in Him.

When worry is in, faith is out. Belief in the absolute goodness of God can sustain the mind and heart even in those deep places of fear and even under the shadow of death. We can accept God's promises for dispelling worry, knowing that He is our Father. Let us not be robbed of a peaceful, happy heart. Let us cast our cares upon the Lord; He cares for us.

Enrichment From the Church: Worry is the advance interest we pay on troubles that seldom come. While traveling away from home for revival, I received the news upon arrival at the church that my son had been rushed to the hospital. The doctors were awaiting my permission to operate. Immediately, I knelt before the Lord in prayer along with the saints and received the assurance that everything would be all right. When I called home after prayer, I was told there was no longer any need for the operation. The X-ray showed the problem had cleared up. God's assurance took care of worry.

Enrichment From the Heart: In all of life's circumstances we know that all things work together for good to those who love the Lord and are the called according to His purpose.

Lord, help us to see that in all things You are working for good. Amen.

Nurture

C. C. Pratt

ACCEPTING GOD'S PROMISES FOR ANXIETY

Scripture: "Therefore I say to you, do not worry about your life, what you will eat or what you will drink; nor about your body, what you will put on. Is not life more than food and the body more than clothing?" (Matthew 6:25).

Enrichment From the Word: Christ has a remedy for anxiety: Do not worry. Do not be anxious (worry) about your life, what you will eat or drink, or about your body, what you will wear. Isn't our life more than food and our body more than clothes? Therefore Jesus says, "Don't worry about your life." If after we have done all that is our duty and within our ability to do we let care about some issue take possession of our mind, we make the mistake the Lord urges against. God knows our needs and has promised to supply all our needs.

Enrichment From the Church: When we are anxious about something, we may feel helpless and trapped by our emotions with no way out. A woman once said, "I can't get rid of this panic inside me. It's a constant threat to me in everything I do." Of course, Christ was able to give her peace instead of panic.

George Mueller said, "The beginning of anxiety is the end of faith, and the beginning of true faith is the end of anxiety."

Enrichment From the Heart: Lord, we confess that our life is compassed about with countless uncertainties. Do not allow these uncertainties to chain us with anxiety. Help us to daily believe Your promises, knowing that Your Word is a certainty we can build our life upon day after day. Amen.

Nurture   December, Week 3

C. C. Pratt

ACCEPTING GOD'S PROMISES FOR PERSONAL INTEGRITY

Scripture: The righteous man walks in his integrity; His children are blessed after him (Proverbs 20:7).

Enrichment From the Word: The parent who lives a Christlike life, who conscientiously performs his duty toward God and man, will bring a blessing on his children who follow his good example, both during his life and after his death.

We can faithfully depend on God for the happy results of a holy life. The Bible describes God as one who shows "mercy to thousands, to those who love Me and keep my commandments" (Exodus 20:6). David prayed on one occasion, "Let integrity and uprightness preserve me" (Psalm 25:21).

Enrichment From the Church: After the Roman governor Pilate had heard the accusations against Jesus and questioned Him, Pilate declared, "'I find no fault in Him at all'" (John 18:38). Because Jesus Christ was and is the supreme example of personal integrity, the world expects a high level of integrity from those who profess to follow Him. When it is revealed that some prominent Christian has committed a grave moral offense, it becomes a headline story in the media of the world. Without question, much harm is done to the cause of Christ when prominent Christians fail to have personal integrity. But let us never forget that most Christians, both clergy and laity, do maintain personal integrity. It would be most unfortunate for us if by focusing our attention on the failures of a few, we lose sight of the many who faithfully follow Christ's example.

Enrichment From the Heart: Lord, fill us with the character of Jesus Christ so we may live with His integrity. And cause us to see that many of our contemporaries are seriously committed to personal integrity through Christlike living. Amen.

Nurture   December, Week 3

C. C. Pratt

ACCEPTING GOD'S PROMISES FOR SPIRITUAL GROWTH

Scripture: As newborn babes, desire the pure milk of the word, that you may grow thereby (1 Peter 2:2).

Enrichment From the Word: Peter exhorted his fellow Christians to hunger for the Word as eagerly as babes hunger for milk. The Apostle was thinking about the Christian's need of spiritual food—pure, simple and nourishing. As we are nourished by the Word, we can "grow in the grace and knowledge of our Lord and Savior Jesus Christ" (2 Peter 3:18). Nourished by the Word and growing in Christian grace and knowledge, we can move toward spiritual maturity.

Enrichment From the Church: As a youth, I knew a minister who was mature in the Lord. His wife forsook him and moved in with another woman's husband. But this minister remained faithful to the Lord; and wherever he met his wife or the man she was living with, he treated them kindly. Before too long, they both were converted. The minister's wife returned to him, and the other woman's husband became a member of the church. The minister's spiritual maturity saved him from rashness and vindictiveness and resulted finally in the salvation of his wife and the other man.

Enrichment From the Heart: The largest room in the world is the room for improvement. As Christians the challenge we face every day is to become more like Christ.

Lord, we know it is not enough for us to want to grow spiritually. Somehow impart to us the zeal to do the things we must to grow in Your likeness. Make us devoted to Your Word and willing to repent and change wherever our life does not measure up to Your ideal. Help us to accept the challenge to keep growing spiritually as long as we live. Amen.

Involvement   **December, Week 4**

Cecil B. Knight

CULTIVATING A PERSONAL BOLD VISION

Scripture: By faith Abraham obeyed when he was called to go out to the place which he would afterward receive as an inheritance. And he went out, not knowing where he was going (Hebrews 11:8).

Enrichment From the Word: Abraham was able to see things that were not physically present because he had a personal vision. He believed what God told him—"I will make you a great nation . . . And make your name great . . . I will bless those who bless you, And I will curse him who curses you" (Genesis 12:2, 3). Yes, he believed, and he was bold and brave in obeying.

Abraham had a bold vision, but he still encountered problem people, people with problems and tension-packed situations. But his bold vision kept him going. He was able to see the permanency of God's covenant with him, and he knew that God was working in his behalf regardless of how things appeared on the surface. A bold vision always produces victory.

Enrichment From the Church: I remember attending the dedication of the Church of God General Offices on May 22, 1968. The facilities were the fruit of commitment and faith—our leaders had a vision. The name General Offices has since been changed to International Offices. Our vision continues to grow.

What plans for ministry, outreach and nurture does God want the church to develop for the future? He reveals His will through His Word and through the thought process and faith of believers. We cultivate a bold vision by believing God—personally . . . implicitly . . . scripturally.

Enrichment From the Heart: Like Abraham, God has given me holy promises regarding His direction and care for my life. By faith and through a bold vision, I will affirm them and act them out in daily life.

Involvement   December, Week 4

Cecil B. Knight

ADDING COLOR TO A BOLD VISION

Scripture: For by grace you have been saved through faith, and that not of yourselves; it is the gift of God (Ephesians 2:8).

Enrichment From the Word: *Grace* has been defined as the spontaneous love and boundless mercy of God freely expressed toward those who are entirely undeserving. Paul said, "By the grace of God I am what I am" (1 Corinthians 15:10).

God's grace adds color to your vision. It guides you in accepting yourself like God made you; in realizing that God is in you shaping you in the likeness of His Son; and in recognizing that in everything you can give thanks.

Enrichment From the Church: The song "Amazing Grace" was written by John Newton in 1758 at the age of 39. The words "that saved a wretch like me" are a true description of his life. But he was changed by God's amazing grace. His testimony is contained on a large tombstone in a small graveyard in Olney, England: "John Newton: Once an infidel and libertine, a seller of slaves in Africa, was by the rich mercy of our Lord and Saviour Jesus Christ preserved, restored, pardoned and appointed to preach the faith he had long labored to destroy." This is a vision with color.

Enrichment From the Heart: Andrew Carnegie had 43 millionaires working for him. They were not millionaires when they came to work for him but had become millionaires by working for him. In response to a question from a reporter on how this happened, he said, "When you work with gold, you must literally move tons of dirt to find a single ounce of gold. However, you do not look for the dirt—you look for the gold!"

You add color to your vision by looking for the best, believing the best and praising God for the best.

Involvement   December, Week 4

Cecil B. Knight

ENLARGING A BOLD VISION

Scripture: Search me, O God, and know my heart; Try me, and know my anxieties; And see if there is any wicked way in me, And lead me in the way everlasting (Psalm 139:23, 24).

Enrichment From the Word: In Psalm 139 we learn that God is a seeing God, a surrounding God, a sustaining God and a searching God. David said, "He knows when I sit down and when I rise up. He discerns my thoughts. He comprehends my path and is acquainted with all my ways. He is aware of all my words. He sees my past and my future" (vv. 2-5, *paraphrased*). Then he said, "Such knowledge is too wonderful for me; It is high, I cannot attain it" (v. 6). The knowledge of God's greatness is wonderful. It thrills us and motivates us to enlarge our vision of Him and to trust Him to reach new heights of Christian commitment and service.

Enrichment From the Church: God works through the members of the local church in relationship to their vision. A bold vision means great growth. A limited vision means restricted growth. Therefore, we need a bold vision. We need a vision of God's ability—"'Is anything too hard for the Lord?'" (Genesis 18:14); a vision of God's availability—He is a very present help, He never slumbers nor sleeps (Psalm 121:3, 4); a vision of God's stability—He never changes, He was, is and ever shall be the same; a vision of God's dependability—Solomon said, "'There has not failed one word of all his good promise'" (1 Kings 8:56). This is the way to spiritual adventure and church growth—a bold vision of the greatness of God.

Enrichment From the Heart: Lord, I want a vision of You like Moses had. Your Word states, "He endured as seeing Him [You] who is invisible" (Hebrews 11:27). I want to see You in Your grace and glory in every situation and opportunity of life so that I can receive Your gifts to living victoriously.

Involvement — December, Week 4

Cecil B. Knight

STAYING IN TOUCH AND IN TUNE

Scripture: Samson called to the Lord, saying, "O Lord God, remember me, I pray! Strengthen me, I pray, just this once, O God, that I may with one blow take vengeance on the Philistines for my two eyes!" (Judges 16:28).

Enrichment From the Word: The name Samson means "sun-man." He was a ray of hope for Israel during a period of oppression. He was born to be a deliverer.

The measure of his usefulness, however, depended on his consecration. When he broke his commitment to God, he lost his power and God's plans were not realized. When he remembered the source and supply of his strength, he was again used by God to destroy the enemy.

Enrichment From the Church: The middle verse in the Bible is Psalm 118:9: "It is better to trust in [or remember] the Lord Than to put confidence in princes." A small boy was heard singing, "Trust and OK." The actual song title is "Trust and Obey"—"Trust and obey, for there's no other way To be happy in Jesus, but to trust and obey." We stay in touch and in tune by trusting God and by remembering what He has done for us.

When we remember, we will be ready—*ready* to give the gospel (Romans 1:15); *ready* for every good work (Titus 3:1); *ready* to feed the flock (1 Peter 5:2); and *ready* for His coming (Matthew 24:44).

Enrichment From the Heart: Lord, I thank You for freedom from sin, freedom to be a new person, freedom to live an abundant life and freedom to receive the promise of eternal life. I want to always remember Your call on my life, and I commit myself to personal purity in Christ, personal positiveness as a Christian, and personal power in the ministry of the church.

Involvement   **December, Week 4**

Cecil B. Knight

PRAISING GOD FOR PRODUCTIVITY

Scripture: But Moses said to God, "Who am I that I should go to Pharaoh, and that I should bring the children of Israel out of Egypt?" (Exodus 3:11).

Enrichment From the Word: God appeared to Moses in a dramatic manner—a burning bush—and gave him a message of hope for Israel. Moses, however, responded in a very undramatic way—"Who am I?" Moses had a poor self-image.

God helped Moses understand he could be productive—that God wanted to work through him to lead Israel out of Egyptian captivity. God said to Moses, "I am who I am and what I am, and I will be what I will be. Say to them, the 'I Am' has sent you and is with you." Moses needed a bold vision of God's power working in him to be productive in His cause.

Enrichment From the Church: What does God want to do through you in the ministry of the Church of God? Your attitude is a key factor. You must believe He is in you and that He has sent you.

Here are five action steps: (1) Believe that you are valuable right now just like you are—let God guide you; (2) develop a burning desire to be successful—don't ever give up; (3) begin every day with clear goals—be a winner; (4) develop spiritual integrity—be trustworthy; and (5) stay alert and yielded—walk in God's will.

Enrichment From the Heart: I want to go out where the burning bushes are. Lord, let me always be looking for Your presence as I travel the road of life. And let me always be spiritually productive.

DAILY BIBLE READING GUIDE
Read the Entire Bible Through in a Year

JANUARY

1	Genesis	1-3
2	Genesis	4-6
3	Genesis	7-9
4	Genesis	10-12
5	Genesis	13-15
6	Genesis	16-18
7	Genesis	19-21
8	Genesis	22-24
9	Genesis	25-27
10	Genesis	28-30
11	Genesis	31-33
12	Genesis	34-36
13	Genesis	37-39
14	Genesis	40-42
15	Genesis	43-45
16	Genesis	46-48
17	Genesis	49-50
18	Exodus	1-3
19	Exodus	4-6
20	Exodus	7-9
21	Exodus	10-12
22	Exodus	13-15
23	Exodus	16-18
24	Exodus	19-21
25	Exodus	22-24
26	Exodus	25-27
27	Exodus	28-29
28	Exodus	30-33
29	Exodus	34-36
30	Exodus	37-40
31	Leviticus	1-3

FEBRUARY

1	Leviticus	4-6
2	Leviticus	7-9
3	Leviticus	10-12
4	Leviticus	13-15
5	Leviticus	16-18
6	Leviticus	19-21
7	Leviticus	22-24
8	Leviticus	25-27
9	Numbers	1-3
10	Numbers	4-6
11	Numbers	7-9
12	Numbers	10-12
13	Numbers	13-15
14	Numbers	16-18
15	Numbers	19-21
16	Numbers	22-24
17	Numbers	25-27
18	Numbers	28-30
19	Numbers	31-33
20	Numbers	34-36
21	Deuteronomy	1-3
22	Deuteronomy	4-6
23	Deuteronomy	7-9
24	Deuteronomy	10-12
25	Deuteronomy	13-15
26	Deuteronomy	16-18
27	Deuteronomy	19-21
28	Deuteronomy	22-24

MARCH

1	Deuteronomy	25-27
2	Deuteronomy	28-30
3	Deuteronomy	31-34
4	Joshua	1-3
5	Joshua	4-6
6	Joshua	7-9
7	Joshua	10-12
8	Joshua	13-15
9	Joshua	16-18
10	Joshua	19-21
11	Joshua	22-24
12	Judges	1-3
13	Judges	4-6

14	Judges	7-9
15	Judges	10-12
16	Judges	13-15
17	Judges	16-18
18	Judges	19-21
19	Ruth	1-4
20	1 Samuel	1-3
21	1 Samuel	4-6
22	1 Samuel	7-9
23	1 Samuel	10-12
24	1 Samuel	13-15
25	1 Samuel	16-18
26	1 Samuel	19-21
27	1 Samuel	22-24
28	1 Samuel	25-27
29	1 Samuel	28-31
30	2 Samuel	1-3
31	2 Samuel	4-6

APRIL

1	2 Samuel	7-9
2	2 Samuel	10-12
3	2 Samuel	13-15
4	2 Samuel	16-18
5	2 Samuel	19-21
6	2 Samuel	22-24
7	1 Kings	1-3
8	1 Kings	4-6
9	1 Kings	7-9
10	1 Kings	10-12
11	1 Kings	13-15
12	1 Kings	16-18
13	1 Kings	19-22
14	2 Kings	1-3
15	2 Kings	4-6
16	2 Kings	7-9
17	2 Kings	10-12
18	2 Kings	13-15
19	2 Kings	16-18
20	2 Kings	19-21
21	2 Kings	22-25
22	1 Chronicles	1-3

23	1 Chronicles	4-6
24	1 Chronicles	7-9
25	1 Chronicles	10-12
26	1 Chronicles	13-15
27	1 Chronicles	16-18
28	1 Chronicles	19-21
29	1 Chronicles	22-24
30	1 Chronicles	25-27

MAY

1	1 Chronicles	28-29
2	2 Chronicles	1-3
3	2 Chronicles	4-6
4	2 Chronicles	7-9
5	2 Chronicles	10-12
6	2 Chronicles	13-15
7	2 Chronicles	16-18
8	2 Chronicles	19-21
9	2 Chronicles	22-24
10	2 Chronicles	25-27
11	2 Chronicles	28-30
12	2 Chronicles	31-33
13	2 Chronicles	34-36
14	Ezra	1-3
15	Ezra	4-6
16	Ezra	7-10
17	Nehemiah	1-3
18	Nehemiah	4-6
19	Nehemiah	7-9
20	Nehemiah	10-13
21	Esther	1-3
22	Esther	4-6
23	Esther	7-10
24	Job	1-3
25	Job	4-6
26	Job	7-9
27	Job	10-12
28	Job	13-15
29	Job	16-18
30	Job	19-21
31	Job	22-24

JUNE

#	Book	Ch.
1	Job	25-27
2	Job	28-30
3	Job	31-33
4	Job	34-36
5	Job	37-39
6	Job	40-42
7	Psalms	1-9
8	Psalms	10-17
9	Psalms	18-22
10	Psalms	23-31
11	Psalms	32-37
12	Psalms	38-44
13	Psalms	45-51
14	Psalms	52-59
15	Psalms	60-67
16	Psalms	68-71
17	Psalms	72-77
18	Psalms	78-81
19	Psalms	82-89
20	Psalms	90-97
21	Psalms	98-104
22	Psalms	105-110
23	Psalms	111-118
24	Psalms	119
25	Psalms	120-127
26	Psalms	128-136
27	Psalms	137-142
28	Psalms	143-150
29	Proverbs	1-3
30	Proverbs	4-6

JULY

#	Book	Ch.
1	Proverbs	7-9
2	Proverbs	10-12
3	Proverbs	13-15
4	Proverbs	16-18
5	Proverbs	19-21
6	Proverbs	22-24
7	Proverbs	25-27
8	Proverbs	28-31
9	Ecclesiastes	1-3
10	Ecclesiastes	4-6
11	Ecclesiastes	7-9
12	Ecclesiastes	10-12
13	Song of Solomon	1-3
14	Song of Solomon	4-6
15	Song of Solomon	7-8
16	Isaiah	1-3
17	Isaiah	4-6
18	Isaiah	7-9
19	Isaiah	10-12
20	Isaiah	13-15
21	Isaiah	16-18
22	Isaiah	19-21
23	Isaiah	22-24
24	Isaiah	25-27
25	Isaiah	28-30
26	Isaiah	31-33
27	Isaiah	34-36
28	Isaiah	37-39
29	Isaiah	40-42
30	Isaiah	43-45
31	Isaiah	46-48

AUGUST

#	Book	Ch.
1	Isaiah	49-51
2	Isaiah	52-54
3	Isaiah	55-57
4	Isaiah	58-60
5	Isaiah	61-63
6	Isaiah	64-66
7	Jeremiah	1-3
8	Jeremiah	4-6
9	Jeremiah	7-9
10	Jeremiah	10-12
11	Jeremiah	13-15
12	Jeremiah	16-18
13	Jeremiah	19-21
14	Jeremiah	22-24
15	Jeremiah	25-27
16	Jeremiah	28-30
17	Jeremiah	31-33
18	Jeremiah	34-36
19	Jeremiah	37-39

20	Jeremiah	40-42	30	Zephaniah	1-3
21	Jeremiah	43-45		**OCTOBER**	
22	Jeremiah	46-48			
23	Jeremiah	49-52	1	Haggai	1-2
24	Lamentations	1-3	2	Zechariah	1-3
25	Lamentations	4-5	3	Zechariah	4-6
26	Ezekiel	1-3	4	Zechariah	7-9
27	Ezekiel	4-6	5	Zechariah	10-12
28	Ezekiel	7-9	6	Zechariah	13-14
29	Ezekiel	10-12	7	Malachi	1-4
30	Ezekiel	13-15	8	Matthew	1-3
31	Ezekiel	16-18	9	Matthew	4-6
			10	Matthew	7-9
	SEPTEMBER		11	Matthew	10-12
1	Ezekiel	19-21	12	Matthew	13-15
2	Ezekiel	22-24	13	Matthew	16-18
3	Ezekiel	25-27	14	Matthew	19-21
4	Ezekiel	28-30	15	Matthew	22-24
5	Ezekiel	31-33	16	Matthew	25-28
6	Ezekiel	34-36	17	Mark	1-3
7	Ezekiel	37-39	18	Mark	4-6
8	Ezekiel	40-42	19	Mark	7-9
9	Ezekiel	43-45	20	Mark	10-12
10	Ezekiel	46-48	21	Mark	13-16
11	Daniel	1-3	22	Luke	1-3
12	Daniel	4-6	23	Luke	4-6
13	Daniel	7-9	24	Luke	7-9
14	Daniel	10-12	25	Luke	10-12
15	Hosea	1-3	26	Luke	13-15
16	Hosea	4-6	27	Luke	16-18
17	Hosea	7-9	28	Luke	19-21
18	Hosea	10-12	29	Luke	22-24
19	Hosea	13-14	30	John	1-3
20	Joel	1-3	31	John	4-6
21	Amos	1-3			
22	Amos	4-6		**NOVEMBER**	
23	Amos	7-9	1	John	7-9
24	Obadiah	1	2	John	10-12
25	Jonah	1-4	3	John	13-15
26	Micah	1-3	4	John	16-18
27	Micah	4-7	5	John	19-21
28	Nahum	1-3	6	Acts	1-3
29	Habakkuk	1-3	7	Acts	4-6

8	Acts	7-9
9	Acts	10-12
10	Acts	13-15
11	Acts	16-18
12	Acts	19-21
13	Acts	22-24
14	Acts	25-28
15	Romans	1-3
16	Romans	4-6
17	Romans	7-9
18	Romans	10-12
19	Romans	13-16
20	1 Corinthians	1-3
21	1 Corinthians	4-6
22	1 Corinthians	7-9
23	1 Corinthians	10-12
24	1 Corinthians	13-16
25	2 Corinthians	1-3
26	2 Corinthians	4-6
27	2 Corinthians	7-9
28	2 Corinthians	10-13
29	Galatians	1-3
30	Galatians	4-6

DECEMBER

1	Ephesians	1-3
2	Ephesians	4-6
3	Philippians	1-4
4	Colossians	1-4
5	1 Thessalonians	1-3
6	1 Thessalonians	4-5
7	2 Thessalonians	1-3
8	1 Timothy	1-3
9	1 Timothy	4-6
10	2 Timothy	1-4
11	Titus	1-3
12	Philemon	1
13	Hebrews	1-3
14	Hebrews	4-6
15	Hebrews	7-9
16	Hebrews	10-13
17	James	1-3
18	James	4-5
19	1 Peter	1-3
20	1 Peter	4-5
21	2 Peter	1-3
22	1 John	1-3
23	1 John	4-5
24	2 John, 3 John, Jude	
25	Revelation	1-3
26	Revelation	4-6
27	Revelation	7-9
28	Revelation	10-12
29	Revelation	13-15
30	Revelation	16-18
31	Revelation	19-22